ALSO BY MARK K. UPDEGROVE

*The Last Republicans: Inside the Extraordinary Relationship
Between George H. W. Bush and George W. Bush*

Indomitable Will: LBJ in the Presidency

*Baptism by Fire: Eight Presidents Who Took Office
in Times of Crisis*

Second Acts: Presidential Lives and Legacies After the White House

INCOMPARABLE
GRACE

INCOMPARABLE GRACE

JFK in the Presidency

MARK K. UPDEGROVE

DUTTON

DUTTON

An imprint of Penguin Random House LLC
penguinrandomhouse.com

LIBRARY OF CONGRESS CATALOGING-IN-PUBLICATION DATA

Names: Updegrove, Mark K., author.
Title: Incomparable grace : JFK in the presidency / by Mark K. Updegrove.
Other titles: JFK in the presidency
Description: [New York, N.Y.] : Dutton, [2022] |
Includes bibliographical references and index.
Identifiers: LCCN 2021015334 (print) | LCCN 2021015335 (ebook) |
ISBN 9781524745745 (hardcover) | ISBN 9781524745769 (ebook)
Subjects: LCSH: Kennedy, John F. (John Fitzgerald), 1917–1963. |
United States—History—1953–1961. | Presidents—United States—Biography.
Classification: LCC E842 .U63 2021 (print) | LCC E842 (ebook) |
DDC 973.922092 [B]—dc23
LC record available at https://lccn.loc.gov/2021015334
LC ebook record available at https://lccn.loc.gov/2021015335

Printed in the United States of America
1 3 5 7 9 10 8 6 4 2

To my wife, Amy Banner Updegrove,
and my sister, Susan Updegrove Crafford,
both of whom share JFK's May 29 birthday
and have given my life such joy.

CONTENTS

Contents

IV. THE PEAK

INCOMPARABLE
GRACE

PROLOGUE

Uneasy lies the head that wears a crown.
—William Shakespeare, *Henry IV, Part 2*

On an early June evening in 1961, President John Fitzgerald Kennedy, less than a week past his forty-fourth birthday, sat grimly in a dark room in the U.S. Embassy in Vienna, his exhausted mind churning. Moments earlier he had come from a dinner at the Soviet Embassy, the last session of a two-day summit between the United States and the Soviet Union. Over those two long days, as news media across the world awaited even the smallest of updates, the ever-composed JFK had finally come face-to-face with the barrel-chested, hot-tempered Soviet premier Nikita Khrushchev, and for perhaps the first time in his life, he worried he was in over his head.

The stakes couldn't have been higher. Since the end of World War II, the two superpowers had been enmeshed in a cold war that defined geopolitics as the world's nations aligned with either the American or Soviet sphere. The threat of nuclear war had become a fact of everyday life as atomic bomb preparedness drills were practiced routinely; the majority of Americans believed a nuclear showdown was imminent. Tensions seethed over the fate of global crucibles: Berlin, the divided German city composed of the free west and communist-controlled east; Laos, the Southeast Asian nation battling a potential takeover by communist insurgents; and Cuba, whose U.S.-backed government had been toppled by rebels two years earlier under the leadership of Fidel Castro.

Expectations for Kennedy's performance had been just as high. As the *Washington Post* wrote on the eve of the summit, "The Soviet hope is that Mr. Kennedy will buckle under to Khrushchev in some form or other. Yet it may be that Mr. Kennedy . . . has the courage to act to protect American interests . . . Nikita Khrushchev notwithstanding." *That* was the American hope.

The curtains in the U.S. Embassy had been drawn so that the presence of James "Scotty" Reston, the Washington bureau chief for the *New York Times,* who had been secretly granted an exclusive off-the-record interview, would go unnoticed by the international press contingent of over 1,500 who waited anxiously outside for a joint statement. When Reston was ushered into the room, the normally upbeat Kennedy appeared drained and unnerved. In the darkness, the president pressed his body into the couch; the brim of a fedora was pulled down over his eyes.

"How was it?" Reston asked.

"Worst thing in my life," Kennedy answered. Khrushchev, he confessed, had "savaged" him.

Reston was taken off guard by Kennedy's candor. "Not the usual bullshit," he scribbled in his notebook, a briar pipe clenched in his mouth. "There is a look a man has when he has to tell the truth."

If there was truth to tell, little of it came out the following day in Reston's front-page story. "President Kennedy, if not pleased, has had his first major experience in 'cold war' diplomacy and has come out of it very well," the last lines read. "He did not expect much and he did not get much, but he went away from here more experienced and he now rates more highly in the estimation of the men who watched these exchanges than he has at any time since he entered the White House."

In fact, as he had admitted to Reston, Kennedy had come out poorly against his shrewd adversary. Kennedy loved what he called "the chess game of power," but he had been outplayed and he knew it. A political cartoon published after the summit conveyed his humiliation: Kennedy and Khrushchev at opposite ends of a chessboard in front of a sign that reads, "The Boy Wonder Versus the Grandmaster," with Kennedy dressed in a schoolboy's uniform sitting atop two large tomes to reach the table, turning to allied Western leaders behind him to report, "Then I moved a pawn and we adjourned . . ."

Just over four months earlier, Kennedy's presidency had begun as promisingly as any since Franklin Roosevelt had taken office in the depths of the Great Depression. Though he had defeated his Republican challenger, Vice President Richard Nixon, by just two-tenths of a percentage point in the presidential election the previous November, Kennedy had quickly captured the imagination and esteem of the American people as he became the youngest president-elect in history at age forty-three. Handsome and charismatic, he radiated glamour unrivaled by any of the men who had preceded him as chief executive, all suited to an evolving television age in which image had become a greater political asset. Indeed, JFK had assumed the presidency with incomparable grace. As Nixon later put it, Kennedy "was one that attracted the people who wanted a young, courageous man in the presidency—and yet one who was suave, smooth, debonair, and graceful. Basically, that was the mark of royalty." Accessorizing his regal aura was his wife, Jackie, who cast elegance and celebrity flair of her own; their two young children, Caroline and John Jr., three years old and two months old upon their father's inauguration; and the vivacious extended Kennedy clan, one of America's wealthiest families. Along with Kennedy, all of them would captivate the media throughout his tenure in office.

Kennedy's luminescent inauguration had only added to his allure, throwing a golden hue on his fledgling presidency. His inaugural speech oratory—*"Ask not what your country can do for you—ask what you can do for your country"*—instantly became an eternal expression of American ideals, while his declaration that the U.S. would *"pay any price, bear any burden, meet any hardship . . . to assure the survival and success of liberty"* was a clarion call to stand up to communist aggression across the world. Civil rights leader and future congressman John Lewis was among the many inspired by the new president. "His whole demeanor and personality gave you a sense of hope and optimism," Lewis said, "a sense that you could do almost anything, that you could go anyplace you wanted to go."

Despite his favorable first days out of the gate, in mid-April Kennedy stumbled with the order of a secret operation of U.S.-trained Cuban exiles to overthrow the Castro regime. The cadres' landing at Cuba's Bay of Pigs was a disaster. Within twenty-four hours, the CIA-led mission had been vanquished by Castro's military, resulting in the deaths of 114 and the capture of more than 1,100 others as the world looked on. It was a devastating defeat for Kennedy.

Yet Americans proved willing to forgive their young president, who publicly owned up to his failure and resolved to do better. Incredibly, his approval rating soared to 83 percent, the highest he would see in the White House. Hardly earned, it was a gesture of good faith; the American people saw JFK's potential.

But Nikita Khrushchev did not. Going into the summit, he considered his Western counterpart to be a callow lightweight, someone who could be bullied and exploited. After two combative days, Khrushchev's perception had only been reinforced. Evidently inured to the prospect of nuclear war, he hammered away at Kennedy as they discussed the trouble spots around the world. When their meetings were over, he sized Kennedy up as "very young and not strong enough. Too intelligent and too weak."

Kennedy sensed that, too. Since entering politics at the age of twenty-nine, he had aspired not only to be president but to be a *great* president, a leader of strength, courage, and vision, the preeminent statesman of his time. He envisioned striding the world stage like the men he considered the century's giants—Franklin D. Roosevelt, Winston Churchill, Charles de Gaulle. But as Kennedy sat languid and beaten before Reston, Khrushchev was departing Vienna newly emboldened.

"[Khrushchev] thought that anyone who was so young and inexperienced as to get into [the Bay of Pigs] mess could be taken," Kennedy confided to Reston. "And anyone who got into it and didn't see it through had no guts. So, he just beat the hell out of me." The president knew that Khrushchev's impression of him would be a "terrible problem." "If he thinks I'm inexperienced and have no guts," he continued, "until we remove those ideas, we won't get anywhere with him."

The question was how.

I

THE TORCH

The Kennedys leave their Georgetown apartment on the morning of
JFK's inauguration, January 20, 1961.
Jacques Lowe, Jacques Lowe Photographic Archive, Briscoe Center for
American History, University of Texas at Austin

TRANSITION

The snow came fast and thick. On the morning of Thursday, January 19, 1961, storm clouds blew up from North Carolina and Virginia in icy gusts, paralyzing the mid-Atlantic states, which saw as much as twenty-nine inches of precipitation as the mercury dived into the low twenties, and then the teens. By day's end, eight inches of snow would blanket Washington, D.C., as the city prepared for the peaceful transfer of power.

Two hours before the snow began to fall, John Kennedy met in the Oval Office with President Dwight Eisenhower, the seventy-year-old incumbent, who would pass on the burden of the office to Kennedy the following day at noon. Even beyond their twenty-seven-year age difference—the greatest America has seen between an incoming and outgoing president—the contrast between them was stark: Kennedy was the tousle-haired picture of young-man-in-a-hurry vitality and ambition, bronzed from a recent stay at his father's Palm Beach estate; Eisenhower was the Kansas farm boy turned stalwart hero of D-Day—pallid, bald, and aged—who wore the mantle of power with reflexive ease. Before repairing to the West Wing, the two men had greeted each other warmly before a gaggle of eager press photographers at the White House's North Portico, flashing the famous smiles that had lit up thousands of campaign posters through the years. All was cordial as they met, belying an undercurrent of tension between them. Among their respective aides, Eisenhower derided Kennedy as "Little Boy Blue," while Kennedy called Eisenhower "that old asshole," a military term reserved by junior officers for the top brass, and, later, "a cold bastard."

This was their second transition meeting. The first, in early December, a discussion on national security matters lasting the better part of an hour, hadn't amounted to much. Remarkably, Kennedy and Eisenhower had crossed paths only once before the transition, a brief encounter in Potsdam, Germany, during World War II when Kennedy was covering the war for Hearst newspapers that Eisenhower couldn't recall. This despite the fact that throughout the entirety of Ike's presidency Kennedy had sat in the U.S. Senate representing his home state of Massachusetts, speaking to the infertility of Kennedy's tenure in Congress's upper chamber.

Regardless, JFK had used his political résumé—six years in the House of Representatives, eight years in the Senate—to launch a successful candidacy for the nation's highest office. On Election Day, he had eked out the sparest of wins against his Republican challenger, Eisenhower's vice president, Richard Nixon, carrying 49.72 percent of the vote to Nixon's 49.55 percent—a margin of just 118,574 votes. The slimmest victory of the twentieth century, it was hardly the mandate Kennedy had hoped for, limiting his ability to deviate markedly from the policies of Eisenhower and nipping at his abundant confidence. "How did I manage to beat a guy like [Nixon] by only a hundred thousand votes?" he asked his aide Kenny O'Donnell incredulously. Still, it had been enough. As

Kennedy himself said after the votes had been counted and his win confirmed the following day, "The margin is thin, but the responsibility is clear."

He had gotten there by pledging to "get America moving again," implicating a supposedly complacent Eisenhower as he hammered away at the "missile gap," a contrivance designed to foster anxiety that the Soviet Union had slowly built up its arsenal disproportionally as the cold war simmered and the president sat idly by. Eisenhower was stung by Kennedy's attacks on his record, and by Nixon's failure to defend him. The old general viewed Kennedy's win as a repudiation of his administration, considering it one of his "greatest disappointments." "All I've done for the last eight years has gone down the drain," he lamented to his son John.

He was wrong. The electorate had simply cast its lot with Kennedy, capriciously tilting the cycle of history in another direction as a means of exercising their own lever in the balance of power inherent in a democracy. With an outgoing approval rating of 60 percent, Ike was nearly as popular with Americans as when he took the presidency in a landslide eight years earlier. At a time when tensions between the U.S. and the Soviet Union were rising, the steady-handed president had kept the cold war from becoming hot, successfully employing a strategy of containment to rein in the ambitions of his Soviet counterpart, Nikita Khrushchev. The hostility between the two superpowers stood in contrast to the halcyon façade that marked the 1950s and the early '60s; an underlying fear of Russian aggression and the spread of communism pervaded the nation and defined the Eisenhower era. But in a dangerous world, Eisenhower, the former supreme allied commander in the greatest of America's foreign wars, had kept the communist wolf from the door.

To be sure, there had been setbacks, especially in Eisenhower's second term. In 1957, the Soviets had stunned the world by launching Sputnik, a satellite not much bigger than a beach ball, spurring alarm that the Russians had gained technological superiority and igniting a space race between the superpowers. The subsequent creation of NASA (the National Aeronautics and Space Administration) did little to instill confidence as the U.S. struggled to catch up, stumbling in early efforts to successfully launch a rocket with American prestige and ingenuity on the line. The following year, revolutionary Fidel Castro led a band of guerrillas to drive out the U.S.-backed regime in Cuba, introducing a communist state to the Western Hemisphere less than a hundred miles off the coast of Florida.

In 1960, Eisenhower's last full year in office, the Soviets shot down American U-2 spy plane pilot Francis Gary Powers on a covert CIA mission to photograph Soviet missile installations in the Russian city of Yekaterinburg. The Eisenhower administration, assuming that neither Powers nor the aircraft had survived the crash, claimed it was a weather plane that had experienced a technical malfunction. The Soviets proved otherwise, revealing to the world that Powers, a member of the CIA's operations team who was very much alive and well, was now their prisoner, and that the downed aircraft was mostly intact, allowing them a firsthand look at American spying apparatus.

After months of interrogation by the KGB, Powers issued an apology along with a confession that he had been engaged in an espionage mission. The incident further strained superpower tensions while providing the Soviets with a public relations windfall. U.S. fears grew that same year when Khrushchev appeared at a United Nations plenary session in New York where he protested an anti-Soviet speech by removing his shoe and defiantly pounding it on the table, bellowing, "We will bury you!"

Domestically, Eisenhower had grappled cautiously with the burgeoning civil rights movement. In the decade before his presidency, promising action had been taken toward racial equality, including a 1941 Executive Order from Franklin Roosevelt to bar discrimination in defense industries and the armed forces based on "race, creed, color, or national origin," followed by Harry Truman's order to desegregate the military in 1948. Still, the postwar years saw a surge in racism, no more so than in the Deep South. A major step forward came in Eisenhower's second year in office with the unanimous ruling on the landmark 1954 Supreme Court case *Brown v. Board of Education*, rendering public school segregation unconstitutional. In 1957, Eisenhower responded to clamorous resistance to racial integration in Little Rock, Arkansas, by calling in the 101st Airborne to ensure the admission of nine Black students at the city's Central High School.

Two years earlier, in 1955, the nation had been introduced to Martin Luther King, Jr., a twenty-six-year-old minister who led a bus boycott in Montgomery, Alabama, after the arrest of Rosa Parks, a Black secretary for the NAACP and seamstress who refused to give up her seat to a white patron. A Supreme Court ruling striking down the segregation of Montgomery's buses came a year later, leading to King's creation of the Southern Christian Leadership Conference (SCLC), an alliance of Black ministers who led new and broader civil rights campaigns in the South.

In October 1960, King was arrested for participating in an Atlanta restaurant sit-in and, after being taken to a DeKalb County jail, was moved in shackles to a rural prison where he would be subjected to hard labor and vulnerable to violence from racist white prison guards and inmates. Only a plea to Georgia's Democratic governor Ernest Vandiver from Kennedy, then in the last days of stumping for the presidency, ensured King's release.

There was also the matter of the economy, which sputtered into recession at the end of Ike's term, with wages stalled, unemployment rising, and gross domestic product down by 5 percent in the last quarter of 1960.

All foreshadowed the trials Kennedy would contend with in Eisenhower's stead: increased hostilities with a menacing, determined Soviet adversary and the threat of the global spread of communism; a flat-footed U.S. space program; the growing demands of equal rights from the Black community against an intractable white majority violently protecting the status quo; and a sluggish economy in need of a lift.

Eisenhower was more than ready to let it all go. But he would be missed. As the editorial board of the *Dallas Morning News* wrote of him on the day of his second meeting with Kennedy, "No man in universal history has amassed so much influence and power without taking one more step: assumption of an imperial diadem or the trappings of dictatorship. It behooves JFK to remember, as we think he does, that neither the U.S. nor the rest of the world is through with Dwight Eisenhower." Nor, in fact, was Kennedy, who understood the value of keeping the redoubtable Ike close then, and in the course of his own presidency. It was Kennedy who had asked for the second transition meeting. As he wrote in a memo to himself later, he did so to reflect "the harmony of the transition," thereby "strengthening our hand." But in truth, he also did it because he knew he would benefit from Eisenhower's counsel.

For forty-five minutes, the pair met alone in the Oval Office. Their conversation began on a somber note, with Ike providing a tutorial on the use of "the Football," the black vinyl bag containing the codes to launch a nuclear attack. The "Presidential Emergency Action Documents," as it was officially known, would be a fixture of Kennedy's presidency, handed off by military aides in eight-hour shifts and always within his reach as commander in chief. Ike then segued into another security measure. "Watch this," he told Kennedy as he picked up a phone, ordering "Opal Drill Three." Within three minutes the presidential helicopter, Marine One, descended on the South Lawn, ready to whisk the president away.

"I've just shown my friend here how to get out in a hurry," Ike quipped as the two men adjourned to the Cabinet Room where they were met by the president's secretaries of state, defense, and treasury, and transition team head, along with their counterparts from Kennedy's team, Dean Rusk, Robert McNamara, Douglas Dillon, and Clark Clifford, respectively.

The first of the four items on the agenda, as requested by Kennedy, was "Trouble Spots." Laos was among those countries on the list. "If Laos should fall to the Communists," Eisenhower warned, "then it would be a question of time until South Vietnam, Cambodia, Thailand, and Burma would collapse"—an allusion to the domino theory, the widespread belief that if the U.S. allowed one nation to yield to communist aggression, others would fall in turn. Laos, he maintained, was "the cork in the bottle," adding, "This is one of the problems I'm leaving you with that I'm not happy about. We might have to fight."

Given the dire situation, Kennedy asked why Eisenhower hadn't already sent in ground troops. "I would have but I did not feel I could commit troops with a new administration coming to power," Eisenhower answered.

Kennedy inquired about whether a coalition government or military action by the Southeast Asia Treaty Organization (SEATO) would work in the region. Neither was a good option, Eisenhower maintained.

As they discussed which of the neighboring nations might

come to the aid of the communist rebels, Kennedy asked, "What about China?" Eisenhower replied that he thought the Chinese would be reluctant to provoke a major war, adding gravely of the situation at large, "It's a high-stakes poker game; there's no easy solution." Kennedy got the impression that Eisenhower was actually enjoying the conversation. So did McNamara and Dillon, who thought the president, to Dillon's mind, got an "inner satisfaction" in laying the onerous problems of Southeast Asia "in Kennedy's lap."

The talk turned to another trouble spot, this one closer to home. On two occasions prior to the meeting, Kennedy had been briefed on a U.S. operation in Guatemala where the CIA was training a band of anti-Castro exiles to stage a coup to wrest Fidel Castro from power. "Should we support guerrilla operations in Cuba?" Kennedy asked Eisenhower.

"To the utmost," Eisenhower replied enthusiastically, recommending "the effort be continued and accelerated," and offering his firm view that the United States "cannot let the present government go on there" as Kennedy took note.

The meeting broke up after about an hour. Just before leaving the Cabinet Room, Eisenhower stole a moment to tell Kennedy that despite the rhetoric of his campaign—a reference to Kennedy's claims of a "missile gap"—the U.S. held a distinct nuclear advantage over the Soviets through its Polaris fleet: submarines with nuclear-missile-firing capabilities that surrounded coastal areas of the Soviet Union. "You have an invulnerable asset in Polaris," he reported to Kennedy, perhaps with some self-satisfaction, "invulnerable."

The interaction resulted in a thaw of sorts between Eisenhower and Kennedy. In spite of his initial reservations, Eisenhower, however grudgingly, was taken by the young man's considerable charm and acute mind. But he worried that Kennedy would be out of his depth in the position he was about to assume. Eight years earlier, when Harry Truman handed the office over to Eisenhower, Truman worried that his successor didn't grasp the enormity of the task before him. So it now was for Eisenhower, who told his diary after their first meeting that he didn't think Kennedy understood the complexities of the job. Kennedy, for his part, held a similar view of Eisenhower. Though he was duly impressed by Eisenhower's "surprising force" of personality and found him to be more up to speed on matters of state than he'd expected, he left with the impression that Eisenhower didn't fully appreciate the power of the office he held.

The president-elect's limousine passed through the black iron gates of the White House just before noon en route to the Georgetown home of a friend, where he would meet with the chairman of the Joint Chiefs of Staff, Lyman Lemnitzer. In less than twenty-four hours Kennedy would be returning, this time with the soon-to-be first lady, Jackie, for the traditional coffee between the incoming and outgoing first couples before venturing together by motorcade to the East Portico of the Capitol for the rites of his inauguration. Then the White House and all that came with it would be his.

As the car made its way through Washington's streets, he sat in the back seat with an aide reflecting on his meeting with Eisenhower. The outgoing president's dispassion as he reported on the momentous issues that crossed his desk gave Kennedy pause. "How can he stare disaster in the face with such equanimity?" he wondered aloud.

"LET US BEGIN"

The blizzard was in full force shortly after Kennedy arrived in Georgetown. By evening it had besieged the capital, with officials describing the situation as "absolutely hopeless." The city became nearly paralyzed, with the *Washington Post* reporting that the resulting traffic jam was "general and truly monumental." On the National Mall, stretching between the Capitol and the Washington Monument, the grass that had been spray-painted green days earlier to give the city an air of spring for Kennedy's inauguration was now covered by over a foot of snow. Thousands of city workers, employing some seven hundred plows and trucks, worked through the night to clear Washington's main arteries for the events to come. At the White House, stranded Eisenhower staffers bunked in makeshift beds throughout the West Wing, while at Constitution Hall only half the National Symphony Orchestra made it for the sold-out inauguration-eve concert, which started an hour later than scheduled and played to a house just one-third full, the bulk of ticket holders unable to make it through the storm.

It wasn't much different across town at the city's National

Guard Armory, where the inaugural gala orchestrated by Frank Sinatra, also a sellout and featuring an eclectic array of stars—Bette Davis, Sir Laurence Olivier, Mahalia Jackson, Leonard Bernstein, Harry Belafonte, Gene Kelly, Nat King Cole, Milton Berle, Jimmy Durante, and Ethel Merman—got off two hours late with the performers playing to a house dotted with vacant seats. Merman, powerless to get back to her hotel to change into the glittery evening dress she had planned to wear, settled for the pedestrian coat and hat she had arrived in for rehearsal. But there was something serendipitous about it all, an excitement that permeated the capital.

Much of it surrounded the soon-to-be first couple. Under the protection of a Secret Service agent's umbrella, Jackie appeared outside the Kennedys' Georgetown townhouse dressed in an ivory silk satin gown that blended with the flurry of snow around her, foreshadowing the glamour that awaited the White House as a legion of camera shutters chittered like a flock of birds. She and her tuxedoed husband attended the concert and gala, where they arrived late even with the pushed-back start times. They wouldn't have made it at all but for the intrepid Secret Service agents who lifted their limousine over a snowbank blocking their passage.

Jackie, who had given birth to the couple's second child, John Jr., through a Caesarean section five weeks earlier, retired for the evening before Sinatra's rambling gala wrapped up, leaving her husband behind to finish it out before he pressed on to a cacophonous get-together hosted by his father at Paul Young's restaurant. "Have you ever seen so many attractive people in one room?" he asked his friend and Navy buddy Paul "Red" Fay. Chief among them was Kennedy himself. One of the attendees, twenty-nine-year-old actress Angie Dickinson, recalled him exuding the "charisma" and "drop dead" good looks of a leading man. (Rumored to be one of Kennedy's paramours, a charge she has long denied, Dickinson recently allowed, "We had a lot of fun thinking about it.") It was 3:48 a.m. before Kennedy arrived back home, and after 4:00 a.m. when his head hit the pillow.

Four hours later, he was up rehearsing his inaugural address down to each inflection, first in the bathtub, then over a breakfast of coffee, eggs, and three strips of bacon. The bacon was a concession by the pope, who gave Roman Catholics in the Washington area a special reprieve from the abstinence of red meat as a penance on Fridays in honor of the ascent of Kennedy as America's first Catholic president. The speech Kennedy practiced had been long in the making. For weeks he had been at his father's estate in Palm Beach, scratching his thoughts on yellow legal pads between meetings and rounds of golf as he puffed on the H. Upmann Petit Coronas Cuban cigars he favored. He saw the oration as the overture of his presidency, the chance to set an uplifting tone around the new generation of leadership that lay ahead.

"I want to say that the American Revolution still is going on, and that this nation is still young and vital," he told a friend a few weeks earlier. His longtime aide Ted Sorensen, the bespectacled Nebraskan who would help craft the speech, was tasked with looking at past presidential orations and marveled at the simplicity of Lincoln's Gettysburg Address, observing that Lincoln avoided using multiple-syllable words over simple ones and "never used two or three words where one word would do."

Intent on healing the divisions of the close election nearly three months earlier, Kennedy dispensed with the idea of exploring domestic themes, which he deemed too partisan. Instead, he chose to concentrate on international issues, with the aim of sounding a message of strength and determination to hold the line against Soviet aggression while imparting his hope for peace in the nuclear age. He saw the office he was about to assume as the bulwark, the last and most potent line of defense, around egalitarian liberty. "We prize our individualism, and rightly so, but we need a cohesive force," he said during his presidential campaign of the need to stand up to Soviet tyranny. "In America, that force is the presidency." The inaugural address would be his cold war manifesto.

He also sought to reemphasize American values with a call for service and self-sacrifice around the nation's greater good. Finally, like Lincoln's Gettysburg masterpiece, he wanted his remarks to be brief. "It's more effective that way," he maintained, "and I don't want the people to think I'm a windbag." He made good on his intention. The final version, just 1,355 words—most of them rendered by Kennedy's own hand—would make it one of the shortest inauguration addresses in U.S. history.

The weather cleared for the occasion, the sky a brilliant blue, the air a bitter twenty-two degrees with arctic blasts up to eighteen miles an hour. Braving the cold, a crowd of twenty thousand, many wrapped in blankets, amassed at the East Front Plaza of the Capitol to look on as the thirty-fifth president took the helm. History would later note the presence of former, incumbent, and future presidents and first ladies spanning just under half a century of White House occupancy: Edith Wilson, Eleanor Roosevelt, Harry and Bess Truman, Dwight and Mamie Eisenhower, John and Jacqueline Kennedy, Lyndon and Lady Bird Johnson, Richard and Pat Nixon, and Gerald and Betty Ford. (The arc would have been four years greater had the winter conditions not prevented the eighty-six-year-old thirty-first president, Herbert Hoover, from flying from Manhattan to Washington.)

At 12:12, Kennedy emerged on the inaugural platform in full

morning dress, which he thought would give him an air of maturity and gravitas: a black cutaway morning coat and tails, a double-breasted gray vest and tie, striped trousers, and a silk top hat perched on his head. Showcasing the "Jackie look" designed to accentuate her youthfulness and portending fashion trends to come, his wife was by his side in an Oleg Cassini–designed A-line coat dress in "greige," a color between gray and beige, and a Halston pillbox hat that would become her signature. The Eisenhowers, decidedly less alluring, accompanied them fresh from having coffee together at the White House. On the short drive they made together to Capitol Hill in a bubble-top limousine, the retiring president took a moment to tell Kennedy that he believed the Russians would refrain from war if America remained strong.

When they arrived at the Capitol, Ike sat on the platform bundled up in a dark overcoat and white scarf, his eyes squinting in the sun. Richard Nixon sat across the aisle, smiling stoically when it was required, alongside Lyndon Johnson, the formidable Senate majority leader turned Kennedy running mate, soon to be inaugurated as vice president by his fellow Texan, House Speaker Sam Rayburn.

Marian Anderson, the renowned African American opera singer who was denied a performance at Constitution Hall by the Daughters of the American Revolution twenty-two years earlier due to the color of her skin, sang a stirring rendition of "America the Beautiful," but the ceremony that followed did not begin promisingly. During an invocation by Boston's Cardinal Richard Cushing, the lectern appeared to catch fire, smoke billowing on either side, the result of a faulty electric motor in place to adjust its height. As soon as the cardinal intoned "Amen," nervous Secret Service agents rushed in to extinguish the fire.

The show went on. Robert Frost, the eighty-six-year-old Pulitzer

Prize–winning poet, rose to the podium to recite a new work titled "Dedication," about Kennedy's election victory. Kennedy was in favor of Frost's participation, with the reservation that the "master of words" might "upstage" him. He needn't have worried. The hatless Frost, wisps of white hair blowing in the breeze, was unable to read the verses due to the blinding sunlight reflecting off the snow. Lyndon Johnson quickly stepped up to offer shade with his top hat. But Frost, commenting, "I'll just have to get through as I can" as laughter murmured from the crowd, soon abandoned the work, instead reciting from memory another of his poems, "The Gift Outright."

Then Kennedy took the stage. Newly sworn in by Chief Justice Earl Warren, he shed his overcoat and top hat and, warmed by an electric heater, resolutely addressed his nation and the world. "Let the word go forth from this time and place to friend and foe alike," his voice rang out in his clipped Boston brogue, exhaling small clouds of mist against the winter air, "that the torch has been passed to a new generation of Americans—born in this century, tempered by war, disciplined by a hard and bitter peace, proud of our ancient heritage—and unwilling to witness or permit the slow undoing of those human rights to which this nation has always been committed, and to which we are committed today at home and around the world."

He continued, his right arm at a ninety-degree angle, his index finger thrusting or hand clenched in a fist gently pounding the lectern for emphasis:

> Let every nation know, whether it wishes us well or ill, that we shall pay any price, bear any burden, meet any hardship, support any friend, oppose any foe to assure the survival and success of liberty. . . .

Finally, to those nations who would make themselves our adversary, we offer not a pledge but a request: that both sides begin anew in the quest for peace, before the dark powers of destruction unleashed by science engulf all humanity in planned or accidental self-destruction. . . .

So let us begin anew—remembering on both sides that civility is not a sign of weakness, and sincerity is always subject to proof. Let us never negotiate out of fear. But let us never fear to negotiate.

Invoking the martyred Lincoln, who a century earlier in his first inaugural address proclaimed, "In your hands, my dissatisfied fellow countrymen, and not in mine, is the momentous issue of civil war," Kennedy asserted:

In your hands, my fellow citizens, more than mine, will rest the final success or failure of our course. . . .

In the long history of the world, only a few generations have been granted the role of defending freedom in its hour of maximum danger. I do not shrink from this responsibility—I welcome it. I do not believe that any of us would exchange places with any other people or any other generation. The energy, the faith, the devotion which we bring to this endeavor will light our country and all who serve it—and the glow from that fire can truly light the world.

He wound down the fourteen-minute oration climactically with the line that would most resonate, ushering in a new age of national commitment and marking the idealistic promise at the dawn of the 1960s:

> And so, my fellow Americans, ask not what your country
> can do for you—ask what you can do for your country.

The line is thought to be borrowed from his prep school headmaster at Choate, who beseeched his students that what mattered most was "not what Choate does for you, but what you can do for Choate." But it echoes the final passage in a stump speech that Kennedy's speechwriter Dick Goodwin had drafted for a campaign swing in Alaska in 1960, which read, "If only we apply to the New Frontier the same dedication and spirit which you applied to the 'Next Frontier.' This is the call of the New Frontier. It is not what I promise I will do; it is what I ask *you* to join *me* in doing." As Jackie wrote to Goodwin later, "It shows the first use of the phrase that later in his inaugural address became 'Ask not what your country can do for you, ask what you can do for your country.'"

Regardless of its origin, the statement was destined to reverberate in history. As much as anything he would say or do, it would define Kennedy's presidency while ranking as among the most memorable of inaugural declarations—on par with Jefferson's "We are all Republicans, we are all Federalists," Lincoln's "With malice toward none, with charity for all," and FDR's "We have nothing to fear but fear itself."

"Jack, you were wonderful," Jackie Kennedy whispered in her husband's ear when he returned from the podium. The public and the press agreed. Nearly three-quarters of Americans approved of the new president's speech. *New York Times* columnist William Safire would later write that it "set the standard by which presidential inaugurals have been judged in the modern era." *Time* magazine wrote that it enjoyed support "from all shades of the political outlook," which was evident from the bipartisan reaction of the dignitaries on the inaugural platform. Eisenhower judged it "fine, very fine," while Harry Truman said, "It was just what the people should hear and live up to." The Congressional leadership was just as enthusiastic; Democratic Speaker of the House Sam Rayburn deemed the oration "better than anything Franklin Roosevelt said at his best—it was better than Lincoln," adding, "I think—I really think—he's a man of destiny," and Republican Senate minority leader Everett Dirksen called it an "inspiring . . . very compact message of hope." Indeed, Kennedy's speech initiated a sanguine streak of activism across the nation. A Gallup Poll taken the following month indicated that 63 percent of Americans said they could personally think of something they could do to better the country, a number that spiked among the nation's youth.

The event broke up a little after noon. The former president and his men dispersed; Eisenhower went off to retirement, journeying by car with his beloved Mamie to their farm in Gettysburg, which abutted the hallowed Civil War battleground, "free—as only private citizens in a democratic nation can be free." Nixon, his political future now uncertain, descended the Capitol steps and drove off, but not before running into Ted Sorensen, to whom he confessed of Kennedy's speech that he wished he had said some of those things. Which part? Sorensen asked. "The part that starts, 'I do solemnly swear,'" Nixon replied. While it may have been said in jest, Nixon left "struck by the thought," as he would later write in his memoirs, "that this was not the end—that someday I would be back here."

The new administration moved on to the celebratory events that awaited. Kennedy and Johnson and their wives attended the inaugural parade that streamed down Pennsylvania Avenue for three long hours, as thirty-two thousand participants—half military, half civilian—marched through the cold for the new commander in chief and his number two, who waved enthusiastically throughout. Then it was on to a record five evening inaugural balls, with Jackie once again peeling off to let her husband continue the revelry. Sometime after midnight, he ended up at the home of a friend, syndicated columnist and Washington insider Joe Alsop, a celebratory cigar burning in hand as he arrived.

He crept back to the White House at four a.m., filing past members of the press gathered to capture him to the last. Hands in the pockets of his overcoat, he exited his limousine flashing one final smile as he strode alone up the stairs of the North Portico of the White House, where he would spend his first night. "Here goes," one reporter heard him say. Then he disappeared into the mansion to sleep in the massive wooden bed Abraham Lincoln had occupied a century before.

"So let us begin anew," Kennedy had said of his fledgling administration sixteen hours earlier. And begun it had. Auspiciously.

THE SECOND SON

Among those who huddled on the platform for the inauguration were sixteen members of the Kennedy family, beaming as one of their own assumed the nation's highest office. The most conspicuous was the brood's seventy-two-year-old patriarch, Joseph P. Kennedy, whose wealth of between $200 and $400 million made him one of the ten richest Americans in the country, according to *Fortune* magazine, and whose unbridled ambition went well beyond his own outsize aspirations. That one of his sons, as he had envisioned, could reach the presidency—the first Roman Catholic to do so—was an audacious notion, even with his considerable prosperity and political connections to fuel the campaign. But Joe Kennedy was nothing if not audacious.

Nearly a quarter of a century earlier, he had been summoned to the Oval Office after President Franklin Roosevelt had learned of Kennedy's interest in two jobs in his administration—and *only* two: secretary of the treasury and ambassador to Great Britain. It was no surprise that Kennedy would want to be treasury secretary. He had known early in his career that it was the banks in America that offered him the best chance of garnering wealth. At age twenty-five, he secured a loan to take over the Columbia Trust Company, a small Boston bank, making him the country's youngest bank president at twenty-five and setting him on his own path to riches. Serving as head of the treasury was a means of exercising power and giving back to his country, both things that stirred Kennedy's passion. But an Irish Catholic from East Boston presiding over the Court of St. James's as ambassador to Great Britain—the most prestigious American diplomatic post? That was something more.

The prospect of Kennedy in the job amused Roosevelt, who shook with laughter at the thought, calling it the "greatest joke in the world." The English had a centuries-long history of spurning Ireland's Catholic populace, depriving them of basic rights, including freedom to worship; voting; and owning land, horses, and guns—and the Catholic religion itself had been illegal in England until just over a century earlier.

Then Roosevelt reconsidered. He owed a debt to Kennedy, who had given his presidential campaign significant financial support and had even written a book titled *I'm for Roosevelt* to boost FDR's 1936 reelection crusade. Plus, there was a certain appeal to appointing someone who wouldn't be swept up into English society, but would instead hold it at a distance, allowing a more detached view of the British government's political leanings as the prospect of war with Nazi Germany loomed over Europe.

If Joe Kennedy was an unconventional choice for the post, so was his interview for the job. Shortly after he arrived in the Oval Office for his meeting, FDR asked him to take down his pants. Kennedy complied, his trousers dropping to the floor.

"You are about the most bowlegged man I have ever seen." Roosevelt laughed. "Don't you know that the Ambassador to the Court of Saint James's has to go through an induction ceremony in which he wears knee britches and silk stockings? . . . When photos of our new ambassador appear all over the world, we'll be a laughingstock."

Embarrassed but undeterred, Kennedy cut a deal. "If I can get the permission of His Majesty's government to wear a cutaway coat and striped pants for the ceremony," he asked, "would you agree to appoint me?"

Roosevelt consented, believing that there was "no way" Kennedy's appeal would come to anything. But within two weeks, Kennedy had pulled strings with the British government to buck protocol and alter the dress code. Shortly afterward, he won the post from the president. Early in 1938, he accepted his charge in front of British royalty in a cutaway coat and striped pants.

It was somehow fitting that Joe Kennedy wore the very same coat and pants as he prepared for the inauguration of his son as the thirty-fifth president. If becoming the ambassador to the Court of St. James's was a milestone in the elder Kennedy's life, witnessing his son ascend to the presidency was the realization of a dream— and a certain expectation of the next generation. From his earliest days of fatherhood, Kennedy had it firmly in his mind that his son would become president. It was all part of the plan. It's just that, initially, it wasn't *this* son.

John Fitzgerald Kennedy, "Jack" as he would become known, was born in Brookline, Massachusetts, on May 29, 1917, the second son of Joe and Rose Kennedy, whose firstborn, Joe Jr., had arrived two years earlier. Seven siblings would follow, produced by their parents from 1918 to 1931—Rosemary, Kathleen, Eunice, Pat, Bobby, Jean, and Ted—making for a family of nine children. Politics ran through the bloodline.

Joe and Rose had grown up in political households, products of Boston's parochial Irish Catholic community, born a little over a generation after virulent prejudice around Catholicism and Irish ethnicity became an open part of American life. The poor and hungry exiles who had come to America's shores to escape Ireland's potato famine in the early and mid-1850s were looked upon as inferior. Classified ads of the time routinely read, "No Irish Need Apply," or similar sentiments, and those stipulating that only "Protestants" or "Americans" would be considered were just as common. But while the Irish continued to be the objects of discrimination, the sheer number of immigrants drove greater acceptance and political consolidation a generation later. Boston elected its first Irish Catholic mayor in 1880, as "Greenbloods" in northeastern cities began amassing local political power by the end of the nineteenth century. The fathers of Joe and Rose were among them.

Born in 1890, Rose grew up the first of six children of the garrulous, twinkly-eyed John "Honey Fitz" Fitzgerald, who won a series of political offices—state senator, U.S. congressman, and mayor of Boston—that kept the Fitzgerald family in the local spotlight, though Rose's reticent mother, Mary, had little interest in politics.

A born showman, Honey Fitz was a fixture in Boston, a man about town whose long-term affair with "Toodles," a cigarette girl, was an open secret. Joe's father, Patrick Joseph "P. J." Kennedy, while not as politically prominent as Honey Fitz, wielded his own power as a Democratic Party insider and "ward boss" in East Boston and in elected posts as a member of the state Senate and House of Representatives. The child of Irish immigrants, P. J. rose from day laborer to successful businessman with a financial stake in two Boston banks, the embodiment of the American dream, allowing his wife and three children a comfortable middle-class life.

Joe and Rose met within the rarified "lace curtain Irish" set of the Boston political elite, with the Kennedy and Fitzgerald families even spending one summer vacation together. Still, when Rose was caught up in a courtship with Joe, Honey Fitz resisted the match, preferring as her suitor another friend of the family, a wealthy contractor he believed to be a better fit. In the end, Rose got her way. She and Joe married in 1914, quickly creating a family and embarking on an epic life together in which they would scale unimaginable heights. But it would come at a cost—tragedy would dog them as an unwanted companion throughout their journey.

While Honey Fitz and P. J. had achieved the outer reaches of what was possible for Irish Americans of their time, Joe's aims went well beyond the world in which he grew up. After he arranged the buyout of the Columbia Trust Company, a Boston newspaper reporter asked him what his future held. "I want to be a millionaire by the age of thirty-five," he replied without hesitation, achieving his goal just as expressly well ahead of schedule.

Shortly after his graduation from Harvard University, he and Rose moved to Brookline, a mostly Protestant middle-class suburb outside Boston, pointing to a desire to break beyond provincial Irish circles in order to advance his career and social standing. The Kennedys wouldn't remain in the middle class for long. In the decade after Jack's birth, Joe built his fortune as a businessman and financier, investing with little regard for ethics or the law in real estate and the booming stock market while capitalizing on the demand for alcohol as a bootlegger during Prohibition. He also invested in the burgeoning movie industry, cofounding the Hollywood studio RKO. By 1927, the family had moved to New York so that Joe could be closer to the country's financial capital, settling on a five-acre estate in Bronxville, a bedroom community just north of Manhattan. More significant was Joe's 1928 purchase of a sprawling compound in Hyannis Port, on Cape Cod, which would become the family's summer retreat and the place they most associated with home. By the time the stock market crashed in 1929, erasing or depleting fortunes overnight, Joe had cashed in his stocks, protecting the family from the economic ruins of the Depression.

Joe's carefully honed public image as an engaged family man was a veneer belied by his protracted absences from the family—mostly lengthy stays in Hollywood as he minded his film interests—and his chronic infidelity, including a longtime affair with actress Gloria Swanson. Day-to-day parenting duties in the bustling, chaotic Kennedy household fell to Rose. Disappointed in her marriage, overcome by the crush of domestic life, and often pregnant or just having given birth, she, too, fled the Kennedy home for long respites, often in Europe, leaving the children in the care of the domestic staff or family. "You're a great mother to go away and leave your children alone," a five-year-old Jack is said to have told her before she embarked on a six-week tour of western states. When home, she was hardly a warm maternal presence. In adherence to the parenting precepts of the time, she neither pampered nor indulged her children, rarely even hugging them. As her brood got older and shuffled off to boarding schools, the Kennedy home in Bronxville was more of a boardinghouse, with children checking in during school breaks wondering which bedroom they would be assigned. Later Jack would reject the notion of raising a big family himself, calling it "institutionalized living, children in a cellblock."

Deeply devoted to her faith, the pious Rose tried to inculcate character in her children through Catholicism, wrangling them to church with her as often as she could. Far less religious, Joe believed character was honed through experience. He encouraged his children to give everything their all, and to play to win. "We want winners," he chided them, spurring their competitiveness. "We don't want losers around here."

As Jack later said, "For the Kennedys it's either the castle or the outhouse, nothing in between." Prevailing in family touch football games and sailing races at Hyannis Port, bringing home As and letters in sports from school—all were chances to shine in the family and prove themselves to their father. Far more demonstrative than his wife, it was Joe who embodied the Kennedy ethos, instilling in his children a certain esprit de corps, an "us against the world" posture that bonded them closely together as the family navigated a world still stacked against Catholics. Rose found her efforts to climb the social ranks in New York often thwarted due to her Catholicism; the Kennedy boys often had scuffles on school playgrounds after being spurned for the same reason. But being a Kennedy was what *really* mattered; nothing was more important than that. Distinction within the family, then, mattered even more.

While accruing wealth was critical to the social ascendancy of the Kennedy family, it was, for Joe, largely a means to an end. He once said he didn't "give a tinker's damn" about business and there wasn't "a member of the family interested" in it, either. Nor did the next generation of Kennedys have much understanding of money. As Jack's prep school roommate Lem Billings put it, "Listening to the Kennedy brothers talk about business was like hearing nuns talk about sex." Instead, the family's focus was on government and public affairs. "I can hardly remember a mealtime," recalled Bobby, "when the conversation was not dominated by what Franklin D. Roosevelt was doing or what was happening around the world. . . . Since public affairs had dominated so much of our actions and discussions, public life seemed really an extension of family life."

By the time the Kennedy family had grown into its full force of nine children in 1931, Joe's own public life had begun expanding in kind. Shortly after FDR took the presidency in 1933, Joe was tapped to head the fledgling Securities and Exchange Commission, a regulatory body to prevent illegal trading, put in place as part of Roosevelt's New Deal. There was some irony in his appointment. Joe had likely profited considerably through the same schemes he was now charged with blocking, but Roosevelt saw Kennedy as the right choice on the grounds that "it takes one to know one."

Joe went on to serve as chairman of the U.S. Maritime Commission in Washington before FDR gave him the nod as ambassador to Great Britain in 1937—bowlegs notwithstanding—advancing him toward his ultimate political aim, nothing less than to become the first Catholic president. But his dream died with his contention that Nazi leader Adolf Hitler should be appeased due to the invincibility of the German military, and that America should stay out of World War II. He resigned from his ambassadorship in late 1940, returning stateside to propagate his isolationist view, putting him at odds with Roosevelt. The Japanese attack on Pearl Harbor in 1941, hurling the United States into the war, sealed his fate. When he vied for a wartime role in the administration, his overture was summarily rebuffed by a bitter FDR. Joe's political ambitions were now foisted entirely on the next generation—especially Joe Jr., to whom he conveyed his dream of becoming president, but his expectations for rampant achievement in the family didn't stop with his oldest son.

Joe Jr. and Jack grew up locked in a perpetual competition,

even as children. In a bike race around their Brookline block, the two boys sped in separate directions with neither giving way as they crashed into each other near the finish line. Joe won the race intact; Jack went to the hospital, where his wounds received twenty-eight stitches. The incident was a metaphor: Throughout adolescence and early adulthood, Joe shined as the picture of promise and accomplishment while Jack often pulled up short, frequently hampered by injuries or ailments that kept him sidelined for long periods. As a high school girlfriend of Jack's recalled, "Joe just kind of overshadowed Jack in everything." Joe Jr.'s nickname, "Young Joe," implying the imprimatur of his father, said it all.

Serious and temperamental, Joe Jr. glided through prep school at Choate in Connecticut, winning the Harvard Trophy for excellence in "scholarship and sportsmanship," before going on to a distinguished tenure at Harvard University, where he pulled down As while excelling in sports—though a letter in football eluded him. Jack struggled in his wake, plagued with health issues. Bobby's quip "If a mosquito bit Jack Kennedy, the mosquito would die" wasn't far off the mark. Shortly after he was born, Jack combated a case of scarlet fever that nearly took his life. His prospects were grim enough that his busy father cut his working hours in half to be by his infant son's bedside, and to attend church every morning to pray for his recovery. Though Jack survived, he suffered from episodes of mysterious pain and inertia that baffled his doctors throughout his early childhood. A spate of illnesses followed, including mumps, measles, whooping cough, chicken pox, and bronchitis, all meticulously documented by Rose, who scribbled his frequent maladies on cards that she kept on file. They carried on into his later years, including a chronic back condition, worsened by injuries sustained in World War II, that often kept him in pain or hospitalized for long stretches. Lem Billings, who would become a lifelong friend, remarked that Jack "had few days when he wasn't in pain or sick in some way," yet he "seldom heard him complain."

Effusive charm, a gently subversive wit, and academic under-achievement marked Jack's high school years. Following his brother to Choate in Wallingford, Connecticut, he ranked in the middle of his class with "gentleman's Cs" that concealed a deeper intel-ligence. "His natural gift of an individual outlook and witty ex-pression are going to help him," the school's headmaster George St. John wrote to Jack's parents. "Jack is not as able academically as his high IQ might lead us to think." Leading a group of a dozen rebellious boys he called "the Muckers," proudly co-opting the label from the headmaster, who reserved it to brand Choate's ne'er-do-wells, Jack faced a serious threat of expulsion, requiring his father to meet with St. John and Jack about the situation. "Don't let me lose confidence in you again," Joe warned his son by letter after the meeting, "because it will be nearly impossible to restore it." By the same token, Joe begrudgingly admired his son's iconoclastic spirit and leadership of the group, traits that reflected the Kennedy ethos. When St. John left the room during their meeting to take a phone call, Joe whispered in Jack's ear that if he had named the group, Jack could "be sure it wouldn't have started with the letter *M*!"

After abandoning plans to attend the London School of Eco-nomics due to illness, Jack enrolled at Princeton, inauspiciously beginning college before dropping out due to a mysterious malady that doctors at first believed to be leukemia. At nineteen, after a long convalescence, he took the path of his father and older brother to Harvard, where, despite a slow start, he made the dean's list by the first semester of his junior year. At his father's urging, he took off the second semester to work at the U.S. Embassy in London and to tour Europe and Russia just before Germany's seizure of Poland, increasing the specter of war.

Jack believed war could be averted, but would later see its initial ravages firsthand when he was dispatched to Scotland to help the American victims from the sinking of the SS *Athenia*, the first British ship to be torpedoed by a German submarine. His experience in Europe led to the writing of his senior thesis, which was published as a book titled *Why England Slept*—borrowing from Winston Churchill's book *While England Slept*—examining Great Britain's unpreparedness during Nazi Germany's truculent rise throughout the 1930s. Critically commended, the book made Jack a bestselling author at age twenty-three, mainly due to the patronage of his father, who purchased thousands of copies to ensure its commercial success.

Despite having failed his physical examinations, Jack followed Joe Jr. into the Navy in October 1941 thanks to his father's intervention. As America plunged into the war after the Japanese attack on Pearl Harbor, both brothers went abroad with the intent of proving themselves. Joe earned his wings as a naval airman with the rank of ensign, and was assigned as a pilot in Europe; Jack was shipped off to the Pacific as a lieutenant to become commander of a small motor-torpedo boat, *PT-109*, charged with liberating the Solomon Islands from Japanese control.

In August 1943, Jack's boat was rammed by a Japanese warship, breaking it in half and killing two of his thirteen-member crew. Jack led his surviving crewmen to a small island several miles away, swimming for hours with the group, including one, severely burnt from the crash, whom he towed to shore by clenching the victim's life vest in his teeth. The castaways were rescued after befriending local islanders, one of whom journeyed by canoe to a U.S. base to deliver an SOS hidden in a coconut. By the end of the year, Jack, now a war hero, was back stateside being treated for back injuries sustained in the incident that would riddle him with pain for the balance of his life.

The recipient of a Navy and Marine Corps Medal for valor and a Purple Heart, Jack later called his bravery in the Pacific "involuntary," adding, "They sank my boat." In truth, he had come by his hero status honestly. While a naval inquiry concluded that Lieutenant Kennedy had showed poor seamanship that led to the ship sinking in the first place, the aftermath was the finest hour of his young and sometimes feckless life, manifesting his leadership and grit under the most extreme of circumstances.

Before the incident, Rose passed on to the family Jack's view that "it would be good for Joe [Jr.'s] political career" if he, Jack, "died for the grand old flag." The comment was revealing of Jack's sardonic humor, but there was some fatalism in it, too. Throughout his life, he had seen his older brother emerge from nearly any situation poised for future success, while he contended with life's thorns, often with his fragile health in question. If either of them was to die on the front lines of war, surely it would be him. But it didn't work out that way. After accepting a dangerous volunteer mission to fly a plane packed with ten tons of TNT to Germany in the summer of 1944, Joe Jr. died when the aircraft exploded mysteriously somewhere over Britain. His body was never found.

It marked a turning point in the Kennedy family. Devastated by the loss of his oldest son and protégé, Joe Sr. locked himself away in his bedroom for days, listening to music and barely eating. "All my plans were tied up with Young Joe," he confided to a friend. "That has gone to smash." In fact, the plans were now heaped on the shoulders of Jack. Now the eldest of the Kennedy children, it was he who would carry forward his father's hope for the next generation. Upon hearing the news of his older brother's fate while lying in recovery for his back injuries at the Chelsea Naval Hospital, Jack knew his own had changed. "The burden now falls to me," he said mournfully.

All of it seemed to be part of a cycle. Pathos bled through the pages of the Kennedy family saga as an endemic part of its destiny, tragedy mingling with triumph as hallmarks throughout its exaggerated vicissitudes. In 1941, Rosemary, who suffered from a mild intellectual disability that compromised her intellectual development and social maturity, underwent a frontal lobotomy that Joe and Rose hoped would alleviate her condition. Instead, the experimental procedure went awry, reducing her to a perpetual child-like state. She was institutionalized in Wisconsin, removing her from the family's orbit for the remainder of her life and irrevocably changing the dynamic in the Kennedy household.

The Kennedys' second daughter, Kathleen, "Kick" as she was known, lost her English husband in the war when he was killed by sniper fire in Belgium. The couple, who met while Kick was in London working for the Red Cross, had been married for just four months. Several years afterward, in the spring of 1948, Kick would lose her own life in a plane crash over France as she flew with a new romantic interest from London to a holiday in the French Riviera, just before they were to meet her father in Paris.

The cycle reflected the patterns of Jack Kennedy's own life, explaining his outlook and behavior. He had borne witness to life's fragility, its tenuousness, and had wrestled with existential crises himself. "There is always an inequity in life," he observed at a press conference in March 1962. "Some men are killed in a war and some are wounded, and some men never leave the country. . . . Life is unfair. Some people are sick and others are well."

Cool and detached, he was pragmatic about fate's mercurial whims; his attitude spoke to the restless, manic pace in which he would go through life—the vitality he exuded, his insatiable intellectual curiosity and quest for adventure and all things new, his sometimes-touching compassion for others and often inexplicable recklessness. *It could all go at any time*, his life's experience whispered in his ear. *Get the most out of it. Don't waste a moment.* "The point is," he once told his friend George Smathers, "you've got to live every day like it's your last day on earth. That's what I'm doing."

RISING STAR

It was only a matter of time before Jack Kennedy ran for political office, an inevitability he likened to "being drafted." As he put it, "My father wanted his oldest son in politics. 'Wanted' isn't the right word. He *demanded* it." Now the oldest son, Jack didn't disappoint. After working briefly as a newspaper reporter upon being discharged from the Navy in March 1945, he exploited his war hero status and his father's money and influence in the Bay State and vigorously pursued a seat in Congress representing the Eleventh District in Massachusetts.

But while it suited his father's ambitions for him, it also fit his. Jack Kennedy didn't see himself going into business or law, "dealing with some dead man's estate . . . or fighting a divorce case." Neither did he see Wall Street as his path; money didn't much interest him. Rather, just as political conversations had dominated his parents' dinner table, it was politics that stirred his imagination. He knew then that the "satisfactions" in politics would be "far greater" than in pursuing something else. He wasn't alone. The postwar period was a time when young people who wanted to make a difference to their country and the world naturally gravitated to the political arena. They had seen what they could do in fighting a world war, saving the world from tyranny, and viewed public service as the best way to make a sustained contribution to America's betterment. Young, ambitious men like Richard Nixon and Gerald Ford, who were part of what would become known as "the Greatest Generation," returned home from the war and threw their hats into the ring almost instinctively.

While the young Jack Kennedy wasn't especially good on the stump—he recalled his father remarking that he was "hopeless"—he was backed enthusiastically by his parents and siblings, who eagerly made his campaign a family affair, and by a team of old hands hired by his father who used every trick in the book to ensure his ultimate win. Congressman Kennedy went on to serve three undistinguished terms in the House of Representatives before launching a bid for the Senate in 1952, winning the seat from his challenger, the ostensibly unbeatable incumbent, Henry Cabot Lodge, Jr., by three percentage points. By Kennedy's own account, he had simply "worked harder." Senator Kennedy's tenure in Congress's upper chamber was no more remarkable than it had been in the lower chamber, adding up to little in the way of legislative achievement. But it didn't much matter; his sights were fixed on a bigger prize.

In 1956, his popularity within the party was enough to make him a close contender to round out the Democratic ticket as its vice presidential nominee. At the party convention in Chicago, Kennedy's name went all the way to the second ballot, where he briefly led the vote tally among convention delegates in a dramatic back-and-forth between contenders before Tennessee senator Estes Kefauver pulled ahead as the top choice, becoming Adlai Stevenson's running mate. Kennedy did much better than he expected, and, believing Kefauver "deserved to win," was not "desolate" afterward. "We did our best," he told his father in a phone call. "I had fun and didn't make a fool of myself." Far from that, he had shined elegantly in the national spotlight, proving that he could be a viable national candidate despite his Catholicism.

By then, the dashing senator, earlier named by the *Saturday Evening Post* as "the most eligible bachelor" in America, had wed the twenty-four-year-old Jacqueline Lee Bouvier in a Newport, Rhode Island, ceremony that became the 1953 social event of the season. In "Jackie"—a nickname foisted on her by the Kennedy clan as a means of purging pretension and compelling informality—Jack had found his social and intellectual match. The pair were introduced by friends Charlie and Martha Bartlett at a 1951 dinner party when Jackie worked for the *Washington Times-Herald* as the "inquiring camera girl." She proved to be a graceful complement to Jack, and a cool, cerebral contrast to the raucous, playful Kennedy sisters and Bobby's wife, Ethel.

"There was no question in my mind, finally, that he was more interested in Jackie than he had been in any other girl," Lem Billings said, adding, "However, he was always interested in girls, so I wasn't actually that sure." As it turned out, he was still interested in girls. While the union put an end to Kennedy's bachelorhood, it didn't abate his womanizing, which would continue throughout the marriage, despite the image that he, like his father, cast as a loyal husband and family man.

Several years into his marriage, Jack nearly lost his life after spinal surgery to relieve his back pain. During his long convalescence, Jackie encouraged him to write and helped to research a book exploring the political courage exhibited by five of Jack's illustrious predecessors in the U.S. Senate. *Profiles in Courage,* written with hefty contributions by Kennedy's Senate aide and chief speechwriter Ted Sorensen, who would receive bonuses through Joe Kennedy's lawyers adding up to a staggering $106,000, was published in late 1956.

"I would rather win a Pulitzer than be president," Jack had told a Pulitzer Prize–winning historian a few years earlier. Though rumors that the book had been ghostwritten swirled in the literary and political worlds, *Profiles in Courage,* with strong lobbying by Kennedy family friend and *New York Times* Washington bureau chief Arthur Krock, would go on to win the Pulitzer Prize for biography in 1957. The notoriety further boosted Jack's profile for his eventual run for the presidency. The same year, the couple had their first child, Caroline. Their second, John Jr., arrived three years later, in 1960, as the Kennedy family prepared for their move to the White House.

In the 1958 midterms, Kennedy breezed his way to reelection in Massachusetts, pulling 73 percent of the vote and exemplifying what *Time* called "the strong Democratic winds" that the magazine speculated "might blow at gale force in 1960." Kennedy was counting on as much, announcing his candidacy for the Democratic presidential nomination against such formidable rivals as Lyndon Johnson, Hubert Humphrey, and Stuart Symington. Vying for the presidency was a natural instinct for Kennedy. For an ambitious politician there was no greater challenge or reward. In early 1960, before embarking on the primary campaign trail, he likened the quest for the White House to that of NFL quarterback Johnny Unitas. "He might find it interesting to play [on] a sandlot team in front of four people," he said, "but he's playing for the [Baltimore] Colts, the best team in the United States, for the world championship." In achieving the presidency, Kennedy would be playing on the biggest stage for the highest stakes.

Through the course of seven hard-fought primaries, the Kennedy machine, which had brought Jack five straight election wins in Massachusetts, kicked into overdrive. The flush Kennedy war chest offered a distinct advantage. Money was poured into the campaign, with Joe declaring at an early strategy session, "We're going to get this thing if it takes every dime I've got." (In response, Bobby quipped, "Wait a minute now. There are others in the family.") Anticipating a run for the White House, Jack drolly acknowledged his father's deep pockets when he spoke at Washington's annual Gridiron Club dinner in 1958. Pulling an imaginary telegram from his father out of his suit pocket, he read, "Dear Jack, don't buy a single vote more than is necessary—I'll be damned if I'm going to pay for a landslide."

But Jack proved an effective campaigner, overcoming the challenges that stood in his way, including his relative youth and his Catholicism. After edging out Humphrey in Wisconsin, which Humphrey was expected to carry as the midwestern son of its neighboring state Minnesota, Kennedy went on to win 61 percent of the vote in poor and heavily Protestant West Virginia. The latter victory was a turning point. Humphrey, who had helped to fund his own campaign effort by tapping into his nest egg for his daughter's impending wedding, pulled from the race, lamenting that he felt like "an independent retailer competing with a chain."

Kennedy went into the Democratic National Convention in Los Angeles in early July 1960 as the easy favorite to capture the nomination, but it was not a done deal. The old guard stood opposed to him as the party's standard-bearer. Eleanor Roosevelt supported a draft of Adlai Stevenson, the party's nominee in the past two election cycles, hoping that the third time would be a charm for the former Illinois governor, while Harry Truman publicly urged Kennedy to beg off due to his lack of maturity and experience. Kennedy deftly responded to Truman's objections with a reasoned argument that if his fourteen years in elected office were "insufficient" to become president, all of the Democratic presidents of the twentieth century to that point—Woodrow Wilson, FDR, even Truman himself—"should have been ruled out" on the same basis.

Despite potential roadblocks, Kennedy fended off a challenge from his nearest rival, Lyndon Johnson, the commanding Senate majority leader from Texas, securing the nomination on the first ballot before nodding to the South by asking Johnson to round out the ticket as his running mate. As he accepted his party's bid before a rapt audience of delegates and revelers, Kennedy made clear the importance of the upcoming election as a New Frontier beckoned. "The New Frontier . . . is not a set of promises—it is a set of challenges," he told them.

> It sums up not what I intend to offer the American people, but what I intend to ask of them. . . . Can a nation organized and governed such as ours endure? That is the real question. . . . Are we up to the task—are we equal to the challenge? . . . That is the question of the New Frontier . . . a choice . . . between the public interest and private comfort—between national greatness and national decline.

Later the same month in Chicago, the GOP crowned the forty-seven-year-old sitting vice president, Richard Nixon, as its presidential designee and as his running mate Henry Cabot Lodge, Jr., Eisenhower's ambassador to the United Nations, whom Kennedy had defeated in their race for the Senate eight years earlier. Throughout the summer, Kennedy and Nixon ran neck and neck in the polls.

In the fall, a series of four televised presidential debates—the first ever—gave Kennedy an edge, given his graceful image and the growing significance of television as a political forum. In the first debate, which aired on September 26 to an audience of some seventy million—nearly 40 percent of the American population—Nixon, gaunt and underweight from a hospital stay for knee surgery, refused makeup to lighten up his five o'clock shadow. When the klieg lights went on, the vice president looked sinister and pasty-faced, his countenance blending into his light gray suit. Kennedy, dressed in a dark suit and suntanned from a recent California campaign swing, appeared cool and confident. While he threw no knockout blow, he was the clear victor. After the debate, he saw a 3 percent boost in the polls, pulling ahead of Nixon for the first time. (The popular notion that Kennedy won the debate among television watchers while Nixon prevailed among radio listeners is mythology with no statistical basis for truth.)

Earlier the same month, Kennedy took on the issue of his Catholicism squarely in a speech to three hundred mostly Republican Protestant ministers in Houston. "I am not the Catholic candidate for president, I am the Democratic Party's candidate for president who happens also to be a Catholic," he explained. "If this election is decided on the basis that forty million Americans lost their chance of being president on the day they were baptized, then it is the whole nation that will be the loser in the eyes of Catholics and non-Catholics around the world, in the eyes of history, and in the eyes of our own people."

In November, Kennedy won the White House with the smallest margin of the twentieth century. Though he had prevailed in spite of his religion, his Catholicism likely contributed to the thinness of his victory. Fifty-four percent of Protestant voters cast their ballots for Nixon—with many in the South and Midwest making religion the deciding factor—as Kennedy squeaked by as the only candidate to that point to win a presidential election without a majority of Protestant voters.

Even then, the election result was in question, coming amid widely reported voter fraud in Illinois and Texas. In one precinct in Chicago's Cook County, 121 votes were counted after only 43 people voted, and in Texas a county of 4,895 registered voters cast 6,138 ballots. "We won but they stole it from us," Nixon privately told a friend afterward. The Republican establishment balked at the irregularities. Eisenhower even offered to help Nixon raise funds for a recount that would have taken months under the guise that the federal government would not "shirk from its duty" to protect the integrity of the electoral system. But in the end, Nixon accepted the result in the interest of governmental stability and continuity, especially with the Soviets watching for weakness and vulnerability.

Exhaustion overcame Kennedy after the election. His mind, normally sharp and quick, was cloudy. The natural enervation after a national political campaign was exacerbated by his ongoing bout with Addison's disease, a disorder of the adrenal glands, often fatal, resulting in low production of cortisol and aldosterone. Talk that Kennedy was afflicted with the malady had been an undercurrent throughout the campaign, nipping at his heels, as he and his team contrived to keep it under wraps. When his press secretary, Pierre Salinger, asked Kennedy how he should address rumors that Kennedy was taking cortisone shots, Kennedy told him to deny them—even as he was giving himself daily injections in the thigh. "I never had Addison's disease; my health is excellent," he insisted when a reporter questioned him about the persistent rumors.

Naturally upbeat and ebullient, Kennedy was worn down with fatigue as he dealt with staffing decisions for his administration.

"Jesus Christ, this one wants this, the other one wants that," he groused to his father in Palm Beach two weeks after the election. "Goddamn it, you can't satisfy any of these people. I don't know what I'm going to do about it." Less than sympathetic, Joe told him that if he didn't want the job he didn't have to take it, reminding him that "they're still counting votes in Cook County."

By mid-December, rested, he had grown comfortable with the notion of taking the nation's helm. "Sure, it's a big job. But I don't know anybody who can do it better than I can," he mused in a reflective moment. "I'm going to be in it for four years. . . . It isn't going to be so bad. You've got time to think. You don't have all those people bothering you that you had in the Senate—besides, the pay is pretty good."

In achieving the presidency, Jack Kennedy had exceeded his father's considerable attainments, just as the old man had done with his own father. Within Kennedy circles, Joe Kennedy was known as "the Ambassador," marking his crowning public accomplishment; Jack Kennedy would be known as "the President." While he was proud of his son, Joe claimed he didn't "feel any different." But the dynamic between the two had changed. Joe, the heavy-handed patriarch, would soon defer to Jack, over time relegating himself to the background, clinging to the shadows and muting any instincts he may have had to bark orders or offer advice. Jack had started to assert himself during his presidential campaign. When Joe called a meeting with the campaign steering committee in October to devise a plan for Jack to pull ahead as he and Nixon were deadlocked in the polls, Jack canceled it. And after Joe repeatedly insisted that inflation should become the predominant issue during a scheduled meeting on strategy, Jack snapped, "You worry about [campaign] financing and I'll worry about the issues."

By the same token, Jack knew how much it meant to his father to see him compete for the country's highest office—and knew he wouldn't be there without him. When friends expressed concern that Joe's active involvement in the campaign might be a liability, Jack put their fears at bay. "He's having the time of his life going around and helping me," he would tell them. "Do you think I can do anything about it—or that I would want to?"

In mid-January, just before Jack began his presidential tenure, Joe considered what it all meant in his surprisingly modest, green-carpeted suite at the Carlyle hotel in New York. "Jack doesn't belong anymore to just a family, he belongs to the country. That's probably the saddest thing about all this," he told *Time*'s Hugh Sidey wistfully. But the Kennedy patriarch saw the urgency in his second son's charge for the New Frontier. "Jack's right," he said, "We have to get moving again. Jack understands this. If we lose the brass ring this time, we are never going to get another chance at it."

Then he added, perhaps just as wistfully, "Jack is the fellow who will give his life to his country."

"THE CENTER OF THE ACTION"

I suppose anybody in politics would like to be President," John Kennedy had said in 1958. "That is the center of the action, the mainspring, the wellspring of the American system." The center of the action: *that* is where Kennedy wanted to be. On the morning of Saturday, January 21, 1961, that's where he found himself.

At ten a.m., the president was in the Oval Office, freshly painted but still barren from the previous day's move, meeting with his first official guest: the thirty-third president. Harry Truman had been as "blue as indigo" when Kennedy had wrangled their party's nomination, grieving that Kennedy and his Republican challenger, Nixon, were "the worst of two evils," while conceding that "the immature Kennedy" was "the best of the two." But, eventually, as he got to know Kennedy during a campaign visit the candidate made to the Truman Library in Independence, Missouri, Truman took a shine to him. Shortly thereafter, he climbed on board the JFK bandwagon, delivering thirteen speeches for him in nine states. Kennedy rewarded Truman with the Oval Office visit, the first time Truman had stepped foot in the White House since he had given it over to Eisenhower eight years earlier. The proximity to the power he'd once held left Truman rife with emotion. He left the White House with tears in his eyes, telling an aide, "Isn't it nice that [Kennedy] would want to bother with an old farmer like me on his first day?"

While the office still had the same ambience of power as when Truman occupied it, JFK's White House organization would bear little resemblance to Truman's—or Eisenhower's, for that matter. For Kennedy, being at the center of power meant just that: *he* was at the center, and he organized his administration accordingly. In the Kennedy White House, the president was Rome—all roads led to him. Rejecting the traditional pyramid structures of his immediate predecessors, he declined to appoint a chief of staff, shunned formality and hierarchy, and, according to Ted Sorensen, paid "little attention to organization charts and chains of command which diluted and distributed his authority." When he wanted to talk to a staff member, he sought him out himself, restlessly poking into offices unannounced as he prowled the West Wing, sending a ripple of anticipation through the building.

What Kennedy wanted above all was action, the ability to get things done with a minimum of bureaucracy and organizational inefficiency. If it created a chaotic atmosphere, with staff members often off-balance or pitted against one another, that's precisely what Kennedy wanted. His special assistant, former Harvard professor Arthur Schlesinger, Jr., who asserted that Kennedy wanted to be a "strong president" in the manner of FDR, called it "a fluid presidency."

The fluidity meant that Kennedy steered clear of large meetings, observing, by his press secretary Pierre Salinger's account, that "their productivity was in inverse proportion to the number of participants." Instead, he would opt for one-on-one briefings, where he could immerse himself in the details of an issue and probe members of his administration with questions, or even more so, by devouring memos that staff members began to produce with as much ferocity as he was likely to consume them. One adviser recalled Kennedy poring through a twenty-six-page memo on economics in ten minutes—he read at a manic pace of 1,200 words a minute—then asking "25 questions about it, intelligent questions." To keep up with Kennedy, aides could expect working days of ten to fourteen hours. As one put it, "The tempo of this administration is fantastic. The President is a fellow who has a foot-long needle in you all the time."

When it came to staffing his administration, Kennedy turned naturally to family. In politics, loyalty is paramount, and in the Kennedy family it flowed naturally through the gene pool. His campaign pledge to "not appoint any relative" to his administration was conveniently put aside to make room in the ranks for Bobby, who had proven himself to be indispensable as campaign manager and protector in chief throughout his brother's political rise, fiercely guarding his interests and earning perhaps the supreme compliment from Joe Sr., who bragged that he was "just as tough as a boot heel."

Any initial concerns Jack had over charges of nepotism were overcome a few weeks after the election. As his friend Abe Ribicoff, the senator from Connecticut who would go on to become Kennedy's secretary of health, education, and welfare, pointed out to him, "I have now watched you Kennedy brothers for five solid years, and I notice every time there's a crisis, you automatically turn to Bobby. You're out of the same womb. There's an empathy. You understand one another. You're not going to be President without using Bobby all the time." The question was in what capacity.

A number of positions had been floated, including subcabinet posts and attorney general, which had been offered to Ribicoff and Adlai Stevenson after Bobby initially declined. But the former options, with the president's brother and closest adviser subordinated by a cabinet official, seemed impractical. The attorney generalship provided a better option; Bobby could run his own organization while being in a position to counsel his brother. At age thirty-five, he would be the youngest attorney general since 1814. Joe Sr., who wanted to give Bobby the same chance for political growth that Jack had been given, left little doubt on where he stood on the matter. "I want Bobby there [as attorney general]. It's the only thing I'm asking for and I want it," the old man demanded.

Initially, Bobby wasn't sold on the idea of riding his brother's coattails into the White House, harboring the notion of diverging onto his own path by running for governor of Massachusetts. Like Jack, he was also concerned about the political fallout of him joining the administration, warning his brother that the newspapers would "kick our balls off." By mid-December, he had overcome his own reservations, writing to columnist Drew Pearson, "I made up my mind today and Jack and I take the plunge tomorrow." At a breakfast with Bobby in his Georgetown townhouse the following morning, Jack, who may have been preaching to the converted, reinforced the need for Bobby to join his administration. "I need someone I can completely . . . rely on, someone who's going to tell me what the best judgment is, my best interest," he said. "There's not another member of the cabinet I can trust that way." Shortly afterward, they made it official with an announcement before reporters gathered outside Jack's front door, but not before the president-elect instructed his younger brother to comb his "damn hair" and refrain from smiling lest the press think he was happy about the appointment. Then, alluding to Bobby's earlier warning, he said, "So that's it, General, grab your balls and let's go."

The backlash in the media was inevitable, including from *Newsweek,* which called the appointment "a travesty of justice." But it quieted relatively quickly. By the time he took office a month later, Jack brushed off the controversy with characteristic wit. "I don't know why people are so mad at me for making Bobby Attorney General," he joked to friends the night of his inauguration, much to Bobby's ire. "I see nothing wrong with giving Robert experience as Attorney General before he goes out to practice law."

Kennedy's brother-in-law Sargent Shriver, the forty-six-year-old husband of his sister Eunice, was tasked with helping to fill the balance of the cabinet. "Shriver knew the kind of man Kennedy wanted," said Harris Wofford, who assisted him in the task. "More accurately, since Kennedy worked well with and respected a wide range of types, Shriver knew the kind *not* wanted: the too ideological, too earnest, too emotional, and too talkative—and the dull."

Dean Rusk, the president of the Rockefeller Foundation and former assistant secretary of state for Far Eastern affairs in the Truman administration, was chosen to be secretary of state. As an overture to the business community and a gesture of bipartisanship, Kennedy reached across the aisle to tap conservative investment banker Douglas Dillon, a Republican, as his treasury secretary. A veteran of the Eisenhower administration, Dillon had served in several posts, including undersecretary of state.

Robert McNamara was chosen as secretary of defense after Kennedy read a *Time* magazine cover story on the forty-four-year-old automotive executive, who just weeks earlier had been named the first outside the Ford family to become the president of the Ford Motor Company. Far from soliciting the job, McNamara told Kennedy the notion of making him the secretary of defense was "absurd"—he could barely tell a nuclear warhead from a station wagon, he confessed later—pleading that he was "unqualified."

Kennedy reassured him. "Look, Bob," he said, "I don't think there's any school for presidents, either." While Kennedy would show little interest in his cabinet secretaries, calling cabinet meetings a "waste of time," McNamara, whom Kennedy considered the smartest man he had ever met, would be an exception, becoming his main adviser on foreign policy along with his national security adviser, McGeorge Bundy, the forty-one-year-old former dean of faculty at Harvard, and Bundy's deputy, renowned MIT economist Walt Rostow.

When it came to his White House aides, Kennedy surrounded himself with the next best thing to family: proven loyalists and longtime friends. Rostow observed that the team Kennedy "wove together represented almost geological layers in Kennedy's experience—old friends from the pre-war days, college friends, the PT boat friends, and these people all respected one another." Youth was another common denominator. Almost all of the staffers were in their mid- to late thirties, representing, as the *New York Times*'s James Reston wrote, "an odd mixture of idealism and cynicism, of liberals and conservatives, of professors and politicians, of Harvard grafted on to the Boston Irish."

Ted Sorensen, tagged by the press as JFK's "intellectual alter ego," would continue to operate as Kennedy's principal aide and speechwriter, just as he had in the Senate. Former California newspaper reporter Pierre Salinger, Kennedy's press secretary throughout the campaign, remained in the post in the White House. Pulitzer Prize–winning presidential historian and Harvard professor Arthur Schlesinger, Jr., filled an ill-defined role as special assistant. When aides asked Kennedy if he was bringing him in to write the administration's official history, Kennedy said he would write it himself, but added, "Arthur will probably write his own and it will be better for us if he's in the White House, seeing what goes on, instead of reading about it in the *New York Times* and *Time* magazine." Schlesinger would serve as a liaison to Democratic Party liberals, many wary of Kennedy, while providing an ongoing gauge for presidential greatness as Kennedy aimed at bending the currents of history like Andrew Jackson and FDR, whom Schlesinger had explored exhaustively in his work.

The Boston Irish contingent, the "Irish Mafia" as they were known by the media, included Kenny O'Donnell, Larry O'Brien, and Dave Powers, friends and colleagues collected during different phases of Kennedy's life, all imbued with the shared Irish Catholic experience—a "persecution thing," Jackie Kennedy called it—that bound them together. O'Donnell, who had initially come into the Kennedy circle as Bobby's Harvard roommate, became the president's no-nonsense appointment secretary, serving as Jack's gatekeeper, adviser, and sounding board. O'Brien, a staffer for Kennedy in Congress, was his congressional liaison, charged with shepherding New Frontier legislation through the Eighty-Seventh Congress, which boasted Democratic majorities in both houses. Powers, an elder in the ranks at age forty-eight, had aided Kennedy as a political jack-of-all-trades since Kennedy's first congressional campaign in 1946. While his official duty was as O'Donnell's deputy, he served the unofficial role of presidential companion; one White House staffer observed that Kennedy was always more "at ease" when Powers was by his side. The same was true for Lem Billings, Kennedy's high school roommate at Choate and closest friend. While the New York advertising executive had no official role in the administration, he was with Kennedy on most weekends and a fixture in the White House, as ubiquitous, according to one staffer, as "a handy old piece of furniture."

If Kennedy emulated Franklin Roosevelt in structuring his White House, it was Roosevelt's prodigious administration that provided a daunting yardstick for his opening weeks in office. FDR had succeeded the laissez-faire Herbert Hoover nearly three decades earlier as the Great Depression swept America, enacting in his benchmark "first hundred days" a flurry of laws aimed at mitigating the economic ravages, all rubber-stamped by a pliant Congress. Kennedy brought the same kind of energy and idealism to the White House, a feeling that a new breeze was blowing through Washington, and that the country, complying with Kennedy's campaign pledge, was "on the move again." In his book *A Thousand Days*, Arthur Schlesinger described the "exhilaration" that accompanied the start of the administration. "The Presidency itself would show how national vitality could in fact be released," he wrote, "not in an existential orgasm but in the halting progression of ideas and actions which make up the fabric of history."

But there wasn't much in the way of legislative initiative to show for it. Despite the fourteen years he had spent beneath the Capitol dome, Kennedy would have little time for his former colleagues in the House and Senate, rarely reaching out to them directly, and, as in his days in Congress, showing only a modicum of interest in legislative sausage making. Nor were there any other visible signs that significant movement was afoot either domestically or on the world stage. In an April issue of the *New Republic*, McGeorge Bundy acknowledged as much. "At this point we are like the Harlem Globetrotters," he said, "passing forward, behind, sideways and underneath. But nobody has made a basket yet."

Still, it didn't seem to matter much. Regardless of the fact that Kennedy and his team hadn't put any points on the board, the image of the young, vigorous president and his dedicated band of acolytes was enough for Americans to *believe* that the country was moving in a positive direction. Image was Kennedy's currency, and he radiated it in spades.

Newsweek wrote that "the new, and untried President—who had been elected by only 49.7 percent of the electorate—now has a great part of the American people behind him." By mid-February, his approval rating topped 72 percent in a Gallup Poll, surpassing those that FDR and Eisenhower had seen in their own first weeks, while Harris had him at a 92 percent favorability rating.

His in-house pollster pointed to the public's perception that he could get things done as his greatest strength. One of the few things he had accomplished in those early days was the creation of the Peace Corps by executive order on March 1, establishing a volunteer force of young people to wage peace and promote advancement in the developing world, reinforcing the youthful idealism and missionary zeal he had conveyed in his inauguration speech.

In addition to the lasting glow of the inauguration, the favorable numbers could be explained, at least in part, by television. Kennedy owed his presidency largely to the medium, and his team ventured that it could continue to be an asset after he took office. His first press conference was made into a live television event, with the venue changing from the cramped Indian Treaty Room of the Old Executive Office Building next to the White House to the spacious new State Department Auditorium. Just five days after Kennedy took office, an estimated sixty-five million viewers tuned in to watch the president make a few brief announcements—a decision to postpone a summit with the Soviets on nuclear test bans until March; an increase in food aid to the famine-stricken population of Congo—before taking thirty-two minutes of questions from the White House press corps. It was hardly programming that would have made for riveting TV for the rhetorically challenged Ike, but it worked for Kennedy, expanding his visibility and showcasing his easy confidence, quick mind, and disarming wit as he beguiled the press and the public concurrently. (In a subsequent press conference, when sternly asked by a female reporter, "What have you done for the women according to the promises of the [party's] platform?" he self-deprecatingly responded, "Well, I'm sure we haven't done enough . . . and I'm glad you reminded me of it.")

Paradoxically, the televised press conferences were also a means of *circumventing* the press, just as FDR had done with radio and Donald Trump would later do on Twitter, allowing Kennedy to take his ideas and messages directly to the people without them being distilled or adulterated by news outlets. As he said half-jokingly to his friend Ben Bradlee of *Newsweek*, "When we don't have to go through you bastards, we can really get our story out to the American people." All told, Kennedy would hold a total of sixty-four press conferences, drawing an average of eighteen million viewers, with 90 percent of Americans watching at least one of the first three, according to a 1961 poll. It spoke to Kennedy's outsize popularity that he also used TV in the first weeks of the administration to impart a special message to the American people, politely asking them to refrain from sending congratulatory letters and telegrams that were overwhelming the White House staff.

Jackie and the children added to the allure. The nation was captivated by the young family in the White House—the first with small children since Theodore Roosevelt, the nation's youngest president at age forty-two, occupied the mansion with his wife and six children at the turn of the twentieth century. Like TR, the

Kennedys, in newspaper parlance, made "good copy," exuding style and glamour that the nation had never quite seen before from a first family. Photos of them were even better. Jackie, as dazzling as her husband, became a radiant though reluctant celebrity as a fashion icon and the country's first mother, tending to her newborn son and three-year-old daughter. The unexpected glimpse of her in equestrian garb in the first days of the administration was enough to spur palpitations throughout the press corps. "You won't be able to go to the men's room for fear of being scooped," one of them lamented.

The addition of Bobby to the administration added to the Kennedy mystique, with Hickory Hill, the six-acre, thirteen-bedroom McLean, Virginia, estate inhabited by Bobby and Ethel and their rambunctious household of seven children and counting (eventually eleven in all) becoming a White House outpost and an extension of the vibrant family brand. So did other members of the family, who had become used to media glare throughout their lives as a matter of course. While Joe stayed consciously out of the limelight, the other members of the family made themselves readily available, much to the delight of the media outlets. The twenty-nine-year-old Ted had political ambitions of his own, angling to fill his brother's Senate seat in 1962, while the Kennedy women, in keeping with the mid-century zeitgeist and family expectations, filled supporting roles. Eunice was the thirty-nine-year-old wife of Sargent Shriver, who would become the inaugural director of Kennedy's Peace Corps. Patricia, thirty-six, fused the worlds of Washington power and Hollywood glamour as the sister of the president and the wife of British actor Peter Lawford, who ran with Frank Sinatra's "Rat Pack," and Jean, thirty-two, the youngest of the Kennedy daughters, was the wife of Stephen Smith, who served as a family consigliere, acting as a political adviser and managing the family fortune.

Possibility and promise bloomed unbridled in those early days of the administration, as the president eased into his new role. Charlie Bartlett, the Pulitzer Prize–winning reporter for the *Chattanooga Times* who had introduced him to Jackie, recalled the "excitement" of a White House dinner he and his wife, Martha, had with the first couple just three days after the inauguration. "I remember [Kennedy] in a mood that night that I don't think I'll ever forget," Bartlett said. "He was just burning with the things he could do." As he had with other early guests, Kennedy eagerly toured them through the mansion, peering into its majestic rooms and marveling along with them at the wonder of it all. When he showed them the Lincoln Bedroom, where he was staying while the presidential bedroom down the hall was being redecorated, Bartlett asked if he had any "strange dreams" the first night he had slept in the sixteenth president's imposing bed. "No," Kennedy replied. "I just jumped in and hung on."

It would prove a useful skill as storm clouds gathered. The torch had been passed, but the fire was to come.

II

THE FIRE

JFK in the Oval Office, 1961

Jacques Lowe, Jacques Lowe Photographic Archive, Briscoe Center for
American History, University of Texas at Austin

"HOW COULD WE HAVE BEEN SO STUPID?"

On one of his first days as president, John Kennedy met a group of diplomats in the Oval Office to bestow the Medal of Freedom on outgoing NATO secretary-general Paul-Henri Spaak of Belgium. It was staged as a quick meet and greet with Kennedy, who would read a brief statement then take leave of the group to get on to more pressing matters. Always in a hurry and often impatient, Kennedy declined to rehearse the brief ceremony. Winging it, he concluded the meeting with a flurry of handshakes and retreated from the office through one of its three interior doors. Then, not knowing exactly where he was, he opened another door and slipped inside. It was a bathroom. The president remained there in quiet solitude until the group eventually left his office. If Kennedy's impetuousness and relative inexperience in his new job had resulted in private embarrassment of no great consequence, he would find in the weeks ahead that it would take a far greater toll—and his humiliation would be quite public.

At eight a.m. on the morning of Wednesday, April 12, 1961, George Thomas, the Black valet who had worked for Kennedy since 1947, gently rapped on the president's bedroom door. "I'm awake," Kennedy replied. A few minutes later, Pierre Salinger called with a bulletin from the Associated Press that began, "The Soviet Union announced today that it had won the race to put a man into space."

Earlier in the day, at 6:07 a.m. local time in southern Kazakhstan, the Vostok 1 rocket was launched into orbit manned by Yuri Gagarin, who circumnavigated the globe before returning back to earth intact. With the reports came exacerbated cold war fears that the Soviets had irrevocably advanced in a quest to dominate the next frontier, first by launching Sputnik in 1957, then by sending two dogs into space in 1960, and now by the orbit of a cosmonaut.

Later in the morning, Kennedy huddled with his vice president in the Oval Office to discuss the matter. Lyndon Johnson had been something of a conundrum for Kennedy. What to do with the hyper-ambitious, bigger-than-life LBJ, whom many in the Kennedy camp—Bobby Kennedy especially—regarded warily? Johnson had been offered the number two spot on the ticket with the expectation that he would spurn it out of pride: Why would the all-powerful Senate majority leader agree to be the number two to his former rival, a Senate backbencher? But to the surprise of many, Johnson accepted, helping to swing the 1960 election by adding southern balance to the ticket. Kennedy knew that Johnson could be a handful, causing initial unease until he resolved to "keep him busy" by tapping him to head the National Aeronautics and Space Council. It was a natural fit for Johnson, who had been a strong advocate for the creation of NASA after the Sputnik launch—"What American wants to go to bed by the light of a communist moon?" he demanded later—and possessed an uncanny knack for getting even the most onerous things done, a skill he would need in the task at hand. Kennedy charged him with determining if and how the U.S. could pull ahead of the Soviets in space exploration.

Central to the exercise was addressing this question: "Do we have a chance of beating the Soviets by . . . a trip around the moon, or by a rocket to the moon, or by a rocket to the moon and back with a man?" Kennedy would soon have his answer.

That afternoon, Kennedy addressed Gagarin's flight in a press conference, acknowledging that it was an "impressive scientific accomplishment," and indicating that he had already sent a congratulatory telegram to Nikita Khrushchev. Then he took questions on a matter closer to home, just ninety miles off the coast of Florida. "Has a decision been reached on how far this country would be willing to go in helping an anti-Castro uprising or invasion in Cuba?" a reporter asked.

"First, I want to say that there will not be, under any conditions, an intervention in Cuba by United States armed forces," Kennedy responded. "This government will do everything it possibly can, and I think it can meet its responsibilities, to make sure there are no Americans involved in any action inside Cuba. . . . The basic issue in Cuba is not one between the United States and Cuba. It is between the Cubans themselves."

In fact, as Kennedy had discovered during the transition, the CIA had been at work preparing a top-secret plan for an invasion of Cuba since the previous fall. The "Cuban Brigade," which would swell to over 1,400 men, was being trained by U.S. forces in the jungles of Guatemala. The plan was to have anti-Castro Cuban exiles storm the island through the Bay of Pigs, where they would be aided by U.S. air support. But its success would rely on attracting other anti-Castro locals on the Cuban mainland, those who would eagerly enlist in an insurrection to drive Castro from power once the invasion was under way. The CIA estimated that roughly a quarter of Cuba's population of just over seven million would support the overthrow of Castro. Eisenhower had endorsed the mission—"To the utmost," he had told Kennedy when asked for his view of the plan during their transition on the eve of the inauguration—and the CIA was just as sanguine, writing of the Cuban exiles, "without exception, they have the utmost confidence in the ability to win."

The utmost? Kennedy wasn't so sure, declining to green-light the mission in repeated security briefings, and, in order to mitigate potential political fallout, insisting that the United States be able to deny any involvement, which meant not allowing the use of any U.S. military equipment or troops. In late March, Arthur Schlesinger had asked him what he thought about "this damned invasion."

"I try to think of it as little as possible," Kennedy said wryly, but, as Schlesinger recognized, it was very much on Kennedy's mind as he wrestled with the plan's central leap of faith that a significant number of Cubans would rally behind an uprising. Was the Cuban dictator as unpopular as the CIA imagined?

But the mission was fast becoming a runaway train. JFK was being pushed by not only the CIA but by the policy he had stated during the presidential campaign, which had generated enough media attention to result in a front-page *New York Times* story headlined "Kennedy Asks Aid for Cuban Rebels to Defeat Castro . . . Rebuts Nixon's Charges of Distortions." If he abandoned the plan, he believed, critics would accuse him of walking away from Ike's commitment to liberate Cuba from Soviet-style communism, while eventually concluding himself that if Cuba wasn't freed from communist tyranny, the domino theory would play out in Central America, bringing the communist threat dangerously close to America's doorstep. How would it look if the president who pledged that his nation would "pay any price [and] bear any burden" for "the survival and success of liberty" allowed communism to spread like a cancer in the Western Hemisphere?

There was also something about the plan, too, a dash of adventure and romance, that appealed to Kennedy's psyche: a dangerous, heroic, and righteous foray against a despotic foe who stood in the way of freedom. Kennedy saw ousting Castro, who had waged his revolution with the promise of liberties that failed to materialize as he flirted with the Soviets, as a "revolution redeemed." Surely the world would see it that way, too.

If the mission sounded as fanciful as a James Bond caper, that made it all the more appealing to Kennedy, who counted Bond's creator, Ian Fleming, as one of his favorite authors. A year earlier, he and Jackie had hosted a dinner for Fleming at their Georgetown townhouse, inviting CIA director Allen Dulles, to whom he had earlier given a copy of Fleming's *From Russia with Love*. Among the topics Kennedy introduced at the dinner was how to wrest Castro from power. Though Dulles begged off at the last minute, sending a CIA stand-in instead, he reached out to Fleming after being briefed about the dinner conversation to talk seriously about how the author's Bond-like ideas could be used to take down Castro.

Yet by early April, as planning for the operation intensified, Kennedy remained hesitant. A key meeting came on the evening of April 4, when Kennedy crammed into a small room on the seventh floor of the State Department with an assortment of officials to discuss the operation. The group included members of Kennedy's cabinet and staff—Bob McNamara, Dean Rusk, Douglas Dillon, Arthur Schlesinger, and Dick Goodwin—as well as Joint Chiefs chairman Lyman Lemnitzer, Allen Dulles, and Dick Bissell, the CIA officer charged with overseeing the so-called Zapata plan.

Also present, at Kennedy's invitation, was William Fulbright, chairman of the Senate Foreign Relations Committee.

Tensions ran high even before the meeting began. Part of it was protocol. The brass wondered why Fulbright was in attendance—it was highly unusual for a member of the Senate to sit in on an executive committee meeting—and they didn't think Schlesinger and Goodwin had any business being there at all. Moreover, Lemnitzer just plain didn't trust Kennedy. The meeting, as they frequently were with Kennedy, was chaotic and disorderly. Those assembled had been mixed on whether the operation would work. Some had expressed their reservations in the days prior. Rusk thought the idea was pure folly. Schlesinger also had serious doubts, as did Lemnitzer, which gave Kennedy particular pause. Likewise, Fulbright had expressed his own concerns.

Bissell briefed the group on the plan's latest incarnation. Goodwin asked why the CIA believed the Cuban people would support the rebels. Bissell assured him the agency's intelligence reports pointed to as much, showing that the Castro regime was "steadily losing popularity" and on the edge of revolt. Kennedy was inclined to believe the analysis.

But Fulbright wasn't buying it, launching into a long critique of the plan. "If one has faith in the human values of the United States," he said, "and if that faith is supported by vigorous and intelligent action, then there is no need to fear competition from an unshaven megalomaniac." The bottom line was that he didn't see the point, adding, "If you succeed, what are you going to do with Cuba? We had it once and we let it go."

Kennedy was getting restless. "Yes or no?" he asked the group. The consensus was yes, the mission should go forward, even if it was a lukewarm sentiment. The only firm no came from Fulbright. Kennedy still wasn't convinced. "Gentlemen, we better sleep on it," he said, breaking up the meeting before turning to Fulbright, adding as a quiet aside, "You're the only one in the room who can say, 'I told you so.'"

By the next day, Kennedy had made up his mind. The mission was a go. He instructed Bissell to "play down the magnitude of the invasion" while cutting air cover by Cuban pilots in half—eight planes rather than sixteen. But the bottom line was that he was in.

The invasion began with a preemptive air strike on April 15, 1961, three days after Kennedy had assured the American people in his press conference that he had no intention of intervening in Cuba. In the coming days, he would come to wish he had stayed true to his word. From the start, the operation seemed doomed. The primitive B-26 bombers the CIA dispatched from Nicaragua, painted to look like Cuban Air Force planes, were ineffective against the Cuban military's aircraft, hitting only five of its thirty-six planes. That left the balance of Cuba's air force to strike the boats transporting the invading Cuban exiles en route from Nicaragua. Moreover, photos of the repainted planes exposed the U.S. as the force behind the operation, making moot any American denials. Sensing disaster and concerned about backlash in the international community, Kennedy called off additional air support.

The invasion began two days later, on April 17. The CIA had severely underestimated the Cuban population's support of Castro and his government. At the Bay of Pigs, few insurgents materialized to aid the invading exiles—Brigade 2506—who were battered by artillery fire. Soon, twenty thousand Cuban troops were on the beach as Cuban warplanes swarmed overhead.

It was all over within a matter of seventy-two hours. A hundred and fifteen of the brigade's troops were killed and another 1,200 were captured by the Cuban army. Kennedy had earlier made clear that he would not provide U.S. military backup for the mission for fear that the Soviets would use it to justify taking military action in Berlin, which could precipitate a war between the superpowers. Yet declassified documents reveal that the CIA had always assumed that the mission in Cuba would fail without U.S. military support, particularly ample air support, and believed the president would send relief as the invasion began to slip. But as it did, so did Kennedy's faith in the CIA and the military brass—and the feeling was mutual. Lemnitzer condemned Kennedy for his passivity, accusing him of "pulling out the rug" on the exiles, contending that it was "absolutely reprehensible, almost criminal."

While Kennedy had seen pain and loss throughout his life, he knew little of defeat. He had never lost a political contest—with the exception of the vice presidential nomination in 1956, which proved a stepping-stone to the national spotlight—and he had never been closely associated with a losing cause. Now, less than three months into his presidency, in his first real test, he'd blundered on the world stage, resulting in the loss of human life and a blow to his reputation. It weighed on him. Lem Billings said Kennedy "constantly blamed himself for the Cuban fiasco," which Kennedy told Ben Bradlee was "the worst experience" of his life.

Jackie recalled her husband fleeing from the West Wing as the news grew worse, retreating to the quiet of his bedroom in the residence. "He started to cry, just with me," she said. "Just put his head in his hands and sort of wept. And I [had] only seen him cry two or three times. . . . And it was so sad, because all of his first hundred days and all his dreams, and then [for] this awful thing to happen. And he cared so much. He didn't care about his first hundred days, but all those poor men who [he'd] sent off with all their hopes high and promises that we'd back them and there they were, shot down like dogs or going to die in jail. He cared so much about them."

The reckoning came quickly. Shortly after the mission, *Time* magazine wrote that Kennedy had been responsible for setbacks "rare in the history of the Republic," while the *New York Times* stated, "it is clear that the expedition has involved the United States in a disastrous loss of prestige and respect. Among high Administration officials there is recognition that a serious miscalculation was made. . . . The reviving confidence of United States allies in its quality of leadership has been shaken."

So was Kennedy's confidence. "He realized he didn't have the magic touch," Ted Sorensen said, "and he realized he had been mistaken by relying on [the judgment of] the military." Less than two weeks after the invasion, on May Day, Castro proclaimed Cuba a Socialist nation, putting it under the Soviet sphere and giving Khrushchev a staging area for his ambitions in the Western Hemisphere. Cuban revolutionary Che Guevara sent Kennedy a message thanking him for the botched invasion. "Before the invasion the revolution was shaky," he wrote. "Now it is stronger than ever."

But the buck stopped with Kennedy. Four days after the fiasco, when asked at a press conference if members of his administration had opposed the plan as had been rumored, Kennedy took the heat. "There is an old saying that victory has a hundred fathers and defeat is an orphan," he said. "I am the responsible officer of this government." Afterward, perhaps because Kennedy had taken responsibility for his actions, Americans rallied around their president. His approval rating soared to 83 percent, with just 5 percent of Americans looking upon him unfavorably after the incident. "It's just like Eisenhower," Kennedy marveled. "The worse I do, the more popular I get."

Eisenhower himself was less forgiving. Kennedy extended an invitation to his predecessor to consult on the matter at Camp David, the presidential retreat in Maryland's Catoctin Mountain Park named for Eisenhower's grandson. It was a calculated gesture, meant to signal to the world that the U.S. was united after the crisis and that the venerable old general, while in retirement, was still engaged and available for counsel. But it amounted to a private trip to the woodshed for Kennedy. "No one knows how rough this job is until after he's in it for a few months," he told Eisenhower during their private one-on-one lunch at Aspen Lodge, followed by a stroll on the grounds of the compound. Ike was having none of it, grilling Kennedy with questions on the failed mission, including why he had declined to provide air support.

"We thought that if it was learned we were really doing this rather than the rebels themselves, the Soviets would be very apt to cause trouble in Berlin," Kennedy explained.

Ike chided him. "Mr. President, that is exactly the opposite of what really would happen. The Soviets follow their own plans, and if they see us show any weakness, then that is when they press us the hardest," he said, then added presciently, "The failure of the Bay of Pigs will embolden the Soviets to do something they would not otherwise do."

Publicly, Ike was more gracious—but just a little. After their meeting, smiling obligingly as they stood side by side, the former and incumbent presidents met with forty-five members of the press. "I'm all in favor of the United States supporting the man who has to carry the responsibility of our foreign affairs," Eisenhower said tepidly. Hugh Sidey, who was there for *Time*, later wrote, "It was the only endorsement that Ike could give Kennedy for the mishandled matter. But it was almost enough. At the moment it meant a lot."

Weeks later, Sidey was on the receiving end of Kennedy's reflections on the Bay of Pigs debacle as they sat in the Oval Office. "I want to know how all this could have happened," Kennedy said calmly, though he was still reeling over the incident. "There were fifty or so of us, presumably the most experienced and smartest people we could get, to plan such an operation. Most of us thought it would work. I know there are some men now saying they were opposed from the start. But five minutes after it began to fall in, we all looked at each other and asked, 'How could we have been so stupid?' . . . I guess you get walled in from reality when you want something to succeed so much."

He was determined not to let himself get so insulated again—nor to let the misjudgments of the military and CIA guide his decisions. During a game of checkers with Red Fay during a weekend in Hyannis Port, he was resolute. "We're not going to plunge into an irresponsible action just because a fanatical fringe in the country puts so-called national pride above national reason," he said. "Do you think I'm going to cause a nuclear exchange—for what? Because I was forced into doing something that I didn't think was proper and right?"

It was an important lesson, one that he would later draw on in the most desperate hour of his presidency—once again in Cuba. The place of his greatest humiliation would become the scene of his greatest triumph. But that was on the horizon. In the meantime, there were immediate trials to come.

"YOU WILL NEVER MAKE IT THROUGH ALABAMA"

On Thursday, May 4, 1961, ten men and three women—seven Black, six white—boarded a bus at the Greyhound Bus terminal in Washington, D.C., bound for New Orleans. The "Freedom Riders," as they were known, planned to travel through the most intractably segregated parts of America in their journey for a scheduled arrival on May 17, the seventh anniversary of the Supreme Court's landmark decision in *Brown v. Board of Education*, outlawing segregation in public schools.

Committed to exposing racial injustice through nonviolent means, the Freedom Riders embarked on a crusade to enforce another Supreme Court decision, *Boynton v. Virginia*, rendered in 1960, which banned segregation in interstate bus stations, but was largely ignored throughout most of the southern states where they were headed. One of the activists, John Lewis, a Black seminary student and future congressman, called the southernmost states on their journey "the belly of the segregated beast." He and his fellow Freedom Riders knew that the "beast" posed a grave threat. So did James Farmer, director of the Congress of Racial Equality (CORE), the organization responsible for planning the campaign. Inspired

78

by Kennedy's messages of hope at the dawn of his administration, Farmer aimed to use the Freedom Rides "to create a crisis so that the federal government would be compelled to enforce the law."

A crisis he got. The bus advanced without incident through Virginia and North Carolina until May 9, when it arrived in Rock Hill, South Carolina, and Lewis and his white colleague, a fifty-five-year-old World War II veteran, were assaulted when they entered a whites-only section of the town's bus station. Worse violence was in store as the group edged deeper into the South. In Atlanta, the Freedom Riders celebrated seven hundred miles at a dinner with Martin Luther King, Jr., before they headed southwest. King was less than celebratory. Whispering to a reporter from *Jet* magazine who was traveling with the group, he warned, "You will never make it through Alabama."

The following day, Sunday, May 14—Mother's Day—the Freedom Riders split up, with seven members boarding a Trailways bus and the rest of the group remaining on a Greyhound. When the latter bus arrived in Anniston, Alabama, forty miles from the Georgia state line, it was met at the station by a white mob of around one hundred, some still in church garb. "Well, boys, here they are," the driver yelled out his window. "I brought you some niggers and nigger-lovers."

The mob charged the bus, slashing its tires, and then followed it by car as it hobbled along, firebombing it after the tires blew, and savagely beating the six Freedom Riders with chains, iron pipes, and baseball bats as they fled the burning vehicle. In Birmingham the same day, the Trailways bus was met just as violently as a rabble attacked the Freedom Riders on board. Local police were not on hand to protect the activists on either bus. On the contrary, the chiefs of police of both Anniston and Birmingham had helped organize the brutality. If not for the warning shots of a highway patrolman dispersing the mob outside Anniston, the activists would likely have been dragged from the scene and lynched. With the lives of the Freedom Riders in jeopardy, James Farmer temporarily suspended the campaign.

President Kennedy learned of the attacks in his bedroom the following morning, taking in a *New York Times* front-page article accompanied by a harrowing photo of the crippled Greyhound bus ominously coughing up a plume of black smoke from its door as dazed passengers looked on. It was the first he had heard of the Freedom Rides.

"Can't you get your goddamned friends off those buses?" he demanded later of his civil rights adviser, Harris Wofford. "Stop them!" As far as he was concerned, the activists were irritants who were damaging America's reputation, especially as he prepared for his first foreign trips as president, a visit with Canadian prime minister John Diefenbaker just two days away, followed by a Paris meeting with French president Charles de Gaulle in late May, and, even more consequentially, a summit in Vienna with Soviet premier Nikita Khrushchev in early June.

Until then, the month had been promising. Ten days earlier, on May 5, Alan Shepard had become the first American in space, completing a fifteen-minute suborbital launch into the heavens that, while not measuring up to Yuri Gagarin's 108-minute orbital flight the previous month, gave NASA a much-needed shot in the arm and Kennedy a little encouragement about the program's future. The Freedom Rides, on the other hand, were an annoying disruption.

"I did not lie awake at night worrying about the problems of negroes," Bobby Kennedy said later, summing up his own attitude toward civil rights activism at the time. Neither did his brother, the president, who was even more detached on the issue. As a senator, JFK had voted "nay" to Eisenhower's 1957 civil rights bill, the first civil rights legislation since Reconstruction, albeit largely impotent but for its symbolism. Though he'd been aware of the racism that plagued much of the country and the segregation that pervaded the South, Senator Kennedy's stance was largely due to political calculus as he eyed his presidential prospects; any overt support of civil rights might offend white voters, especially in the southern states, traditional Democratic strongholds.

By the 1960 campaign, however, his mindset had changed. He won the support of many southern Blacks by coming to the aid of Martin Luther King, Jr. After an arrest at an Atlanta restaurant sit-in, King had been jolted awake in his jail cell in the middle of the night, thrown into a sheriff's car, and driven three hundred miles to a rural Georgia prison in the heart of Ku Klux Klan country, where brutal, racist prison guards and white inmates potentially put his life at risk. Andrew Young, a key lieutenant to King, called it "the roughest" experience of King's life. A call of support by Kennedy to King's wife, Coretta, recommended by campaign aide Harris Wofford, led to Kennedy arranging for King's release through a plea to Georgia's Democratic governor Ernest Vandiver. King's father, Martin Luther King, Sr., said he never knew of any white man who "called a negro woman when her husband was in prison." It was enough for the influential Atlanta clergyman to switch his allegiance from Richard Nixon to Kennedy, promising "a suitcase full of votes" from the African American community.

Kennedy also made inroads by pledging to do away with segregation in federally subsidized public housing with "a stroke of a pen." His progressive stances paid off. He would go on to pick up 70 percent of the Black vote, a boost from the 63 percent the Democratic ticket garnered in 1956, which would make a difference in swing states like Illinois, Michigan, and New Jersey. Like

James Farmer, many in the civil rights movement took heart in Kennedy's election and in his ostensible idealism. "He didn't mention race or civil rights in his [inauguration] speech," Lewis wrote later, "but I assumed that was simply a matter of political expediency. I believed that *he* believed in what we all believed in—the Beloved Community."

If so, it was slow in revealing itself in his presidency. While Kennedy established the Committee on Equal Employment Opportunity in March, headed by Lyndon Johnson, he declined in his first months in office to make good on the executive order he'd promised to end segregated federal public housing with one presidential signature. "Where's the PEN, Mr. President?" Lewis and other civil rights soldiers asked impatiently, some sending him pens in an "Ink for Jack" drive. Once again, Kennedy's hesitancy had to do with political pragmatism. Powerful southern Democrats, all toeing the line on segregation, controlled much of Congress, holding eleven of nineteen committee chairmanships in the House, and two-thirds in the Senate. Kennedy was reluctant to make waves, especially so soon into his presidency. Nor did he seem to have any moral conviction over the cause.

"Knock, knock," Kennedy said drolly to Pennsylvania governor David Lawrence during a visit to Philadelphia, co-opting a popular joke of the time around fear of Blacks moving into white neighborhoods.

"Who's there?" Lawrence asked dutifully.

"Iza."

"Iza who?"

"I's ya next-door neighbah!"

Most Americans didn't see the urgency in pushing civil rights, either; 64 percent were opposed to the Freedom Rides, according to a Gallup Poll conducted shortly after the crisis in Alabama, versus 24 percent who supported them.

It was foreign policy that interested Kennedy, anyway, not domestic issues. In the nuclear age, there was, in Kennedy's mind, greater urgency in it. "Domestic policy can only defeat us. Foreign policy can kill us," he said. Reaching out to prominent Republicans after the Bay of Pigs fiasco, he confided to Richard Nixon, "It really is true that foreign affairs is the only important issue for a president to handle, isn't it? I mean, who gives a shit if the minimum wage is $1.15 or $1.25 in comparison to something like this?"

While the minimum wage was a far less morally charged issue than civil rights, the latter amounted to a presidential inconvenience for Kennedy, one that he hoped to kick down the road. But as much as he may have wanted the burgeoning civil rights movement—including the Freedom Riders—to quietly go away, it would become a focal point of his administration, a growing, simmering crusade that threatened to boil over at any moment. "He got constantly more committed than he was," Burke Marshall, assistant attorney general in the civil rights division, said of Kennedy. "Until the end of 1963, every big demonstration . . . was a [political] problem for the president, so that affected the way [attorney general] Bob Kennedy would look at it. I mean, he would look at it as a problem."

But no president, Kennedy would learn, can dictate the issues that cross his desk. The Freedom Riders forced Kennedy's hand on civil rights. When it became clear that Farmer was intent on resuming the anti-segregation campaign in the wake of the violence, it fell to the president to ensure their protection and that of their supporters. Kennedy would have to deal directly with the situation or risk violence spreading from Alabama throughout the southern states.

To that end, Bobby Kennedy dispatched his closest aide at the Department of Justice, John Seigenthaler, a southerner, to monitor the situation in Montgomery, Alabama's capital. Soon after his arrival, Seigenthaler came to the aid of two young women who were being attacked by a horde of over a thousand outside the city's Greyhound station; he claimed he was a federal agent, only to be knocked in the head with a lead pipe and kicked by the mob as he lay unconscious on the street for nearly a half hour before being taken to the hospital with a cracked skull. John Lewis was also beaten unconscious, and nearby another young Black activist was drenched with a flammable liquid and set on fire.

On Sunday, May 21, Martin Luther King, Jr., arrived in Montgomery to lend support to the Freedom Riders. Just a few years earlier he had lived there as a young minister, rising to national prominence as the leader of the Montgomery bus boycott, igniting the modern civil rights movement before returning to his hometown of Atlanta to head up the SCLC and its nonviolent assault on systemic racism across the South. That evening, intent on showing his support of the Freedom Riders, the thirty-two-year-old King was due to speak at a mass gathering at the city's First Baptist Church, bringing with it the prospect of further violence. Bobby Kennedy's pleas to King not to go went unheeded.

King grudgingly admired the Kennedys and shared much in common with them. Like them, he had grown up privileged (at least by the standards of the African American community) as the son of a redoubtable father. "Daddy" King had given him a convertible upon his graduation from high school and summers in Martha's Vineyard, which came along with princely expectations for his future success. Like the Kennedys, too, King, according to longtime friend Stanley Levison, felt some guilt around the affluence in which he was raised, spurring a responsibility to give back.

But King thought Kennedy's northeastern privilege meant insulation from matters of race that pointed to a certain ignorance. "He really knew almost nothing on race," Andrew Young said of Kennedy. "[The Kennedys] didn't even have Black maids. They didn't know any Black people. . . . I doubt he had a Black friend before he went into the White House." According to Young, King believed that Kennedy wanted to "do the right thing" on civil rights and "had a real appreciation for his sensitivity," but saw his lack of experience around issues of race as holding him back. Young contended that Kennedy hadn't been exposed to virulent prejudice and equated Black oppression to how the Irish were treated in the middle of the nineteenth century, "which wasn't anything like slavery" and the systemic inequality and deep-seated bigotry that came in its wake.

King, moreover, demanded to be treated with respect, and he didn't feel it from the Kennedys. It was telling that while inside-the-Beltway civil rights leaders like Roy Wilkins, the head of the NAACP, had received invitations to Kennedy's inauguration, King had not, a slight that rankled not only him but others in the movement. After the Bay of Pigs, he railed against Kennedy. "I think our country has done not only a disservice to its own citizens but to the whole of humanity in dealing with the Cuban situation," he said. "For some reason, we just don't understand the meaning of the revolution taking place all over the world." That included the nonviolent revolution King was mobilizing at home, methodically exposing cracks in the country's inherent ideal of equality.

The Kennedys, meanwhile, considered King a rabble-rouser, an agitator stoking the fires of an already volatile situation. As white liberals from the Northeast swept into Montgomery in the wake of the initial violence, Bobby dismissed them—and King, too—as "honkers." "It took guts for the first [Freedom Riders] group to go," he maintained, "but not much for the others." Still, with Alabama's governor, John Patterson, declining to send in the state's National Guard to protect King and his flock, Bobby sought to make good on his promise to King to safeguard the civil rights advocates, sending several dozen U.S. marshals to the scene as King addressed some 1,500 parishioners at the First Baptist Church on Sunday evening.

Trouble came almost immediately. First Baptist was surrounded by an angry throng of over three thousand whites, brandishing everything from baseball bats and bicycle chains to Coca-Cola crates and garden implements, trapping King and his followers inside. They set a parishioner's car ablaze and hurled rocks through the church's stained-glass windows, the shards of which rained down on the congregants who huddled against one another for cover. King could feel the wolves at the door. The fifty U.S. marshals sent by Bobby to protect the parishioners were hardly sufficient to keep them at bay. King worried that the mob would burn the church to the ground. From the basement, he called the attorney general, who had gone directly to his office at the Justice Department from a game of touch football at Hickory Hill as the situation worsened. When would help arrive? King demanded; there was fear in his voice. Bobby promised that U.S. marshal reinforcements were on the way. "If they don't get here immediately," King warned, "we're going to have a bloody confrontation." Presently, six hundred additional U.S. marshals arrived as the two men spoke, pulling up in red, white, and blue trucks marked "U.S. Mail." But the crisis was far from over.

As it played out, the president was at Glen Ora, the pastoral four-hundred-acre weekend home the Kennedy family used in Middleburg, Virginia, forty miles from Washington, where Jackie could indulge her equestrian passions. Ostensibly disengaged, he tracked the situation and actively made decisions through an open line with Bobby, whose office at the Justice Department had become a makeshift war room. Earlier JFK had phoned Governor Patterson, a supporter in his presidential campaign, to get assurances that the Freedom Riders and their supporters would be shielded from violence. The governor declined to return the call.

Bobby reached Patterson later, after midnight. Patterson said that he had mobilized the Alabama National Guard, which could defend everyone but King. The federal government would have to be responsible for him, he said. Who said so? Bobby asked. Patterson claimed it was the guard's adjutant general, who commanded the unit. "Have him call me," Bobby snapped. "I want to hear a general in the United States Army say that he can't protect Martin Luther King." Patterson pulled back; it was he, not the general, who said the guard couldn't protect King.

That was enough for Bobby, who, along with his brother, was looking for a way for the state of Alabama rather than the federal government to be on the hook for the protection of those in the church. Content to leave the situation in Bobby's hands, the president retired for the evening. Bobby withdrew the marshals, leaving the guard in place as the only thing between those in First Baptist and the mob outside. It wasn't much comfort to those in the besieged church. The guardsmen, many waving Confederate flags, trained their rifles on them, holding them as captives. Livid that the marshals had yielded to the guard, King once again called Bobby. "You betrayed us," he yelled through the receiver.

Bobby shot back, "Now, Reverend, you know just as well as I do that if it hadn't been for the United States marshals, you'd be as dead as Kelsey's nuts right now." King was confused by the mangled version of the Boston Irish colloquialism "as tight as Kelsey's nuts," denoting stinginess. He turned away from the phone and asked those around him, "Who's Kelsey? Anyone know Kelsey?"

The crisis abated at daybreak. Slowly throughout the early morning hours the mob had broken up, until the streets outside were eerily quiet. The Justice Department arranged for the release of the parishioners, who were led out of First Baptist into the dim light of dawn, the air suffused with the remnants of tear gas. Though the immediate danger had passed, discord and distrust between the Kennedys and King and the civil rights community would intensify.

Almost immediately, the Freedom Riders resumed their campaign, once again defying the wishes of the Kennedys, who urged them to call it off and patiently wait for reform to take hold. "Wait means 'Never,'" King told *Time* magazine. As the number of Freedom Riders swelled to over three hundred, the inaugural springtime Freedom Rides evolved into "Freedom Summer," and the dog days were made hotter throughout the South with the threat of violence hanging balefully over every bus route and depot.

In the president's first formal statement after the crisis, he wrote that the violence was "a source of deepest concern to me" while expressing "hope" that "any persons . . . would refrain from any action which would in any way tend to provoke further outbreaks." That, of course, included the civil rights advocates. Privately, he fumed after a White House meeting with Harry Belafonte and a group of liberals, including the dean of Yale Law School, who encouraged him to show "moral leadership" on the issue of segregation. Upon their departure, he groused, "Doesn't he know I've done more for civil rights than any president in American history?" Those in the movement, however, didn't see it that way. "The Kennedys wanted [it] both ways," said Roy Wilkins. "They wanted to be our friends and they wanted to break the movement." But it became clear that the movement would not be broken.

The attorney general's own first statement in the wake of the violence was more forthright. As his brother prepared for critical meetings abroad with Khrushchev, Bobby believed that King and others had prolonged the crisis in Alabama, giving America's cold war enemies a propaganda boost. His fear, he said, was that "continuing international publicity about ugly race riots would send the leader of the free world into European palaces with mud on his shoes."

SHOWDOWN IN VIENNA

With or without the riots the Freedom Riders had prompted, Kennedy already had "mud on his shoes"—at least in the mind of Nikita Khrushchev. The world had been watching when Kennedy blundered in Cuba, but no one more so than the leader of the Soviet Union. Though Americans were inclined to give Kennedy the benefit of the doubt around the debacle, Khrushchev, as Eisenhower had predicted, sensed opportunity and moved to seize it. "I don't understand Kennedy," he confided privately to his son Sergei as the Bay of Pigs operation played out disastrously. "What's wrong with him? Can he really be that indecisive?" Mikhail Menshikov, the Soviet ambassador to the United States, judged that Kennedy's inexperience meant that he "would never amount to a good president." Similarly, Khrushchev's son-in-law Aleksei Adzhubei, a Soviet journalist who had been exposed to the Kennedy brothers, had sized them up as "little boys in short pants." Kennedy, Khrushchev concluded, was weak.

Certainly, Kennedy had been weakened by the Bay of Pigs, which had diminished his ability to act resolutely on the world scene. Shortly after the failed foray, he was informed that the U.S.-backed nation of Laos was teetering on the brink of a communist takeover, as he had been warned during the transition, bringing with it a greater threat of a communist tide flowing into other parts of Southeast Asia—Burma, Cambodia, or Thailand. "We would have troops in Laos right now if it weren't for the Bay of Pigs," he told Ted Sorensen. Instead, he opted for a diplomatic solution, tapping former New York governor Averell Harriman, who had coordinated the Lend-Lease program in World War II, to oversee a neutralization agreement before turning the situation over to a UN force to ensure a coalition government. It was a way for Kennedy to save face: declining direct unilateral military intervention in Laos, which could incite a showdown with the Soviets, but not cutting and running. "If we have to fight in Southeast Asia, let's fight in Vietnam," he told Dean Rusk, as they discussed U.S. strategy in the region. "The Vietnamese, at least, are committed to fight. Vietnam is the place."

Kennedy knew the stakes. "There are just so many concessions that one can make to communists in one year and survive politically," he said. "We just can't have another defeat this year in Vietnam." Accordingly, the president ramped up U.S. support. By the end of April, he had boosted the number of U.S. military advisers in Vietnam from 685 to 785, while more than doubling the size of South Vietnam's Civil Guard by authorizing an increase from 32,000 to 68,000. Additionally, he sent U.S. Special Forces to train the South Vietnamese Army in counterinsurgency warfare and commissioned a study on expanding the size of the South Vietnamese Army by 30,000.

After the setbacks of April, Kennedy's staff recognized that changes needed to be made to his loose, chaotic White House in the interest of preventing further blows to the administration. On his way back from his late-May visit to Canada, where he had severely injured his back during a tree-planting ceremony, intensifying the pain that was an inherent part of his daily life, Kennedy was given a surprisingly blunt memo from McGeorge Bundy reflecting the views of members of the senior White House staff.

Bundy, who wrote that he hoped the president would be in a "good mood" upon reading it, offered suggestions that he believed would be "useful" for him going forward. While maintaining that the president had made the White House "a center of energy," he expressed "fear" from "old-timers" that "because of Cuba we may turn back to cautious inactivity." "We do have a problem of management," he asserted. "Centrally it is a problem of your time."

> You should set aside a . . . regular time each day for national security discussion and action. . . . We can't get you to sit still. . . . Calling three meetings in five days is foolish—and putting them off for six weeks at a time is just as bad. . . . Right now it is so hard to get to you with anything not urgent. . . . About half of the papers and reports you personally ask for are never shown to you because by the time you are available you clearly have lost interest in them. . . . If we put a little staff work on these and keep in close touch, we can be sure that all your questions are answered. . . . Will you try?

While he may have tried, hope of him sitting still was never fully realized. Kennedy accepted some changes, allowing more briefings and formal meetings, but his natural restlessness and erraticism continued to bedevil staffers.

———

By all indications, the spring of 1961 was not the time for a chastened John F. Kennedy to meet with Nikita Khrushchev, engaging in a media spectacle that would capture the attention of the world. But Kennedy saw it differently. He understood that his "Cuban mistake" had given his Soviet counterpart license to "get tougher and tougher," which could precipitate "crises in all parts of the world." Accordingly, he wanted to meet Khrushchev as soon as it could be arranged. "Getting involved in a fight between the Communists and anti-Communists in Cuba or Laos was one thing," he explained to Kenny O'Donnell. "But this is the time to let [Khrushchev] know that a showdown between the U.S. and Russia would be entirely something else again." In mid-May, the two sides agreed to an American-Soviet summit in Vienna—neutral territory—on June 3 and 4, just three weeks away.

Prior to his departure, Kennedy gave his second address to a joint session of Congress. Far from shrinking in the wake of the events of April, he rose to new challenges. Encouraged by the successful suborbital flight of Alan Shepard, and by assurances from Lyndon Johnson that NASA could quickly find its way, which came with the vice president's contention that "dramatic accomplishments in space" were "a major indicator of world leadership," JFK aimed for the moon. "If we are to win the battle that is now going on around the world between freedom and tyranny," he told the nation,

> the dramatic achievements in space which occurred in recent weeks should have made clear to us all, as did the Sputnik in 1957, the impact of this adventure on the minds of men everywhere, who are attempting to make the determination of which road they should take. . . .

I believe that this nation should commit itself to achieving the goal, before this decade is out, of landing a man on the moon and returning him safely to the earth. No single space project in this period will be more impressive to mankind, or more important for the long-range exploration of space; and none will be so difficult or expensive to accomplish.

It was a bold ambition. A little more than a week before his summit with the Soviet premier, Kennedy had thrown down a cold war gauntlet, upping the ante in the escalating space race in which the U.S. was manifestly lagging.

John Kennedy talked a lot about "guts," who had them, who didn't. If he deemed one to have guts, it was the ultimate tip of the hat, naturally in keeping with the premium the Kennedys put on toughness and personal courage. The Russians valued those things, too. Over centuries, the country's vast, open frontier brought with it a history of savage invasion by foreign powers and an inclination among the insecure Russian people toward authoritarian leadership, unyielding strongmen who would guard against an attack by outside forces and ensure national order. Someone like Nikita Khrushchev.

As the summit in Vienna approached, Kennedy knew he had to show his own guts to his Soviet adversary, intent that Khrushchev not "misunderstand Laos and Cuba as an indication that the United States is in a yielding mood" around Berlin. The divided city, a Western outpost a hundred miles into East Germany accessible by West Germans only by a rail line and the autobahn, a long narrow strip of highway, stuck in Khrushchev's craw. Mixing metaphors, he called it "a bone in my throat," vowing to "eradicate this splinter from the heart of Europe." Kennedy's greatest fear was that Khrushchev would move to wrest control of West Berlin, precipitating the possibility of war. At the very least, Khrushchev was expected to make a move to block off the East Berlin sector boundary as a means of choking off the embarrassing migration of East Germans into West Germany.

On May 29, Kennedy attended a dinner at the Boston Armory to celebrate his birthday. "I am only 44, but I have lived in my 44 years through three wars," he told those assembled. "No one can study the origins of any of these three struggles without realizing the serious miscalculations, the serious misapprehensions, about the possible actions of the other side which existed in the minds of the adversaries which helped bring about those wars."

Kennedy sought to use the meeting with Khrushchev to avoid catastrophic miscalculations that would result in the cold war becoming hot. That meant establishing a dialogue in which the two men made their nation's vital interests clear and worked toward détente by not challenging the current geopolitical balance of power. Kennedy, in other words, needed to reinforce America's resolve around Berlin in the interest of keeping Khrushchev's global ambitions in check.

"Your job, Mr. President, is to make sure Khrushchev believes you are a man who will fight," Charles de Gaulle reminded Kennedy during his visit to Paris a few days later, his first European stop before the meeting in Vienna. De Gaulle didn't believe the Soviets would go to war over Berlin but saw the importance of Kennedy remaining firm over the issue. "Stand fast when Khrushchev summons you to change the status of Berlin. This is the most useful service you can render the world," he said. Like others, the lanky and cantankerous seventy-year-old French leader had his doubts. After Cuba, he thought "the young man" to be "somewhat fumbling and overeager," but, to the surprise of the staffs of both men, and perhaps of de Gaulle himself, he was suitably impressed by Kennedy.

Just before departing for France, Kennedy also received advice in New York from Averell Harriman, who implored him to "have fun" with Khrushchev. "Remember, he's just as scared as you are," he said. "He'll try to rattle you, frighten you, but don't pay any attention to that." It was a tall order. Additionally, compounding any anxiety Kennedy harbored over the meeting was his back pain, which had become pronounced since he had thrown it out shoveling dirt in a tree-planting ceremony in Ottawa several weeks earlier.

On June 3, 1961, after a short hop from Paris aboard Air Force One, Kennedy arrived in Vienna to a reception of seventy thousand fervent Austrians, who lined the streets in the rain to catch a glimpse of the American president. Only the day before, the sun had shone bright over the city, yet substantially fewer people—fifty thousand—had come out to greet Khrushchev, who had arrived from Moscow by rail. The summit was a media spectacle, with 1,500 reporters striving to capture every moment and nuance, conveying all the drama of a showdown between gladiators. If crowd size was any indication, Kennedy had handily won the first round.

The advantage also went to Kennedy later in the day as the swarm of press photographers captured their first handshake outside the American ambassador's residence before their meeting. After nervously pacing the front halls in anticipation of Khrushchev's arrival, Kennedy glided down the front steps like a Hollywood headliner as the premier's black Chaika approached.

Khrushchev emerged from the car resembling, at best, an aging character actor, squat and unsightly, exuding all the elegance of a rusted fireplug. Twenty-three years separated the men, as did nine inches in height, with the six-foot, 175-pound JFK towering over his Eastern rival, who stood at a portly five foot three. "How are you?" Kennedy smiled as he extended his hand. "I'm glad to see you."

Withdrawing into the ambassador's prosaic gray stucco residence for their conversation in the home's music room, Kennedy soon lost the edge. The meeting started off amiably enough, with the two men sitting with aides in a circle of chairs, exchanging pleasantries and professing their aim to understand each other.

"We cast the deciding vote for you when you beat that son-of-a-bitch Nixon," Khrushchev boasted.

"How?" Kennedy asked.

"We waited to release the [U-2] spy pilots until after the election. So Nixon could not claim he knew how to deal with the Russians."

Kennedy asked that Khrushchev not spread the story around. "If you tell everybody that you like me better than Nixon, I'll be ruined at home," he said with a laugh.

But the small talk was soon put aside for weightier matters. As they adjourned to a table to continue their discussion, Khrushchev, true to his pugnacious form, soon bore into Kennedy, rocking him back on his heels by steering the conversation into a no-win ideological debate about their respective political systems, one for which Khrushchev was far better prepared and that Kennedy's advisers had urged him to avoid. Khrushchev enumerated the United States' past failures and violations of trust with the USSR, accusing Kennedy of promulgating policy aimed at the "liquidation of the Communist system." Kennedy said it was the other way around, that the Soviet Union wanted to "liquidate the free system in other countries." Khrushchev punched right back, insisting, "The Soviet Union is against implanting its policy in other states." In the initial exchanges, Kennedy came across as off-kilter, slightly dazed. Khrushchev, the son of a Ukrainian coal miner who had dropped out of school at the age of fifteen to work as a pipe fitter in a factory, could come off publicly as clownish, but he was no bumpkin. As Kennedy expected, he was sharp and well prepared.

Kennedy tried to redirect the conversation toward their mutual benefit in establishing détente, warning against the kind of "miscalculation" that he had spoken about a few days earlier, one that could spark a war. "*Miscalculation?*" Khrushchev responded incredulously, seizing the word and repeating it rabidly. "All I ever hear from your people . . . is that damned word 'miscalculation,'" he said, insisting that his nation could not ensure that Soviet ideas would not spread beyond the borders of existing communist states but that they would "not start a war by mistake." The word "miscalculation," he demanded, should be "buried in cold storage" and never used again.

Lunch brought a welcome bit of comic relief. Kennedy inquired about the two medals pinned to Khrushchev's chest, one of which, Khrushchev informed him, was a Lenin Peace Prize medal. Kennedy turned to Khrushchev's interpreter; "Tell him I hope they never take it away from him," he quipped. Later, upon lighting a cigar after a lunch of beef Wellington, Kennedy accidentally dropped a lighted match behind Khrushchev's chair before snuffing it out with his foot. "Are you trying to light me on fire?" Khrushchev asked, feigning alarm as he drew on a dry vodka martini. Kennedy insisted he was not. "Ah," Khrushchev barbed, "a capitalist, not an incendiary."

After lunch, the two men resumed their conversation by taking a walk on the grounds of the residence, with Khrushchev, according to Kenny O'Donnell, who witnessed them from a second-floor window in the residence, "snapping" at Kennedy "like a terrier and shaking his finger." They returned to the music room, where they sat on pink damask chairs and continued their exchange. In an attempt to clarify what he had been trying to state earlier, Kennedy went back to the delicate subject of miscalculations, actions that could lead to a catastrophic nuclear war. He conceded his own miscalculation with the Bay of Pigs, which, he said, was "more than a mistake. It was a failure." Kennedy was hoping the confession would prompt Khrushchev to lower his guard and engender a more convivial and productive dialogue. When it didn't, Kennedy said, "We admit our mistakes. Do you ever admit you're wrong?"

The strongman wasn't going to concede any personal blunder or vulnerability to his adversary. "Certainly, in a speech before the Twentieth Party Congress, I admitted all of Stalin's mistakes," he replied.

"Those were Stalin's mistakes, not yours," a frustrated Kennedy pointed out.

They turned to the subject of Laos, with Khrushchev warning, "If the United States supports old, moribund, reactionary regimes, then a precedent of intervention in internal affairs will be set, which might cause a clash between our two countries."

Kennedy considered the premier's remarks. "We regard . . . Sino-Soviet forces and the forces of the United States and Western Europe as being more or less in balance," he said.

This was exactly what Khrushchev wanted to hear: heartening recognition that they were roughly equal powers, which he construed as a deterrent against the United States waging war with the

Soviet Union, an admission he would crow about for the remainder of his years and that incensed the U.S. Joint Chiefs of Staff, further straining the relationship between them and Kennedy. The premier of the Soviet Union was now standing on equal ground with the president of the United States.

The day's meetings ended at 6:45 p.m. As Arthur Schlesinger put it mildly later, "it had been a rough day" that left Kennedy "impressed by Khrushchev's vitality, his debating skill and his brutal candor," but at the same time "depressed by the blank wall of dogma" that he found virtually impenetrable. That evening, as Kennedy relieved his throbbing back in a hot bath, he told Dave Powers, "I'm trying to remind myself: the next time you're talking to Khrushchev, don't mention miscalculation."

The bantam Soviet leader, as it turned out, was just getting started. He saved his most aggressive assault for the following day, as the two sides convened midmorning at the Soviet Embassy, a large rectangular palace once inhabited by Austrian archduke Franz Ferdinand, whose assassination touched off the First World War. The venue was fitting, as the danger of war—one far more devastating in the nuclear age—hung forbiddingly over the balance of the summit, threatening to end humanity itself.

During lunch, in an effort to impart the dangers of a war between the superpowers, Kennedy gave the premier a model of the USS *Constitution*, the U.S. Navy frigate commissioned in 1797 and nicknamed "Old Ironsides." Kennedy noted that the ship's weaponry could reach only half a mile. In previous generations, he reminded Khrushchev, wars could be fought without obliterating entire populations. There was no such certainty in the latter half of the twentieth century. To that end, Kennedy tried to pursue the

issue of disarmament, only to be stymied by Khrushchev, who refused to give ground on allowing U.S. inspections of Soviet missile
sites, claiming the visits would be used as a means of espionage.

The pair then went on to address the elephant in the room, the
smoldering question of Berlin, which had been touched on only
lightly to that point. Khrushchev called it "the most dangerous
spot in the world," claiming that the Soviets were going to "perform an operation . . . to eliminate this . . . ulcer." It would come
in the form of a peace treaty creating the "free city" of West Berlin, over which East Germany, the German Democratic Republic,
would have sovereignty, rendering void all previous conditions
around the city, including Western occupation. U.S. troops would
be allowed into the city under certain conditions, he claimed, just
as Soviet troops would. The premier made no bones about his
position: If the U.S. didn't sign the treaty, the USSR would sign
it alone. Afterward, the Soviets would consider any violation of
East German sovereignty an act of war.

Kennedy thanked Khrushchev for his directness. He then made
it clear that the U.S. occupied Berlin due to "contractual rights"
negotiated after World War II and would defend Berlin "at any
risk." Khrushchev didn't budge. His decision was "irrevocable";
with or without the United States, the Soviet Union would sign a
binding agreement by the end of December. "It is up to the U.S.
to decide whether there will be war or peace," the premier said
defiantly. "If that is true," the president responded, "it will be a
cold winter."

Throughout the two days in Vienna, JFK had, in his words, been
treated by Khrushchev "like a schoolboy." As Jackie said later,
Khrushchev had exhibited "naked, brutal, ruthless power" and

"thought he could do what he wanted with Jack," who had gone to Vienna "with lovely illusions that they could all work together." Instead, Khrushchev rattled Kennedy just as he had hoped, leaving the summit with the upper hand.

Kennedy, for his part, left with a chilling view of his Russian counterpart. In diplomatic meetings, Dean Rusk pointed out, the word "war" was rarely uttered. Yet Khrushchev had used the word repeatedly, ostensibly indifferent to the prospect of nuclear holocaust. "I never met a man like this," Kennedy told Hugh Sidey aboard Air Force One as the president moved on to London the following day. "I talked about how a nuclear exchange would kill seventy million people in ten minutes, and [Khrushchev] looked at me as if to say, 'So what?'"

JACKIE

Jacqueline Lee Bouvier first cast her wide-set brown eyes on the White House in 1940. During a trip to Washington from her native New York, she and her mother took a public tour of "the People's House," occupied at the time by Franklin and Eleanor Roosevelt. By then, young Jacqueline had already achieved some distinction, sweeping a national junior equestrian championship in her state the same year, prompting the *New York Times* to write, "The occasions are few when a young rider wins both contests in the same show." But whatever awe the grandeur of the old house may have inspired in others on the tour, it eluded the precocious eleven-year-old, who "shuffled through," underwhelmed by its style and décor. She believed she could do better. Just over two decades later, now thirty-one years old and known worldwide as "Jackie," she would have her own chance to make her mark on the White House—and on the role she had assumed. As soon as she took up residence, she was determined to make it the "prettiest house in America" and, according to a Kennedy family member, to be "as great a First Lady in her own right as Jack is a President."

If there had been a bright spot in President Kennedy's overseas state visits in the spring of 1961, it was the first lady, who glittered across Europe, starting with the first couple's arrival in Paris, where half a million people lined their ten-mile route into the French capital, chanting, "Vive Jacqueline!" The evening prior, French television had aired a fifteen-minute interview that the first lady had done from Washington in which she spoke in impeccable French—cultivated in a formative year she'd spent in France as a college junior—expressing her love of the nation's culture and ingratiating herself to its people. "Paris Has a New Queen," a French newspaper headline gushed the day after her arrival. Charles de Gaulle was equally taken with her. While the French president was, according to Ted Sorensen, "intransigent, insufferably vain . . . and impossible to please" in talks with the president, who failed to dissuade de Gaulle from developing a nuclear weapon, he was downright smitten with Jackie. "Mrs. Kennedy knows more about French history than most French women," he told Kennedy approvingly. Her reception by Khrushchev in Vienna was just as fulsome. "First Lady Wins Khrushchev, Too," read a headline in the *New York Times*, which would later write of the first couple's visit to London, "In the pubs, the talk is more of 'Jackie' . . . than of her husband and international politics."

The president went along self-effacingly with his wife's overshadowing presence—at least publicly. Before leaving for Vienna, he declared to a group of reporters, "I don't think it inappropriate to introduce myself to this audience: I am the man who accompanied Jacqueline Kennedy to Paris, and I have enjoyed it."

"Jack wanted more than looks," said Jackie's designer, Oleg Cassini, whose frocks for the first lady made up the bulk of the nearly two truckloads of luggage accompanying the Kennedys on their trip. "He wanted courage, accomplishment. He wanted a champion, a star."

It was apparent that Jacqueline Bouvier was a star nearly from the beginning. Born in 1929, the first child of John Bouvier III, a wealthy stockbroker of French descent, and Janet Lee, a New York socialite, she rode her first horse well before she was out of diapers, and in elementary school was characterized by one teacher as "a darling child, the prettiest little girl, very clever, very artistic, and full of the devil." Her preteen years were divided between New York City and East Hampton, a wealthy enclave near the tip of Long Island. By 1942, her mother had divorced the philandering Bouvier and married Hugh Auchincloss, a lawyer and heir to the Standard Oil fortune, bringing Jacqueline and her sister Lee to live at Merrywood, Auchincloss's home outside Washington, D.C., with summers at Hammersmith Farm, his vast estate in Newport, Rhode Island. Jacqueline and Lee, two years her junior, attended high school at Miss Porter's, an elite all-girls boarding school in Farmington, Connecticut, where Jacqueline won plaudits for her literary skills. As she later explained it, "Lee was the pretty one. So, I guess I was supposed to be the intelligent one"—this notwith-standing her designation by a local newspaper as the "Debutante of the Year" for the 1947–48 social season during her senior year, an indication of her poise and elegance, and a cool, placid natural beauty that didn't leave her lacking in male attention. But her stated ambition the same year in Miss Porter's yearbook "not to be a housewife" made a bigger statement. She was looking for more.

She attended Vassar College in upstate New York before mov-ing on to a junior year in Paris that she called her "happiest and most carefree." "I learned not to be ashamed of a real hunger for knowledge," she wrote later of the experience abroad, "something I had always tried to hide." Afterward, she transferred to American University in Washington, where she graduated with a degree in French literature in 1951. The same year, she beat out 1,280 contestants to win *Vogue* magazine's Prix de Paris, a promise that included penning an essay on "People I Wish I Had Known." She declined the prize offering her a position as junior editor in Paris when her mother objected to her leaving the U.S. Instead she went on to her first job as the "inquiring camera girl" at the *Washington Times-Herald*, making $42.50 a week.

In December 1951, she accepted a marriage proposal from John Husted, Jr., a modestly successful New York–based stockbroker, with the *New York Times* early in the following year announcing a June wedding. The writing on the wall, though, came with a missive she dashed off to him from Washington shortly into their betrothal. "Don't pay any attention to the drivel you hear about me and Jack Kennedy," she wrote. "It doesn't mean a thing." Soon afterward, she brought the engagement to an end, suggesting that she "may not be the most appropriate person" for him, and paving the way toward an open courtship with Kennedy. She and the junior senator from Massachusetts would marry in 1953 in an opulent wedding at Hammersmith Farm, a signature Kennedy event tailored to attract the national media's gaze. (Husted, for his part, would pursue a successful career as a stockbroker and member of the New York Stock Exchange, marrying happily and settling with his wife in Bedford, New York, where they raised two children.)

"How perfect it is to be married," Jackie wrote as her Acapulco, Mexico, honeymoon wound down. The marriage would hardly remain perfect. Just a few years later, as Jack's political star rose in the wake of nearly securing the vice presidential nomination, Jackie, fed up with her husband's serial philandering, was reportedly ready to pack it in. "I'm never going back," she said to Peter Ward, a British friend, several times during an excursion to France late in the summer of 1956. According to a 1960 *Time* magazine profile on the Kennedys, Joe offered her $1 million to remain in the marriage. (Afterward, she called her father-in-law and jokingly asked, "Only one million? Why not ten?") The money, which she allegedly accepted, may help explain why she stuck things out. Moreover, since her youth, she had wanted to be "part of a great man's life." However flawed, she found one in her husband. "Jack could have had a worthwhile life without me," she said, "but mine would have been a wasteland and I would have known it every step of the way." Her mother, Janet, recognized her "introvertness [*sic*], stiffness" and the difficulty she had in showing her feelings, but added that she and Jack were "very close to each other and understood each other wonderfully. He appreciated her gifts and she worshipped him and appreciated his humor and kindness."

In a letter to a journalist after the election in 1960, Jackie called Kennedy's life, like hers, an "iceberg." "The public life is above water—& the private life is submerged," she wrote. "I flatter myself that I have made his private life something he can love & find peace in."

If anyone was able to thaw the cool Jack Kennedy, at least as much as anyone could, it was her. "Jackie was the only woman I saw him show affection to," Dave Powers said. Kennedy respected Jackie; he admired her. When he once asked why women—including his wife—were so drawn to Adlai Stevenson, his paunchy, "half-bald" ambassador to the United Nations, he was told by a member of Stevenson's staff that Stevenson "conveys the idea that women are intelligent and worth listening to."

"Well, I don't doubt what you're saying," Kennedy said half-jokingly, "but I'm not willing to go to those lengths." Jackie was an exception.

Inherent in her married last name was the family business of politics, which Jackie—a "born and reared" Republican who became a Democratic convert in marriage—saw as "sort of my enemy as far as seeing Jack was concerned." She treated politics as a necessary evil, something that helped to define her husband but that she held at a distance, perhaps holding her nose at the same time. During JFK's political rise, she rarely campaigned for him; when she did, she declined to contrive a generic, plasticized politician's-wife persona geared toward relatability. Instead, she remained true to herself, not flaunting her privileged background but not hiding it, either. She simply allowed herself to be who she was: white-gloved and whispery, refined and reserved. In many ways, she was antithetical to Ethel Kennedy, described by a family friend as "more Kennedy than thou," and to the Kennedy sisters, all of whom exuberantly threw themselves into political supporting roles—hosting teas, pressing the flesh on the hustings, beaming vivaciously for the cameras. Jackie instinctively held back, knowing, as she said in the third person, that "your hair, that you spoke French, that you didn't just adore to campaign, and that you didn't bake bread with flour up to your arms" was a "liability." But, she added, "Jack never made me feel that I was a liability to him."

When the Kennedys reached the White House, the tables had fortuitously turned. As was apparent in Europe in the spring of 1961, Jackie Kennedy, distinctive and authentic, was now an indisputable asset. "All the things that I'd always done suddenly became wonderful," she said, "because anything the first lady does that's different, everyone seizes on [it]—and I was so happy for Jack, especially now that . . . he could be proud of me. . . . Because it made him so happy—it made *me* so happy."

Her husband's pride was also felt by the nation, which embraced her as she fast became a cultural export, projecting poise and urbanity that had not before been seen from a modern first lady; she was an international icon and a youthful emblem of the American brand. Her quest to "restore" the White House was backed by

Congress, which appropriated $50,000 for the effort, a sum that was augmented over time by private donations of money, art, and furnishings amounting to hundreds of thousands of dollars. It became her lofty goal to make the White House the envy of the world, so much so that the French, who epitomized style in her view, would be "ashamed of Versailles." The effort allowed for the transformation of the mansion into a chic, stately display of the best of American art and antiques. "Everything in the White House must have a reason for being there," she said. It wasn't a frivolous matter of redecorating, she argued, it was "a question of scholarship."

In 1962, eighty million American viewers tuned in to CBS for the first lady's televised tour of the newly made-over White House. The previous year she'd founded the White House Historical Association and created a White House guidebook so that the public could better understand the house's history and heritage, as well as the presidents and first ladies who had come before. Visitors flooded White House tours, with the president boasting to his wife at the end of one particularly busy day, "We had more people today than the Eisenhowers had in their first two years."

The first lady's cultivated sensibility flowed over into entertaining. The White House became a showcase for American arts and humanities, as the Kennedys welcomed artists, musicians, writers, and scholars, turning the mansion into a sort of royal court rivaling those of Europe. In the Kennedys' first year alone, a cavalcade of talent, almost all white and male—poet Carl Sandburg, composers Igor Stravinsky and Leonard Bernstein, ballet choreographer George Balanchine, filmmaker Elia Kazan—strode through the White House doors as honored guests. In early 1962, the *New York Times* wrote, "Not since Thomas Jefferson occupied what was then known as the President's Palace has culture had such good friends in the White House."

But despite her desire to be "more than just a housewife," her priority, "to take care of the president" and their children, was decidedly more traditional. "If you bungle raising your children," she explained, "I don't think whatever else you do well matters very much." Signs of a young family surrounded the White House: a swing set and trampoline stood on the South Lawn, and a preschool was established in the White House with young children coming and going on weekdays. In addition to attending her husband, Jackie devoted much of her time to Caroline and John Jr., zealously guarding their privacy and striving to give them as unaffected a childhood experience as circumstances would allow. "We better get out of the way pretty quick, things get pretty sticky when Jackie's around," Kennedy said when a photographer snapped photos of the kids that he knew were advantageous to him politically. He also knew that his family was a diplomatic asset. Letitia Baldrige, the White House social secretary, said, "One of the greatest hits made with state visitors was having the children introduced to them. . . . The president would always make sure that [Mrs. Kennedy] would be there with the children . . . which the president knew was important and relaxing to a state visitor."

Jackie would find, as would other first ladies, that she had more family time with her husband as president than she did during his Senate days. Weekends were often spent at Glen Ora, where the Kennedys could get away from the prying eyes around the White House gates. Though the president's interests and frenetic pace were ill-suited to the bucolic life of the Virginia countryside—he would have far preferred the active, aquatic life in Hyannis Port—the house was a concession to Jackie, a place where she could spend quiet time on horseback. "He liked to see me ride," she said. "He always said Daddy told him 'Keep her riding and she'll always be in a good mood.'"

Still, hers was hardly a conventional marriage, at least by the standards of the era. She and Kennedy often vacationed separately, with Jackie taking extended holidays alone or with her sister in Italy and Greece, and retreating to their four-bedroom cottage in Hyannis Port with the children from early summer until well into October, leaving the president stag in Washington. During the balance of the year, she often set out for Glen Ora for extended weekends, arriving before and leaving after her husband. "Good night, Mrs. Kennedy, wherever you are," became an inside joke at the White House, echoing comedian Jimmy Durante's signature television sign-off, "Good night, Mrs. Calabash, wherever you are."

Like his father before him, Kennedy cultivated the image of an engaged family man, with photographs of him and his frolicking children—Kennedy scooping them up in his arms or playing along with them—coveted by newspaper and magazine editors who quickly turned them into newsstand gold. While his paternal delight and affection were genuine, the children were rarely with their father more than momentarily before they were whisked away by nannies at the clap of his hands.

If the press didn't capture *that* JFK, nor did they expose the rampant and reckless womanizer we now know him to have been, which stood in far greater contrast to the family-man persona. Though, according to Charlie Bartlett, Kennedy had vowed to tamp down his extramarital sexual escapades as president, he failed to make good on his intentions. His sexual appetite was ramped up by daily cortisone shots for his back, and was fed all too readily by friends and acolytes eager to indulge him by finding willing partners: socialites, movie stars, White House secretaries and interns, and high-end prostitutes—anyone would do. It proved demoralizing for his Secret Service agents. One of them, Larry Newman, recalled, "You were on the most elite assignment in the

Secret Service, and you were there watching an elevator or door because the president was inside with two hookers."

J. Edgar Hoover, the longtime FBI director and Washington fixture who had meticulously kept the capital's most powerful people under his thumb by amassing incriminating intelligence about their sexual peccadillos, had deeper concerns. All too willing to let Kennedy know what the FBI had discovered, ostensibly for Kennedy's own political protection, Hoover generated a memo for the president titled "Judith E. Campbell: Associate of Hoodlums," which disclosed that Campbell, one of Kennedy's paramours, was also the mistress of mob bosses Sam Giancana of Chicago and John Roselli of Los Angeles. What isn't clear is whether Kennedy knew at the time that the CIA had secretly enlisted Giancana and Roselli as paid assassins in a hapless plot against Fidel Castro.

Just as disturbing on moral grounds was Kennedy's ongoing sexual relationship with Mimi Beardsley, a nineteen-year-old White House college intern who lost her virginity to Kennedy just four days into the job. Beardsley, who lacked secretarial skills, including an ability to type, conducted an eighteen-month affair with Kennedy, often traveling with him, where her sole responsibility was to wait for presidential trysts. On one especially troubling occasion, Kennedy directed her to perform oral sex on Dave Powers, over thirty years her senior, as Kennedy amusedly looked on.

To be sure, JFK had grown up learning philandering at the feet of the master, Joe Kennedy, Sr., who had affairs as a matter of course throughout his long married life, some long-term, most fleeting. "Be sure to lock the bedroom door," Jack would say, smiling waggishly at female visitors to Hyannis Port. "The ambassador has a tendency to prowl at night." Jack's friend Bill Walton recalled, "[Jack] was totally open about what a wicked old man [Joe] had been. He didn't defend him in any way. It may have rendered [Jack] as being more promiscuous himself as a result of this pattern but . . . none of us has enough evidence to know what caused that."

In the hypercompetitive, testosterone-infused Kennedy family, unbridled womanizing seemed as much about keeping score as it did the thrill of the conquest. After losing his virginity to a white prostitute in a Harlem brothel at age seventeen with Lem Billings in tow, Kennedy seemed intent on proving himself, documenting his sexual adventures with locker room bravado through a series of letters to Billings. "I can now get tail as often and as free as I want which is a step in the right direction," he boasted as a twenty-year-old.

It was a game that continued into adulthood. "I don't know how it is with you, Harold," he told the British prime minister Harold Macmillan in between meetings on nuclear arms. "If I don't have a woman for three days, I get a terrible headache." (The monogamous prime minister later sternly took him to task for "spending half" of this time "thinking about adultery.") One of Kennedy's favorite books, *Melbourne*, about the life of one of Macmillan's nineteenth-century predecessors, Lord Melbourne, depicts him and his political contemporaries nobly rendering their public duty during the day and romping in sexual abandon at night and on decadent English manor house weekends, almost as a right of the privileged class. JFK seemed to see his extramarital activities the same way, as his right. "The chase was more fun than the kill," he told Vivian Crespi, a friend of both Jack and Jackie, who maintained that Jack's escapades were "recreational, not emotional," rationalizing that "men of that type need a release."

Jackie appeared to condone her husband's philandering in the same way. If she didn't turn a blind eye to his extramarital affairs, it was at least a knowing one. She accepted it, according to Frank Finnerty, a Washington cardiologist and friend in whom she periodically confided, as "an intrinsic part of his life," a "vicious trait" that he had "undoubtedly inherited" from his father. According to Finnerty, she was not "mad or obsessed" about his sexual exploits and was aware of the women with whom he had had dalliances, including actress and sex symbol Marilyn Monroe, who "seemed to bother her the most." During a White House tour for a reporter from *Paris Match*, Jackie pointed out a young woman in the West Wing secretarial pool, commenting matter-of-factly in French, "And this is the woman my husband is supposed to be sleeping with."

That the revelation was offered to a French reporter was significant; Jackie the Francophile seemed to subscribe to the more open-minded view of marital infidelity held by the French. She had not only been mindful of the legendary womanizing of her father, who began cheating on Jackie's mother forty-eight hours into their marriage, but crowed about his sexual exploits during her days at Miss Porter's, where her father was gleefully received by Jackie's schoolmates during visits to the school. "Black Jack" Bouvier, as he was known, possessed a roguish charm that she also found in her husband. "She wasn't sexually attracted to men unless they were dangerous like old Black Jack," Kennedy friend Chuck Spalding claimed.

Andrew Cavendish, the Duke of Devonshire and onetime brother-in-law to Kick Kennedy, observed, "[Jack] Kennedy is doing for sex what Eisenhower did for golf," suggesting that Kennedy's exploits were an open secret among select insiders. True to Kennedy's compartmentalized makeup, he flaunted it to some and hid it from others. "We're a bunch of virgins, married virgins,"

Fred Dutton, the secretary to the cabinet, said. "And he's like God, fucking anybody he wants to anytime he feels like it."

Aides like Dave Powers and Kenny O'Donnell not only knew about Kennedy's proclivities but helped procure women; others like Arthur Schlesinger were kept in the dark. So were members of the press corps, with the exception of close personal friend Charlie Bartlett, whom a columnist called "a tomb of secrets."

"Like everyone else, we had heard reports of presidential infidelity, but we were always able to say we knew of no evidence, none," recalled Ben Bradlee, who would later discover that his sister-in-law, Mary Pinchot Meyer, was among Kennedy's paramours. CBS News anchor Walter Cronkite wrote in his memoir, "None of the White House correspondents I know claimed at the time to have any evidence of John Kennedy's alleged bedroom escapades. Most will tell you today that they knew about the rumors but were never able to come up with enough evidence to go with the story." It was also a condoned, if not fully accepted, part of the life of the power elite of Washington in mid-century America. As Cronkite explained, "In the sixties the Washington press, like the media elsewhere, operated on a rule of thumb regarding the morals of our public men. The rule had it that, as long as his outside activities, alcoholic or sexual, did not interfere with or seriously endanger the discharge of his public duties, a man was entitled to his privacy."

What to make of JFK's *Mad Men*–era licentiousness in the unyielding light of the twenty-first-century "#MeToo" world into which we have evolved? Kennedy's record as president points to his ability to discharge his public duties largely uncompromised. But there is a moral failing that can't be ignored. The revelations of

Mimi Beardsley in particular reflect more than just a privileged, middle-aged playboy freely indulging in the pleasures of the flesh he saw as his right. When the reports about Beardsley were revealed in Robert Dallek's 2003 biography of Kennedy, *An Unfinished Life*, journalist Hugh Sidey, who revered Kennedy despite the many salacious revelations and rumors that had dribbled out about him in the years after the assassination, was taken aback, causing his dispirited reevaluation of Kennedy. "I think the guy had a problem," he said incredulously. The most powerful man in the free world's objectification and exploitation of a nineteen-year-old intern goes well beyond the common consensual extramarital sex of the time, pointing to the most disturbing recesses of Kennedy's complex, multilayered psyche; his negligence and callousness can't be rationalized by a wayward paternal influence or the mid-century zeitgeist.

Regardless, the president and Mrs. Kennedy weathered whatever storms his philandering may have brought to bear in their marriage, which strengthened during his years in the presidency as she tapped her aesthetic talents and refined sensibility to make a lasting contribution to American life. It allowed the country to realize the singularity that her husband had seen in her all along. She called the thirty-four months they spent in the White House "our happiest years."

THE WALL

Sirens wailed in the small hours after midnight, adding to a cacophony that included the clamor of jeeps, trucks, and Russian-made tanks rolling ominously down cobblestone streets. As the din rose, East German troops fanned out through the city, some setting up makeshift checkpoints as others lined the porous twenty-seven-mile border of West Berlin, which the previous month alone had seen the migration of more than thirty thousand East Germans. By daybreak on the morning of Sunday, August 13, 1961, it was done. East Berlin awoke to a hastily constructed thirteen-foot-high barbed wire and cinder block wall that now divided the city, gray and somber, from its vibrant sister to the west, a blockade that would grow more forbidding with upgrades over time. It would become known as the Berlin Wall, or simply the Wall, a potent symbol of communist tyranny.

Discharged early from Sunday mass due to the summer heat, the president was fifteen minutes into a sail on his boat the *Marlin* in Nantucket Sound off the coast of Hyannis Port when he was called back to shore with reports of the development. The news was no great surprise. Khrushchev's situation, Kennedy knew, was "unbearable" as East Germans were "hemorrhaging" out of the city. Since 1945, over four million had escaped the German Democratic Republic—many of them highly skilled professionals—with the numbers escalating month after month. "The entire East bloc is in danger," Kennedy told Walt Rostow days before the wall went up. "He has to do something to stop this. Perhaps a wall. And there's not a damn thing we can do about it."

Kennedy was also of the mind that he could rally Western alliance powers to take action only if Khrushchev made a move against West Berlin, not East Berlin. Despite Khrushchev's initial apprehension that it would be too provocative, a wall, it seemed, was almost an inevitability. Two weeks before it went up, William Fulbright had seeded the notion of the East Germans building a barrier between the cities on national television, wondering aloud on a news broadcast why the GDR "didn't close the border," asserting his belief that they "have a right" to do it.

In fact, Kennedy was coming around to the idea of a wall bordering East Berlin himself. "Why would Khrushchev put up a wall if he really intended to seize West Berlin?" he asked Kenny O'Donnell rhetorically later. "There wouldn't be a need for a wall if he occupied the whole city. This is his way out of a predicament. It's not a very nice solution, but a wall is a hell of a lot better than a war."

On July 25, Kennedy used a televised address to the nation to draw a clear line in the sand for Khrushchev at the foot of West Berlin. Mindful that the Soviets had attempted to cut off Western access to the city during a tense standoff in 1948, prompting Harry Truman to order the fifteen-month-long Berlin Airlift, Kennedy called Berlin "the great testing place of Western courage and will, a focal point where our solemn commitments stretching back over the years since 1945, and the Soviet ambitions now meet in basic confrontation." He warned, "We do not want to fight, but we have fought before. We cannot and we will not permit the Communists to drive us out of Berlin either gradually or by force."

To that end, Kennedy welcomed the wall as a means of defusing the threat of war. Though the theory is unproven, historian Michael Beschloss has suggested that Bobby Kennedy may have indicated to Georgi Bolshakov, a midlevel diplomat at the Soviet Embassy in Washington and undercover Soviet military intelligence operative whom Bobby would use as a back channel to Moscow, that the U.S. would not challenge the Soviets militarily if a wall went up between the east and west sectors.

As he was briefed telephonically by Dean Rusk in Washington on August 13, fresh from being summoned back from his sail, Kennedy took the news in stride. While irate that U.S. intelligence didn't see it coming, he was heartened by the fact that no Soviet troops were involved in the maneuver and that access hadn't been choked off to West Berlin, which saw no disruption. Seeing nothing that needed to be done in the immediate term, Kennedy was soon back on board the *Marlin*, gliding on Nantucket Sound. "Okay, go to your ballgame," he told Rusk at the close of their call, knowing his secretary of state had planned to go to Griffith Stadium to watch the Washington Senators play the New York Yankees. "I'm going sailing."

While it may have solved a problem for Kennedy, defusing for the moment the threat of a greater conflict, his ostensible acceptance of the wall drew fears among West Berliners that America had abandoned them. Three days after the wall went up, *Bild*, a large-circulation West German newspaper, ran a front-page story headlined, "The East acts—and what does the West do? The West does NOTHING!" Not nothing, exactly. Kennedy had ordered 1,600 American troops from the Army's Eighth Division into the city, carefully monitoring their safe passage across the one hundred miles of autobahn from West Germany into West Berlin. He also dispatched Lyndon Johnson to West Berlin as a diplomatic gesture, where upon arrival Johnson declared the "gallant" city had "become an inspiration to the entire world."

But Kennedy's response fell well short of West Berlin mayor Willy Brandt's demand that the wall be met by American tanks and that Kennedy register a formal protest at the United Nations. A candidate for West Germany's chancellorship, Brandt suspended his campaign for the moment and took his concern directly to the Western allied commanders of the United States, Great Britain, and France. "The Berlin Senate publicly condemns the illegal and inhumane measures by those who are dividing Germany," he said. "The cold concrete stakes that cut through our city have been driven into the heart of German unity and into the living organism of our single city of Berlin."

Kennedy's acquiescence further alienated him from the military's top brass, including Lyman Lemnitzer, now suspicious of Kennedy nearly to the point of hostility. The chairman of the Joint Chiefs of Staff privately condemned Kennedy's passivity in the matter, judging the West's approach to the cold war to be "hopeless, helpless and harmless." But by and large, criticism of Kennedy in the matter was as muted as Kennedy's response.

As the year closed, the public seemed willing to give Kennedy a pass not only for the Berlin Wall but for the foreign policy disasters that had preceded it, granting him an approval rating of 79 percent. Part of his popularity owed to a recovering economy. Just ten days into his presidency, Kennedy had warned Congress that "the American economy is in trouble." By the end of the year, it was on the uptick. An infusion of domestic and military deficit spending by the administration, in adherence to widely held Keynesian economic theory that advocated using federal stimulus to combat recession or counter inflation, allowed for modest economic growth in 1961 and paved the way for a prosperous new year, which would see a gross domestic product boost of just over 6 percent.

As important as his actions, though, was Kennedy's image. "Reporters liked Kennedy for being instinctively graceful and natural," recalled Ben Bradlee, "physically unable to be programmed or corny." Yet it was hardly instinctive. Conscious of the infamous photo op of Calvin Coolidge awkwardly sporting a Sioux feather headdress as being one of the only things people remembered about Coolidge, Kennedy worked diligently to craft his own image, forgoing the hokey "man of the people" contrivances that were a go-to standard for many of his predecessors.

The graceful persona he projected, his youthful "vigor" and elegant style, made Kennedy the most interesting and celebrated man in America within a matter of months after his election. Part of his allure was an air of mystery. "No one ever knew John Kennedy, not all of him," Charlie Bartlett contended. Kenny O'Donnell and Dave Powers, Kennedy's close friends and aides since his days stumping for Congress in the midforties, paradoxically titled their 1972 memoir of their time with him *Johnny, We Hardly Knew Ye*. That was the way Kennedy wanted it. Even to intimates he revealed different shades of a complicated, sometimes contradictory nature, never showing any of them the entirety of who he was. As Jackie said, "He really kept his life so [*sic*] in compartments." He remained enigmatic even to her.

The president's immense popularity resulted in the emulation of much of America and the launch of consumer trends. Demand for cigars rose as a result of Kennedy's two-a-day habit, and the sale of men's hats and button-down collared shirts plummeted due to the fact that he rarely wore them. A Georgetown bookstore's increased newsstand sales of 400 percent were attributed to a spike in readership among a public imitating Kennedy's voracious appetite for the written word. (Arthur Schlesinger called Kennedy "a fanatical reader . . . not only at normal times and places but at meals, in the bathtub, sometimes even when walking.") In early 1962, a poll among college students had Kennedy surpassing matinee idols to top the list of men with the greatest sex appeal.

If the public was besotted with Kennedy, he in turn was consumed by the news media's coverage of him. He actively worked members of the press—*New York Times* columnist Arthur Krock called it "social flattery"—laying on his profuse charm to bring them to his side. Generally, it was an easy sell. As Kennedy biographer Richard Reeves wrote, "John Kennedy's life was sequential seduction and there were few complaints from the seduced."

That didn't mean he always liked what the press wrote. Without question, Kennedy saw the value of a free press. In a late 1962 press conference, NBC reporter Sander Vanocur, reminding Kennedy that he had once said he was "reading more and enjoying it less," asked him whether he still read the news avidly. Kennedy responded by calling the news media "an invaluable arm of the presidency as a check on what's going on in the administration." Comparing it to the totalitarian system in which Khrushchev operated, "which has many advantages as far as being able to move in secret," he added: "There isn't any doubt that we could not do the job at all in a free society without a very, very active press."

But reporters writing an unfavorable article about the administration could expect it to be challenged vociferously by members of Kennedy's team. "They remind me of the ballplayer who yells at the umpire after a strike call," said a veteran reporter. "The batter has no hope of changing the ump's decision, but he hopes to soften him up for the next pitch."

It also applied to Kennedy, who wasn't shy about expressing his own views. His friendship with Kennedy notwithstanding, Ben Bradlee found himself frozen out by the White House when an August 1962 *Look* magazine story titled "Kennedy vs. the Press" quoted him as saying of Jack and Bobby, "It's almost impossible to write a story they like. Even if the story is quite favorable to their side, they'll find one paragraph to quibble with." A thaw between the president and Bradlee came a month later when Bradlee wrote a *Newsweek* piece refuting rumors that Kennedy had been previously married to a Palm Beach socialite named Durie Malcolm. The White House gave Bradlee FBI documents disproving the story only after Bradlee agreed to show the president the story before it was published, the only time Bradlee would consent to such a provision.

Kennedy may have been most concerned about the coverage in *Time*, the behemoth newsmagazine that commanded national attention each week. Every Sunday night, before copies were stuffed into mailboxes and stacked on newsstands across the country, the president was served up a fresh issue directly from the printer. Frequently, he took exception to its coverage. When *Time* incorrectly reported that Kennedy had posed for the cover of the men's fashion magazine *Gentlemen's Quarterly*, widely regarded as a gay publication—a "fag rag," Bobby Kennedy called it—he berated *Time*'s White House reporter Hugh Sidey, calling it "a lie." "I'm getting sick and goddamned tired of it," he told Sidey. "People remember people for one thing. . . . People are going to remember me because I posed for the cover of *Gentlemen's Quarterly*." (An image of Kennedy appeared on the cover of *Gentlemen's Quarterly* in March 1962 with the heading "New Fashion Frontier," but Kennedy did not pose for the magazine.)

Often Kennedy took his complaints directly to Henry Luce, the magazine's owner and editor. Like almost everyone else, it seemed, Luce, a moderate conservative, found himself drawn to Kennedy. "I don't agree with Kennedy on most things. But I like him," he said. His affinity for Kennedy may have helped to explain why, in late December, *Time* named him as its "Man of the Year," its annual designation for the newsmaker who, for better or for worse, had made an impact on the year. In Kennedy's case, it was clearly for better. "He took over the [presidency] with a youth-can-do-anything sort of self-confidence," the magazine wrote. "He learned better; but learn he did. And in so doing he not only made 1961 the most endlessly interesting and exciting presidential year within recent memory; he also made the process of his growing up to be President a saving factor for the U.S. in the cold war."

But *had* the newly tested, more experienced Kennedy provided a "saving factor" in the cold war? Without a doubt, the resolution of the Berlin crisis alleviated the tension that posed the greatest threat of a nuclear exchange between the superpowers. It allowed Khrushchev to solve the immediate problem of western migration that had become a festering sore for the Soviet Union and the communist sphere while not being directly provocative toward West Germany and the Western powers. But had it pacified the Soviets' global ambition? Did Khrushchev see Kennedy any differently than the "weak," inexperienced leader he had been before the Berlin Wall went up? That remained to be seen.

Joe Kennedy was inclined to agree with *Time*. Though the controversial Kennedy father was kept prudently at arm's length from the White House, rarely consulted by his sons as they toiled at the business of state, he was a keen observer. "I tell you, Hugh," he told Sidey before the year ended, "Jack is the luckiest guy I know. He could fall into a pile of manure and come up smelling like a rose. The Bay of Pigs and the other things were the best lessons he could have gotten and he got them all early. He knows what will work and what won't, who he can trust and who he can't, who will stick with him and who will not."

A blow, however, came before the year was out. On December 19, 1961, during a round of golf in Palm Beach, Joe suffered a massive stroke that would later leave him almost entirely paralyzed on his right side and largely unable to speak. The bigger-than-life, effusively positive Kennedy patriarch who embodied the family's vitality and ethos, fueling the ambitions of his sons, would be reduced to the life of an invalid whose only intelligible word was *no*.

The president had just returned to the White House from Florida earlier that morning when Bobby called to tell him of their father's illness. He looked stunned. "Dad's gotten sick," he told Pierre Salinger. Presently, he, Bobby, and their sister Jean boarded Air Force One and rushed from Washington to Palm Beach to be at his bedside. There Bobby took charge, ordering doctors to keep him alive, fighting for his life; Lem Billings recalled Joe being "one breath away."

Joe Kennedy would live through the entirety of his son's presidency, becoming one of only four presidential fathers to do so. But his days of being an active participant in the life of the president, who perhaps trusted him more than anyone, were over. By then, Bobby had already stepped in to fill the void.

III

THE BRINK

At the height of the Cuban Missile Crisis, JFK and members of his
ExComm team meet on the West Colonnade outside the Oval Office,
October 29, 1962.

Cecil Stoughton, White House Photographs, JFK Library

THE BROTHERS KENNEDY

It couldn't have been easy for Robert Francis Kennedy. Buck-toothed and pint-sized—he would never grow taller than five nine—Bobby was called "the runt" by his father, dwarfed and outshined by his two older brothers, whose sheen was blinding. Not much was initially expected of him. "Bobby? Forget it," Eunice said when someone singled out Bobby for praise in the family. "Let's talk about the other boys." Even his mother fretted that he was "girlish," perhaps the worst insult for a boy in the virile, red-blooded Kennedy family.

Throughout his formative years, he struggled to distinguish himself, serving as an altar boy to please his pious mother, yet taking boxing lessons and later making the varsity football team at Harvard through sheer grit to prove himself to his demanding father. Kenny O'Donnell, his Harvard teammate, said, "I can't think of anyone who had less right to make varsity than Bobby. If you were blocking him, you'd knock him down, but he'd be up again going after the play. He never let up. He just made himself better."

A sensitive loner by nature, Bobby compelled himself to be

tough. As a boy in Hyannis Port, frustrated that he couldn't yet swim like his older siblings, he hurled himself off a sailboat into Nantucket Sound to force himself to do so as an existential necessity. Instinctively, Joe Jr., Bobby's idol, leapt to his aid, bringing him safely back on board as Jack, who held his brother at a distance, watched from the beach, uncertain as to whether the act reflected his younger brother's acute bravery or utter stupidity.

Jack's blasé attitude toward Bobby didn't much change as they got older. When his father suggested that the twenty-year-old Bobby help run Jack's 1946 campaign for Congress, Jack resisted, acerbically telling a friend, "I can't see that sober, silent face breathing new 'vigor' into the campaign." His nickname for Bobby, "Black Robert," said it all, and throughout Bobby's young adulthood, it fit. As Jack would discover, though, the toughness and diligence Bobby had shown on the football practice field at Harvard could turn into a take-no-prisoners ruthlessness that would be beneficial to Jack throughout his political career. Bobby made himself indispensable as Jack's hatchet man, earning his brother's confidence and respect with hard work and unyielding loyalty.

The same toughness came into play in advancing Bobby's own career. After graduating from Harvard with a degree in government in 1948 and earning his law degree from the University of Virginia in 1951, he went on to serve as a junior lawyer in the Justice Department. Two years later, a phone call from Joe Kennedy to Wisconsin Republican senator Joseph McCarthy cinched Bobby a position as assistant counsel on McCarthy's Senate Permanent Subcommittee on Investigations, whose anti-Communist crusade had played out perniciously by that time. (Though Kenny O'Donnell would later claim that "Bobby didn't know McCarthy from a cord of wood," McCarthy was a Kennedy family friend who had gone out on dates with Pat and Jean. While Bobby resigned from the committee after six months due to the investigation's excesses and would later renounce it while acting as chief counsel for the Democratic minority, McCarthy's moral absolutism spoke to Bobby's inherent sanctimony.)

Toughness also defined Bobby's two-year stint as chief counsel on the McClellan Committee, named for Arkansas senator John McClellan and charged with investigating labor racketeering. There Bobby was given broad leeway to interrogate witnesses, which he did with characteristic pugnacity, including the grilling of Jimmy Hoffa, the notorious head of the Teamsters Union who would become a lifelong enemy.

But when Jack's career beckoned, those turns were quickly put aside. At twenty-six, Bobby diligently managed his brother's Senate campaign—tie loosened, sleeves rolled up—driving the staff to do more but outworking everyone under him to help maneuver Jack's underdog win against Henry Cabot Lodge, Jr. When Jack vied for the presidency eight years later, it naturally fell to Bobby to run the show. There was really no other choice.

Once Jack was elected president, it was Joe Kennedy who had insisted that Bobby become Jack's attorney general, just as he had always defined the roles the two would play. As RFK biographer Evan Thomas wrote, Joe's view was: "Jack was noble. Bobby was tough. Jack was the visionary. Bobby the enforcer. Jack's job was to move forward. Bobby's to cover his back." If the religious Bobby was a crusader, never shying away from a fight, he found his greatest cause to that point in his life in serving his brother. Despite his initial resistance to joining the administration in order to launch his own political career, which would become the narrative that he and the family would put forth, it seemed a foregone conclusion that Bobby would aid his brother in the White House. "For many reasons I believe it is the only thing I could do," he told Drew Pearson a little over a month after his brother's election victory. Family always came first, nepotism be damned.

Shortly after he took on the job, however, Bobby's responsibilities were extended well beyond the halls of the Department of Justice and its thirty-two thousand employees. When things went awry for Jack with the Bay of Pigs, signaling trouble for his presidency, he turned instinctively to Bobby to help turn things around, regretting not involving him in the operation from the beginning. It was a turning point.

"Up until that time, Jack more or less dismissed the reasons his father had given for wanting Bobby in the cabinet as more of that tribal Irish thing," Lem Billings said. "But now he realized how right the old man had been. When the crunch came, family members *were* the only ones he could count on. Bobby *was* the only person [in the administration] he could rely on to be absolutely dedicated. Jack would never have admitted it, but from that moment on the presidency became a sort of collaboration between them."

Jack tasked a committee to become known as the Cuba Study Group—composed of Bobby, CIA chief Allen Dulles, the Joint Chiefs' admiral Arleigh Burke, and retired general Maxwell Taylor—with looking into what went wrong. Bobby burrowed dutifully into the task, spending long hours at the CIA and in a windowless office at the Pentagon while also attending to his immediate duties as attorney general.

"All of us involved made mistakes," he concluded, reflecting the consensus of the group. "The President has taken responsibility, but it was everybody's fault." Along with Jack, Bobby's wariness of careerists across government became more pronounced as he saw their decisions colored by their own interests, avoiding risks that might jeopardize their chance to ascend the rungs of the civil service ladder rather than acting for the good of the president and the country at large. It was hardly the kind of bold thinking the Kennedys envisioned for the New Frontier. Likewise, the Kennedy brothers grew distrustful of the military brass. As the president told a White House guest, "The first thing I'm going to tell my successor is to watch for the generals, and to avoid feeling that just because they were military men, their opinions on military matters were worth a damn." At Bobby's recommendation, Taylor would go on to work in the White House to provide the president with his own military counsel. Within the White House itself, Bobby advocated for more direct and candid dialogue with top aides.

As the administration moved beyond the Bay of Pigs, Bobby's role expanded further. Behind the scenes, he continued to be his brother's chief protector, covering up affairs with mafia moll Judith Exner and Ellen Rometsch, a high-end prostitute believed by the FBI to be a spy for the East German government. But increasingly, his public profile was rising. In February 1962, he and Ethel embarked on a monthlong, eleven-country tour around the world where he met with heads of state on behalf of his brother, signaling his expanding importance and influence in the administration as the president's international surrogate and raising questions about his own political future. The title of a February 1962 *U.S. News & World Report* cover story on Bobby put the question squarely: "Bobby Kennedy: Is He the 'Assistant President'?"

As Robert Kennedy circles the globe, representing this country abroad, speculation grows in Washington. How powerful is the role of the President's younger brother? What part does he play in shaping presidential decisions? . . . Is he being groomed to take over the Presidency himself, succeeding his brother? . . . Digging for answers to such questions, you find 'Bobby' Kennedy's influence in almost every corner of the Government. . . . The younger Kennedy is circling the globe carrying credentials second only in importance to those of the President himself.

The role of presidential surrogate was nothing new. Other presidents had tapped alter egos who acted on their behalf, traveling the world with their proxy. Woodrow Wilson had Edward House, nicknamed "Colonel" despite having no military background, who acted as his "executive agent," helping him to secure the Democratic nomination for president in 1912 and acting as his diplomat in chief during World War I. Likewise, Harry Hopkins was a critical adviser to FDR, assisting in the hatching of the New Deal during the Depression and becoming his international ambassador-at-large during World War II. In the later years of the administration, Hopkins became a literal White House insider, taking up residence in the Lincoln Bedroom for nearly four years.

But Bobby Kennedy did House and Hopkins one better. No president before John Kennedy had tapped a family member to join his cabinet and so manifestly relied on him as a member of the administration. Bonded by blood and inextricably bound by family loyalties and shared ambitions, the president and attorney general became almost synonymous. "We're both cryptic," the president said; they communicated "by osmosis." While their interactions were relatively infrequent—in-person meetings once or twice a week, phone calls every other day or so—Bobby was unquestionably the president's closest adviser, the one he turned to immediately when a crisis erupted.

"Get Rusk on the phone. Go get my brother," he barked to an aide upon hearing the news that the Berlin Wall had been built. "Don't kid anybody about who is the top adviser," Lyndon Johnson observed. "Bobby is first in, last out. And Bobby is the boy he listens to." Arthur Schlesinger called Bobby "his brother's total partner" who "more than anyone else enabled the President to infuse the government with the energy and purpose of the New Frontier."

The two differed in personality and temperament. *U.S. News* quoted an unnamed Kennedy insider as saying that Bobby, more than Jack, was "prone to look at things more as black or white, particularly in sizing up personalities. The President is more tolerant in his judgement of people." In its own February 1962 cover story on Bobby, titled "More Than a Brother," *Time* wrote, "Bobby lacks his brother's easy grace, he is earthier, bristling in his loyalties, implacable in his enmities." Ben Bradlee said that "Jack Kennedy admired above all his brother's toughness," a trait he didn't share to the same extent. But increasingly the Kennedy brothers were becoming two halves of the same whole.

As to rumors that there were family plans afoot for him to succeed his brother in the presidency, Bobby dismissed them out of hand as "so obviously untrue." But, as *Time* pointed out, "If he does not want to become President, it is safe to say that he wants his brother to become a great President, assisted by a great Attorney General. Meanwhile, as President John Kennedy . . . [has] long known, [and] as the U.S. has come to realize . . . Bobby Kennedy is a power in his own right." That much was undeniable.

The ambitions of Ted Kennedy, the youngest of the Kennedy brood, were as obvious in 1962 as his candidacy to fill the Senate seat his brother had vacated upon winning the presidency, kept warm by Jack's friend Ben Smith. The Kennedy men were split on whether the thirty-year-old Ted, just three years out of law school at the University of Virginia and presently serving in Massachusetts as the assistant deputy attorney for Suffolk County, should seek higher office. Jack and Bobby were opposed to it on the grounds that it would complicate things for them politically. But Ted wanted it. More important, so did Joe Kennedy. Before his stroke, the Kennedy father had told his older sons, "You boys have what you want now, and everyone else helped you work to get it. Now it's Ted's turn. Whatever he wants, I'm going to see he gets it." That was all it took; capitulating, Jack said, "I don't want him to run and Bobby doesn't want him to run either. But if he's going to do it, we don't want him to lose."

Edward Moore Kennedy was destined to go into the family business of politics. His 1932 birth was met by President Herbert Hoover with a bouquet of flowers and a congratulatory note to his mother—with five cents postage due. Moreover, Ted was a political natural, gregarious and aspiring, and imbued with a vivacious, easygoing nature and the strong Kennedy jaw and winning smile. Rounding out his profile were his attractive wife, Joan, the debutante daughter of a New York City ad executive, and their two small children. During his brother's presidential run, Ted had shown his political chops by overseeing the thirteen western states, tirelessly stumping on Jack's behalf and earning the admiration of his two brothers, who claimed that no one had worked harder. He brought the same ethic to his own campaign in the Bay State, his right hand expanding half an inch from a profusion of handshaking on the hustings as he worked to defeat his Democratic rival for the nomination, the state's attorney general, Eddie McCormack.

The campaign hit a snag when the *Boston Globe* revealed that Ted had been thrown out by Harvard in 1951 for cheating, having talked a classmate into taking a Spanish exam for him. (After a two-year stint in the Army, he was readmitted to Harvard, where he graduated with a degree in history and government in 1956.) Jack, who had tried in vain to prevent the piece from running by arranging an arm-twisting Oval Office meeting with the article's writer, remarked, "We're having more trouble with this than the fucking Bay of Pigs."

It turned out to be an apt analogy. Just as Jack had risen from the ashes of the Bay of Pigs more popular than ever, the younger Kennedy not only survived the scandal but walked away with 70 percent of the primary vote in September, with the Kennedy machine revving up for the general election in November. Yet as Jack and Bobby expected, their brother's political emergence came with its own fallout. After the primary win, the *New York Times* wrote that the victory was "demeaning to the dignity of the Senate and the democratic process." Republican National Committee chairman William Miller was less kind. "We're going to take a lot of votes all over the country out of this," he maintained, "because people are going to think twice about the dynasty issue now. It was bad enough making Bobby attorney general. But even that wasn't the joke this one is."

If it was a joke, the Massachusetts voters were in on it. In November, Ted walked away with an easy win over his Republican challenger, George Cabot Lodge II, in the heavily Democratic state's general election, laughing all the way to Washington. Whatever shortcomings his résumé may have had, they were more than overcome by the Kennedy charisma and celebrity mystique. Despite America's resistance to political dynasties and warnings of

"Kennedyism," it became increasingly clear in 1962 that the Kennedys were an irrepressible political force, with Jack poised for eight years in the White House, widespread chatter that Bobby and Ted—an heir and a spare—were waiting in the wings for their turns, and a gaggle of Kennedy progeny being prepared to carry the torch for the next generation.

KEEPING THE PEACE

John Kennedy had a simple wish for how he wanted to be remembered. "All I want people to say about me is what they said about John Adams," he allowed: "'He kept the peace.'" Born into wealth and privilege, Kennedy had little understanding of economic hardship. When asked while running for the presidency what he remembered about the Great Depression, Kennedy responded with surprising candor. "I have no firsthand knowledge of the Depression," he told Hugh Sidey, conceding that his family had "one of the great fortunes in the world" and that the only understanding he had of it came later in the reading he did at Harvard. "My experience is war," he said. "I can tell you about that." Kennedy had seen the grim ravages of World War II up close. The formative experience shaped him, and he saw no good in it. "All war," he wrote in 1943, "is stupid."

World War II had exacted a devastating toll on his family, claiming the lives of his older brother and his brother-in-law, as well as two of his closest friends. Afterward, the Kennedys took nothing for granted. "It turned my father and brothers and sisters and I upside down and sucked all the oxygen out of our smug and comfortable assumptions," he wrote in 1947 to a friend in the State Department. "Now, after all that we experienced and lost in the war, we finally understand that there is nothing inevitable about us."

He did, on the other hand, see the inevitability of war, and he was certain that a nuclear conflict between the United States and the Soviet Union would lead to mutually assured destruction, a term used so often at the time that it earned the acronym MAD. Informed by the books he had devoured by history's great military strategists, he concluded, "Ever since the longbow, when man had developed new weapons and stockpiled them, somebody has come along and used them. I don't know how we escape it with nuclear weapons."

But he was determined to try. As he embarked on his second year in the presidency in an increasingly dangerous world, alleviating the threat of nuclear holocaust would become Kennedy's most important pursuit—and his greatest challenge. Four nations—the United States, the Soviet Union, the United Kingdom, and France—had successfully developed nuclear weapons by 1961, with China and Israel close to achieving their own nuclear capabilities and the danger lurking that other nations, including rogue states, would follow, heightening the possibility of a nuclear conflict. In a press conference late in his presidency, Kennedy expressed his view that by the next decade the United States would have "to face a world in which 15 or 20 or 25 nations" may have nuclear weapons. He made it plain that he regarded nuclear proliferation as "the greatest possible danger and hazard." In his January 11, 1962, State of the Union address, Kennedy put the issue of nuclear disarmament front and center:

> World order will be secured only when the whole world
> has laid down these weapons which seem to offer us

present security but threaten the future survival of the human race. That armistice day seems very far away. The vast resources of this planet are being devoted more and more to the means of destroying, instead of enriching, human life. . . . This nation has the will and the faith to make a supreme effort to break the log jam on disarmament and nuclear tests—and we will persist until we prevail, until the rule of law has replaced the ever dangerous use of force.

Any hopes of immediate disarmament he may have had were dashed later in the month when the Conference on the Discontinuance of Nuclear Weapon Tests, attended by representatives from the United States, the United Kingdom, and the Soviet Union, and held nearly continuously in Geneva since the fall of 1959, was suspended on January 29, 1962, without a trilateral agreement. The culprit was the Soviet Union, which balked at on-site verifications by a control commission made up of scientists from each of the nations to determine whether seismic activity was caused by an earthquake or an illicit nuclear test; the Soviets deemed instrumental verification sufficient.

Just over two weeks later, portending the demonstrations that would later become a hallmark of the 1960s, hundreds of students came together outside the White House gates to protest nuclear testing. But they were in the minority. A January 1961 Gallup Poll reflected the support of the American public for nuclear testing by a ratio of two to one, a reflection of the very cold war fears Kennedy had stirred during his presidential campaign by promoting the notion of a "missile gap," with the USSR surpassing the United States militarily.

After the ill-fated summit in Vienna, during which Khrushchev dismissed Kennedy's overtures toward arms reduction, and later Kennedy's challenge in a September 1961 address to the United Nations "not to an arms race, but a peace race," the Soviets resumed atmospheric nuclear tests. Before the year was out, they would conduct thirty-one atmospheric tests, including the testing of a bomb four thousand times more powerful than the one the United States dropped on Hiroshima in 1945 to force an end to World War II. Under pressure to keep up, Kennedy had little choice but to continue the U.S.'s own testing, which he resumed in April 1962.

A bigger problem for Kennedy was the hawkish Pentagon brass, which mounted pressure to continue U.S. testing and the proliferation of the American nuclear arsenal, asserting their belief, unlike Kennedy's, that a nuclear showdown with the Soviets would not necessarily end in mutual destruction. Less than a decade earlier, the Korean War had ended in stalemate, leaving a bitter taste in the mouths of the military establishment; five-star general Douglas MacArthur had vainly advocated the use of atomic weaponry to bring the conflict to a conclusive end, just as the United States had done in the Second World War. Instead, his commander in chief, Harry Truman, relieved him of his command, straining relations between the White House and the military. Not only did the military higher-ups under Kennedy not trust him, they were determined not to give him sole control over first-strike nuclear decisions. NATO commander General Lauris Norstad and Air Force generals Curtis LeMay and Thomas Power openly challenged White House directives that limited their authority around nuclear decisions.

The distrust or disdain they had for Kennedy was reciprocal. From the start of his presidency, Kennedy harbored worries that the Joint Chiefs of Staff would push the world into nuclear apoca-

lypse, and he remained deeply suspicious of the Pentagon brass—
especially after the Bay of Pigs. Arthur Schlesinger recalled Kennedy
examining cables Joint Chiefs chairman Lyman Lemnitzer had sent
the president during an inspection tour of Laos, and exclaiming,
"If it hadn't been for the Bay of Pigs, I might have been impressed
by this." As Schlesinger saw it, "JFK's war hero status allowed him
to defy the Joint Chiefs." He blamed Eisenhower for leaving him
with "a bunch of old men" as his top military brass, including
Lemnitzer, whom he considered "a dope." It spoke volumes that
he worried less about Khrushchev's launch of a nuclear warhead in
a surprise attack than the Pentagon brass taking rogue action that
might result in catastrophe.

Given the jingoism of the Joint Chiefs and Kennedy's inherent
cautiousness, it was no surprise that they saw Vietnam differently,
with the Joint Chiefs advocating the dispatch of up to two hundred thousand troops to engage directly in combat alongside
South Vietnamese soldiers. Without question, Kennedy saw the
strategic importance of Vietnam as a bulwark of Western resolve
over the spread of communism in Southeast Asia, where in 1954
the United States had signed on to the Southeast Asia Treaty Organization (SEATO), a pact with nine mostly–Southeast
Asian nations pledging to defend the region from communist aggression.

The cold war—"a global civil war" Kennedy called it in his 1962
State of the Union address—was at its height, and America's cred-
ibility around the world would be at risk in not actively taking a
stand against communist insurgency. Sensitive to being perceived
as weak on communism by the right wing at home, Kennedy also
saw Vietnam's political significance. But he resisted the notion of

sending American combat soldiers to Vietnam's shores. Instead, he bolstered support of the government of South Vietnam's president, Ngo Dinh Diem, through "Operation Beef-Up." True to its name, the policy authorized a twofold increase in South Vietnamese military assistance in 1962, including escalating the number of U.S. military advisers from 3,205 at the close of 1961 to over 9,000 by the end of 1962, while secretly granting them greater involvement in South Vietnam's military efforts and allowing for the introduction of chemical weapons: napalm, defoliants, and herbicides. Though falling well short of the military's recommendations, Kennedy's policy exceeded those of his own advisers, Maxwell Taylor and McGeorge Bundy, whose dire reports after an inspection tour in South Vietnam prompted greater urgency from the administration.

The administration's investment in Diem was not without risks. His regime was rife with corruption, with Diem shoring up political power by making military and local government appointments based on loyalty over competence. There was also the growing disaffection over the Roman Catholic Diem's systematic oppression of the country's majority Buddhist population. Between 10 and 11 million of South Vietnam's 14.5 million people considered themselves Buddhists, while Roman Catholics, the nation's ruling class, numbered less than 10 percent. During an early 1963 visit, a high-level U.S. State Department official said, "The thing that bothers me about this government is that the only people who are for it are the Americans." Charmed by Diem during a visit to South Vietnam in May 1961, Lyndon Johnson hoisted a champagne flute during a diplomatic reception, toasting Diem as "the Winston Churchill of Asia," while privately harboring reservations over Diem's increasing totalitarianism and the general inefficiency of his government. But, for the moment at least, the pro-Western Diem was the Kennedy administration's best bet in fending off communist insurgency. "Shit," Johnson replied when asked by a journalist later if he was sincere in likening the South Vietnamese president to Churchill, "Diem's the only boy we got out there."

By the midpoint in Kennedy's presidency, the bet seemed to be paying off. In 1962, bolstered by the helicopters and tanks provided by the U.S., the Army of the Republic of Vietnam (ARVN) was successful in thwarting the communist threat without relying on U.S. combat troops. Diem's strategic hamlets program, allowing for the fortification of small, rural villages throughout the country to repel communist military forces and reduce political influence, seemed to be working. The stabilization of South Vietnam gave Kennedy enough hope that he ordered Robert McNamara to begin the withdrawal of U.S. military advisers by the end of the following year. That was, of course, assuming the situation held. In 1962, there was reason to believe that it would.

"WE CHOOSE TO GO TO
THE MOON"

The life of New York almost stood still," wrote the *New York Times* on February 20, 1962. As many as nine thousand people crammed into Grand Central Station, standing shoulder to shoulder in silence as they watched black-and-white images from Cape Canaveral, Florida, flicker on huge television screens—the largest static crowd, police said, ever to amass in the station's forty-nine years. Students throughout the city were liberated from classes and ushered into cafeterias to watch the TVs that had been set up for the day, as pedestrians walked with transistor radios cupped to their ears or crowded into bars, diners, or the television sections of department stores to watch with employees who had suspended work to join them. For the first time in the New York City Transit Authority's history, the subway's loudspeaker system was used for an announcement unrelated to the prosaic business of public transport. "Colonel John H. Glenn, Jr., has just taken off in his rocket for orbit," the disembodied male voice crackled throughout the line at 9:36 a.m. "Please say a prayer for him."

The balance of the country was no different. Over 100 million Americans tuned in to see if Glenn would become the third

American in space—following the suborbital lobs of his fellow "Mercury Seven" astronauts Alan Shepard and Gus Grissom the previous year, both lasting less than fifteen minutes—and the first to reach Earth's orbit. Far more viewers watched around the world. That was the point. In keeping with the openness at the core of American democracy, John Kennedy had made the conscious decision to televise the mission. It wasn't to be done clandestinely, as the Russian space flights had been, revealing only their triumphs, but transparently.

But the risk was an embarrassment for all the world to see. Ten times Glenn's mission had been scheduled; ten times it had been scrubbed, due to weather or technical malfunctions. All the while, the Soviets dominated the space race largely uncontested, boasting technological superiority with two successful orbital launches, including their latest in August 1961 as cosmonaut Gherman Titov rounded the earth seventeen times during the course of his twenty-four-hour flight. Cartoons in the Soviet newspapers mocked NASA's delays, including one of a bearded Atlas rocket at Cape Canaveral in a barber's chair awaiting a shave.

In Washington, John Kennedy awoke early and turned on his bedroom television set at 7:15 a.m., muting the sound as he ate his breakfast with Jackie and pored over his morning newspapers before heading to the small dining room in the West Wing, where he, Lyndon Johnson, and congressional leaders watched Glenn's *Friendship 7* capsule lift off promisingly. Glenn, the forty-year-old former Marine pilot, was the ideal face for the American space program: a churchgoing, clean-living all-American hero-in-the-making who looked like he had been plucked from a box of Wheaties. "If only he were a negro," quipped Johnson, imagining the boon to civil rights and spurring a laugh from Kennedy.

Toward the end of its four hours and fifty-six minutes, the

mission hit a snag. An indicator light in mission control signaled a problem with the spacecraft's heat shield, in place to protect the capsule from burning up upon reentering the Earth's atmosphere. Had it come loose or broken off? If so, it would mean almost certain death for Glenn during reentry. Tension descended on the West Wing. Kennedy canceled a planned congratulatory phone call to Glenn while he was in orbit, which would have been seen as a morbid exercise if the mission were to go wrong. Happily, it turned out to be a false alarm. After a harrowing reentry, with the cool-headed Glenn manning control of the cramped, sweltering capsule manually in order to keep a retro-rocket in place to better secure the heat shield, the flight came to a spectacular end. *Friendship 7* splashed down safely in the Atlantic near Bermuda after circling the globe three times, pushing speeds of over 17,000 miles an hour in the course of its 75,000-mile journey. While the United States had not pulled ahead of the Soviets, it had successfully entered the next leg in its quest for the moon. "We have a long way to go in this space race," Kennedy said in a statement after the flight. "But this is the new ocean, and I believe the United States must sail on it and be in a position second to none." After a slow start, America was in the game.

Kennedy was thrilled by the adventure of it all. Two days later, he traveled down to Cape Canaveral to greet Glenn before bringing him, Alan Shepard, and Gus Grissom back to Washington on Air Force One to award Glenn the NASA Distinguished Service Medal. During the bulk of the ninety-minute flight, the president sat in the plane's forward cabin with the three astronauts. Aides saw clearly that he didn't want to be disturbed with other matters. He wanted to talk about space—not the technical aspects but the experience itself, barraging Glenn with questions about his flight.

He was drawn by Glenn's courage under fire. Shepard, in turn, was taken by Kennedy's pioneer spirit.

In the late summer, Kennedy brought the same spirit to the nation. The year prior, before a joint session of Congress, he had audaciously proclaimed his administration's aim to reach the moon before the end of the decade, resulting in Congress's approval of a year-over-year increase in NASA's budget of 89 percent, and then 101 percent the following year. But he had yet to rally the nation behind the undertaking. That changed memorably with a presidential visit to Houston on September 12. On a bright afternoon, after touring NASA's Manned Spacecraft Center, Kennedy addressed a crowd of some forty thousand in the football stadium at Rice University. His speech, written by Ted Sorensen, was an eloquent expression of the race to the moon as a distinctly American proposition, a fulfillment of our destiny as a nation.

> The exploration of space will go on whether we join in it or not. And it is one of the great adventures of all time. And no nation which expects to be the leader of other nations can expect to stay behind in this race for space. . . . We mean to be a part of it. We mean to lead it. . . . But why, some say, the moon? Why choose this as our goal? And they may ask why climb the highest mountain? Why, 35 years ago, fly the Atlantic? Why does Rice play Texas?

Kennedy had handwritten the reference to Rice playing Texas into the typed speech, a savvy politician's pandering nod to the football-crazed Texans before him, who whooped their approval. He continued in quintessential fashion: the thrusting right hand, youthful dynamism, and distinct Boston-accented cadence, which echoed metallically through the stadium's loudspeakers.

> We choose to go to the moon. We choose to go to the moon in this decade and do the other things, not because they are easy, but because they are hard, because that goal will serve to organize and measure the best of our energies and skills, because that challenge is one that we are willing to accept, one we are unwilling to postpone, and one which we intend to win.

He closed by calling the moon shot "the most hazardous and dangerous and greatest adventure on which man has ever embarked."

And yet, adventure and the test of the human spirit—indeed, the *American* spirit, as he defined it—were just happy by-products of JFK's commitment to the United States' dominance in space. If his foreign policy was hewed in response to cold war pressures, so, too, was the space program. Ultimately, like his commitment to keep communist insurgency in check in Vietnam, it was about ensuring that the USSR would not overtake the U.S. militarily, technologically, or ideologically. "I think the United States cannot permit the Soviet Union to become dominant in the sea of space," he said in an informal press conference in June. "There are many military implications to it which are still yet unknown." And, as he had said in his policy address to Congress the previous year, reaching the moon was a crucial step toward winning "the battle that is now going on around the world between freedom and tyranny."

Kennedy made that plain two months later in a tense but crucial November 21 Cabinet Room meeting with NASA officials, including James Webb, the agency's administrator, in which the group

JFK in his Senate office in 1959, prior to his bid for the White House, sitting in a rocking chair that would later become a symbol of his presidency.

Jacques Lowe, Jacques Lowe Photographic Archive, Briscoe Center for American History, University of Texas at Austin

The Kennedy family (*left to right*): Bobby, Jack, Eunice, Jean, Joe Sr., Rose, Patricia, Kathleen, Joe Jr., and Rosemary at their Hyannis Port compound, September 1931.
Richard Sears, JFK Library

Nearly thirty years later, the Kennedys and their spouses gather in Hyannis Port to celebrate a day after JFK's narrow presidential election victory, November 9, 1960.
Jacques Lowe, Jacques Lowe Photographic Archive, Briscoe Center for American History, University of Texas at Austin

JFK, Jackie, and Caroline Kennedy, July 1958.
Jacques Lowe, Jacques Lowe Photographic Archive, Briscoe Center for American History, University of Texas at Austin

The Kennedys take a break at an Oregon diner during a campaign swing, November 1959. Jackie declined to contrive a relatable political wife's persona, instead remaining true to herself.
Jacques Lowe, Jacques Lowe Photographic Archive, Briscoe Center for American History, University of Texas at Austin

LBJ, RFK, and JFK meet during the Democratic National Convention in Los Angeles, July 14, 1960. RFK's contempt for LBJ was returned in kind.
Jacques Lowe, Jacques Lowe Photographic Archive, Briscoe Center for American History, University of Texas at Austin

JFK campaigns in Kansas, in the fall of 1960.
Jacques Lowe, Jacques Lowe Photographic Archive, Briscoe Center for American History, University of Texas at Austin

JFK watches election returns in Hyannis Port with members of his campaign staff and the Kennedy family as RFK emblematically stands behind him, November 8, 1960.
Jacques Lowe, Jacques Lowe Photographic Archive, Briscoe Center for American History, University of Texas at Austin

JFK and Dwight Eisenhower in their second transition meeting, January 19, 1961. JFK's false charges of a "missile gap" with the Soviets stoked fears among Americans that the USSR had gained technical superiority in the Cold War.
Abbie Rowe, White House Photographs, JFK Library

JFK takes the oath of office from Chief Justice Earl Warren,
January 20, 1961.
United States Army Signal Corps Photographs, JFK Library

The Kennedys arrive at the
Inauguration Ball at the
National Guard Armory in
Washington.
*Abbie Rowe, White House
Photographs, JFK Library*

On his first full day as president, JFK greets his first guest, Harry Truman, outside the West Wing, January 21, 1961.
Abbie Rowe, White House Photographs, JFK Library

Five days after taking office, JFK holds his introductory press conference as president, drawing over sixty-five million television viewers, January 25, 1961.
Abbie Rowe, White House Photographs, JFK Library

JFK and his brother-in-law Sargent Shriver prepare to meet the inaugural group of volunteers for the Peace Corps, which would become an embodiment of Kennedy's "Ask not . . ." ideal, August 28, 1961.
Abbie Rowe, White House Photographs, JFK Library

Early in his presidency, JFK meets with the Joint Chiefs of Staff. He regarded the military brass warily, especially after they and the CIA put "national pride above national reason" by advocating the botched Bay of Pigs incursion.
Jacques Lowe, Jacques Lowe Photographic Archive, Briscoe Center for American History, University of Texas at Austin

After the Bay of Pigs, JFK meets with Dwight Eisenhower at Camp David, April 22, 1961. Eisenhower warned him that the mission's failure would "embolden the Soviets."
Abbie Rowe, White House Photographs, JFK Library

In their first state visit together, Jackie upstages her husband during their stop in France, reflecting her international celebrity, May 31, 1961. "Paris Has a New Queen," a French newspaper headline gushed.
Jacques Lowe, Jacques Lowe Photographic Archive, Briscoe Center for American History, University of Texas at Austin

JFK and Nikita Khrushchev meet at their much-anticipated summit in Vienna, June 3, 1961. After it concluded, JFK privately confessed that he had been "savaged" by Khrushchev, who left believing that JFK was "too intelligent and too weak."
(above) US Department of State, JFK Library; (left) Jacques Lowe, Jacques Lowe Photographic Archive, Briscoe Center for American History, University of Texas at Austin

Martin Luther King Jr. gets arrested in Montgomery, Alabama, in 1958, as his wife, Coretta Scott King, looks on. King's nonviolent campaign for civil rights would be a constant in JFK's presidency, pushing JFK to take a more active stand.
Charles Moore, Charles L. Moore Photographic Archive, Briscoe Center for American History, University of Texas at Austin

JFK and John Glenn inspect Glenn's *Friendship 7* capsule after Glenn's triumphant orbital flight, February 23, 1962. Despite the Soviets' lead in the space race, Kennedy boldly called for the US to reach the moon by the end of the decade.

Cecil Stoughton, White House Photographs, JFK Library

JFK meets with Roger Blough *(left)*, the president of U.S. Steel, and labor leader David McDonald. A year earlier, JFK had successfully gone to "war" with Blough to prevent a hike in steel prices that would lead to an inflationary economy.

Cecil Stoughton, White House Photographs, JFK Library

JFK campaigns in Buffalo prior to the 1962 midterm election, which yielded the best midterm result for Democrats since 1934. While he paradoxically considered himself to be "the antithesis of a politician," he also believed he "fit the times."

Cecil Stoughton, White House Photographs, JFK Library

JFK and his closest advisor, RFK, huddle outside the West Wing on October 3, 1962. Bonded by blood and shared ambitions, the president and attorney general became almost synonymous, communicating, JFK said, "by osmosis."
Cecil Stoughton, White House Photographs, JFK Library

JFK addresses the nation on the buildup of missiles by the USSR in Cuba, which would bring the two superpowers to the brink of nuclear war, October 22, 1962.
Cecil Stoughton, White House Photographs, JFK Library

At the height of the Cuban Missile Crisis, JFK, flanked by Secretary of State Dean Rusk (*right*) and Secretary of Defense Robert McNamara (*left*), meets with his National Security Council, ExComm, on October 29, 1962. JFK's triumph over the USSR in the crisis owed to his restraint and equanimity.
Cecil Stoughton, White House Photographs, JFK Library

Student civil rights demonstrators get blasted by weaponized fire hoses in Birmingham, Alabama, in 1963. National media coverage of the "direct action" campaign would show the brutal systemic racism that pervaded the South.

Charles Moore, Charles Moore Photographic Archive, Briscoe Center for American History, University of Texas at Austin

Alabama governor George Wallace stands in the doorway at the University of Alabama to prevent the integration of Black students, June 11, 1963. That evening, JFK spoke to the American people, elevating the civil rights crisis as "a moral issue."

Shel Hershorn, Shel Hershorn Photographic Archive, Briscoe Center for American History, University of Texas at Austin

Martin Luther King Jr. delivers his soaring "I Have a Dream" speech, culminating in the March on Washington for Jobs and Freedom, August 28, 1963.

Flip Schulke, Flip Schulke Photographic Archive, Briscoe Center for American History, University of Texas at Austin

Immediately after the March on Washington, JFK and LBJ meet with organizers, including Martin Luther King Jr., John Lewis, A. Philip Randolph, and Whitney Young.

Cecil Stoughton, White House Photographs, JFK Library

JFK peers into East Berlin from the Berlin Wall's "Checkpoint Charlie," June 26, 1963. Nikita Khrushchev called the divided city "the most dangerous spot in the world."
Cecil Stoughton, White House Photographs, JFK Library

In December 1961, JFK meets with Henry Cabot Lodge Jr., who would become his ambassador in South Vietnam. The Kennedy Administration backed South Vietnamese president Ngo Dinh Diem, but by late 1963, Lodge believed the war was unwinnable with Diem in power and a coup against him was inevitable.
Robert Knudsen, White House Photographs, JFK Library

JFK signs the Nuclear Test Ban Treaty, his proudest presidential accomplishment, October 7, 1963.
Cecil Stoughton, White House Photographs, JFK Library

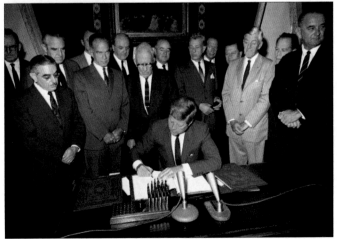

Always happiest when he was on the water, JFK enjoys a sail on the Nantucket Sound, September 1963.

Abbie Rowe, White House Photographs, JFK Library

A week after the loss of their prematurely born son, Patrick, the Kennedys relax in Hyannis Port with their children and family dogs, August 14, 1963. The death of Patrick further bound the public to JFK and Jackie while deepening the relationship between the two of them.

Cecil Stoughton, White House Photographs, JFK Library

JFK meets with LBJ in the Oval Office, September 17, 1963. The same month, while sailing with friends, Kennedy asked, "How do you think Lyndon would be if I got killed?"

Abbie Rowe, White House Photographs, JFK Library

The Kennedys after touching down in Houston during their visit to Texas, November 21, 1963.
Cecil Stoughton, White House Photographs, JFK Library

The following morning, the Kennedys arrive at Dallas Love Field, November 22, 1963.
Cecil Stoughton, White House Photographs, JFK Library

RFK, Jackie, and Ted Kennedy at President Kennedy's funeral services, November 25, 1963.
Jacques Lowe, Jacques Lowe Photographic Archive, Briscoe Center for American History, University of Texas at Austin

The White House portrait of John F. Kennedy. Artist: Aaron Shikler, 1970.
White House Collection/White House Historical Association

debated the future of the U.S. space program. The president asked Webb if a manned mission to the moon should be NASA's top priority.

"No sir, I do not. I think it is *one* of the top priority programs," Webb said frankly, asserting that "several scientific disciplines" had converged around space exploration, including satellite communications and weather prediction, and should be pursued with equal determination.

"Jim, I think this *is* the top priority," Kennedy countered. "I think we ought to have that very clear. . . . This is important for political reasons, international political reasons and for . . . whether we like it or not, in a sense a race. . . . If we go up second to the moon, it's nice but it's like being second any time. . . . So, I think we have to take the view that this is the top priority of it. It certainly is mine."

Webb and members of his team continued to push back, questioning whether a lunar landing was even scientifically possible. Kennedy didn't budge. "The policy ought to be that this is the top priority of the agency and one of two—except for defense—the top priority of the United States," he insisted. It wasn't the moon shot itself—"I'm not that interested in space," he confessed to the group—but the endeavor as a vehicle to show American resilience and resolve to overcome the Soviet Union. "The only justification for [the cost of] it, in my opinion," Kennedy said, "is because we hope to beat them and demonstrate to the entire world that starting behind, as we did by a couple years, by God we passed them."

Being the first to the moon, the leader in the space race, also served Kennedy's objectives as a keeper of the peace. There was a moral imperative in it. "Space science, like nuclear science and all technology, has no conscience of its own," he said at Rice. "Whether it becomes a force for good or ill depends on man. And only if the United States occupied a position of preeminence can we help decide whether this new ocean will be a sea of peace or a new terrifying theater of war."

Landing on the moon, though, wouldn't come cheap. Between 1960 and 1973, NASA—between the Mercury, Gemini, and Apollo manned space programs—would spend $28 billion. Resistance around the moon shot abounded. Liberals in Congress saw it as crowding out important domestic programs and far too expensive to warrant any return on investment. Among others, William Fulbright urged Kennedy to put the money he had allocated to space behind education. "Bill, I completely agree with you," Kennedy told him. "But you and I know that Congress would never pass that much money for education. They'll spend it on the space program, and we need those billions of dollars in the economy to create jobs." Without question, efforts around manned space missions were a windfall for the economy. During the course of Kennedy's administration alone, NASA's ranks jumped from 16,500 to 28,000, while the agency's contractors ballooned from less than 60,000 to over 200,000.

Still, when the pace of the Soviets' space efforts slowed and his concern about the budgetary impact of America's own efforts began to mount as public support waned, Kennedy expressed private uncertainty about the program. In a September 1963 phone conversation between Kennedy and Webb, the positions of the two around the space program seemed to invert, with Kennedy questioning the effort and Webb reinforcing its value. By then, NASA had launched three additional orbital flights; Glenn's triumph was followed by the successful missions of Scott Carpenter, Wally Schirra, and Gordon Cooper, whose May 1963 ride—Project

Mercury's last launch—took him around the earth twenty-two times in thirty-four hours. Kennedy proclaimed Cooper's flight "one of the great victories of the human spirit," as NASA began gearing up for Project Gemini, the next phase of the space program. Fretting that orbital space flight had "lost a lot of its glamour," Kennedy thought that public interest might be reignited if the Russians, who had failed to up the ante, achieved "some tremendous feat."

"Why should we spend that kind of dough to put a man on the moon?" he demanded of Webb. "We've got to wrap around in this country, a military use for what we're doing and spending in space. If we don't, it does look like a stunt."

Webb reassured him. "While you're president, this is going to come true in this country," he said firmly. "You're going to have both science and technology appreciating your leadership in this field, without a doubt in my mind. . . . And, I predict you are not going be sorry—no sir—that you did this."

Kennedy's concerns were largely rhetorical. Both men knew the die was cast. Kennedy had told the world that America had chosen to go to the moon—and there was no going back.

"GOING FOR BROKE"

U nder normal circumstances, John Kennedy didn't get angry for long. His passions stirred briefly, then cooled, the broad smile quickly returning to his face. Even in the double-dealing business of politics, he tended not to get worked up or hold grudges. Often, he was the first to extend a hand to a foe after the heat of battle. But in the early spring of 1962, his anger flared.

On the afternoon of April 11, as Kennedy strode to the podium in the State Department for his thirtieth press conference, his usual joviality—the slight smile, the rakish head nod acknowledging those in the press corps, the wry quip—was conspicuously missing. As he stepped to the microphone, his indignation was palpable. "Simultaneous and identical actions of United States Steel and other leading steel corporations, increasing steel prices by some $6 a ton," he began bitterly, "constitute a wholly unjustifiable and irresponsible defiance of the public interest."

Just a dozen days earlier, the United Steelworkers of America had settled a contract with U.S. Steel in which the parties agreed to a ten-cent-an-hour hike in fringe benefits in lieu of a wage increase. The "non-inflationary" agreement, in Kennedy's words, would ensure that steel prices, which had not increased since 1958, would remain flat, and that the nation's steel mills would continue to hum along with the economy at large. Kennedy, who feared inflation would get in the way of the sustained economic growth that he saw as key to a successful presidency, and his re-election, had urged corporate America to refrain from price increases in keeping with the *"Ask not . . ."* sacrifices he had beseeched all Americans to consider as a contribution to the greater good.

U.S. Steel was the third-largest corporation in America, and it, along with its competitors in the steel sector, had significant influence on the economy as a whole. When the dispute between the industry's management and labor had been resolved—aided and encouraged by the Kennedy White House—he could breathe a sigh of relief. With the 1961 recession now past and the threat of inflation reduced, the economy was poised to continue to expand unimpeded.

All that changed on April 10. During a late afternoon Oval Office meeting arranged hastily at the request of Roger Blough, the fifty-eight-year-old president of U.S. Steel—the country's largest steel producer—and the chairman of Kennedy's Business Advisory Council, Blough handed Kennedy a four-page mimeographed press release. U.S. Steel, it informed him, had raised the price of steel by 3.5 percent to $6.00 a ton. The move set things in motion for its competitors. By late the following day, Bethlehem Steel Corporation, the country's second-largest steel company, along with four other large steel interests representing 85 percent of steel production, would follow suit.

Kennedy seethed as he read the announcement. "I think you're making a mistake," he told Blough direly. "You double-crossed me." After Blough was shown the door, Kennedy was more direct with the aides he convened in the West Wing to discuss the crisis. "He fucked me," he said. "They fucked us, and we've got to try to fuck them."

His secretary of labor, Arthur Goldberg, who had worked with the steel companies toward their late March agreement with the union, put it even more bluntly: "This is war."

War it was—and the outcome was by no means inevitable. In order to combat the threat of inflation, Kennedy would battle with the most powerful players in the steel sector, men whom Kennedy's father had warned him were "pricks." Reflecting on the situation later, Kennedy said that if he had "made a speech about it and then failed . . . that would have been an awful setback. There is no sense in putting the office of the presidency on the line on an issue and being defeated."

The bellicose tenor Kennedy struck in his April 11 press conference made it clear that he had no intention of going down in defeat. He used the balance of the thirty-one-minute session to excoriate Blough and his counterparts, leaving no question on where he stood. "At a time when restraint and sacrifice are being asked of every citizen," he said, "the American people will find it hard—as I do—to accept a situation in which a tiny handful of steel executives whose pursuit of private power and profit exceeds their sense of public responsibility can show such utter contempt for the interest of 185 million Americans."

Roger Blough, whose $300,000 annual salary was over a hundred times the median American income of $2,800, watched the president silently from a conference room at U.S. Steel's corporate offices in New York. Mounting his defense, he called his own press conference, justifying the actions of the steel companies in the interest of competitiveness. Just as the White House wasn't buying it, neither was much of official Washington, which became a hive of activity to compel big steel to roll back the price hikes. Kennedy's allies in Congress opened up four antitrust investigations, while the Pentagon pulled back steel purchases from U.S. Steel and granted them to smaller companies that hadn't imposed the increases.

"Going for broke," Bobby Kennedy set in motion his team at the Department of Justice to determine if antitrust laws had been breached by steel executives while enlisting FBI agents to check newspaper reports of a Bethlehem Steel shareholder meeting that suggested that the company's sudden price shift was the result of collusion with U.S. Steel. One overzealous agent stirred a Philadelphia reporter from his bed at three a.m. to badger him with questions.

At the White House, Arthur Goldberg, Robert McNamara, and Douglas Dillon called executives and officials across the country to mount pressure on the steel executives as Kennedy threatened to continue to use the bully pulpit to pound away at their greed.

The steel executives, looking for a way out, groped for a compromise. Goldberg and Clark Clifford, the Washington power broker whom Kennedy had tapped to manage his transition, were dispatched to New York, where Blough dangled an olive branch at a meeting at the Carlyle hotel, proposing to meet in the middle. Clifford called Kennedy with Blough's offer. "Blough and his people want to know what you would say if they announce a partial rollback of the price increases, say 50 percent," he said.

"I wouldn't say a damn thing," Kennedy replied, unmoved. "It's the whole way."

Shortly afterward, he got his wish. Bethlehem Steel was the first to back down publicly, stating that it would rescind its increase. The move put U.S. Steel on its heels. Blough learned that his chief competitor had caved during his meeting with Clifford and Goldberg, before, "pale and shaken," according to Clifford, he took leave of the men to huddle with his team. At 5:30 p.m., nearly forty-eight hours to the minute after he had handed his statement to Kennedy in the Oval Office announcing he would impose a price increase, Blough released another one, rolling it back for the sake of "relations between government and business." Clifford reached Kennedy by phone as the president was touring the USS *Northampton* at Naval Station Norfolk in Virginia. "We have met the enemy and they are ours," Clifford reported. "They have capitulated, Mr. President."

Kennedy's triumph was short-lived. Immediately, he was castigated for executive overreach, charged with employing fascist tactics to bend the steel industry to his will. The *New York Herald Tribune* was among those who took him to task, running a scathing op-ed and a cartoon that had Pierre Salinger returning from a trip to the USSR and informing the president, "Khrushchev said he liked your style in the steel crisis."

"The fucking *Herald Tribune* is at it again," Kennedy said when he saw the coverage, promptly ordering the cancellation of the White House's twenty subscriptions, a move that only turned up the heat for Kennedy.

The episode had calmed down by the middle of the following month, even becoming parody when Kennedy celebrated his forty-fifth birthday prematurely with a splashy May 19 Democratic Party fundraiser before an audience of fifteen thousand at New York's

Madison Square Garden. Jack Benny, Maria Callas, Harry Bela-fonte, Henry Fonda, Ella Fitzgerald, and Kennedy brother-in-law Peter Lawford were among the celebrities who helped mark the occasion. But they were mere footnotes. It was Marilyn Monroe who stole the show.

In an iconic fusion of Washington and Hollywood glamour unmatched before or since, Monroe shimmied into a hint of dress—nude colored and backless—that she called just "skin and beads." Even that may have been an understatement. The pricy Jean Louis creation, composed of scant silk gauze and a galaxy of rhinestones, clung to her like scales on a goldfish, and had to be hand-sewn onto the bombshell, delaying the proceedings. When she finally emerged, Monroe, who would be dead of a barbiturate overdose at age thirty-six just three months later, crooned to the tune of Bob Hope's signature song, "Thanks for the Memory":

> *Thanks, Mr. President,*
> *For all the things you've done,*
> *The battles that you've won*
> *The way you deal with U.S. Steel*
> *And our problems by the ton*
> *We thank you so much.*

More indelible, though, was her breathy, seductive version of "Happy Birthday," which was as scandalous as her dress. After taking the microphone from Monroe, Kennedy, who attended the event stag, said ironically, "I can now retire from politics having had 'Happy Birthday' sung to me in such a sweet, wholesome way."

The day before the president's actual birthday, however, he got a reminder that the cost of the steel industry showdown was lingering in the form of a rap on him as anti-business. On May 28, after slowly declining since Kennedy's election, the Dow Jones Industrial Average plunged nearly 6 percent, the highest one-day drop since 1929's "Black Friday" precipitated the Great Depression. "The stock market careened downward yesterday," wrote the *Wall Street Journal* the following day, "leaving traders shaken and exhausted." The market correction was called the "Flash Crash," or, more pointedly, the "Kennedy Crash." "When the market went down, it's the Kennedy stock market," Kennedy griped; "when it goes up, it's the free enterprise systems."

A survey conducted in June revealed that just over half of six thousand business executives thought Kennedy to be "strongly anti-business," while another 36 percent saw him as "moderately anti-business." Kennedy strove to do better, reaching out to corporate America in the following months while making a tax cut a domestic priority to prime the pump of the stalled economy. And when the steel industry put a rate increase in place the following year, it went unchallenged by the Kennedy White House.

"In winning the victory [against U.S. Steel]," wrote Arthur Schlesinger later, "Kennedy answered the question with which the business community had confronted every activist Chief Executive since [Andrew] Jackson: 'Who is President anyway?' He delivered his answer at a cost, but the cost of not answering would have been greater." Kennedy now took his place among progressive presidents who had used the bully pulpit to battle capitalist forces in the name of the greater good. Jackson, encouraged by the support he received in his populist 1832 reelection bid, had taken out the Second Bank of the United States. Theodore Roosevelt had mounted a trust-busting assault on monopolies including J. D. Rockefeller's Standard Oil, and Woodrow Wilson continued the crusade, drawing the ire of big business by creating the Federal Trade Commission to keep large corporations in check. But the U.S. Steel episode would reinforce a lesson Kennedy would learn throughout his tenure in office, just as his predecessors had learned in theirs: There are no final victories in the presidency.

OLE MISS

In the early fall of 1962, Louis Martin, known as the "Godfather of Black Politics" and John Kennedy's only African American adviser, told the president something he didn't want to hear. Despite the fact that the civil rights movement had quieted since the bloody Freedom Rides of the spring and summer of 1961, the restless stirrings of Blacks striving for civil rights in the Jim Crow South were once again about to bring tensions to a boil. "Negroes are getting ideas they didn't have before," Martin said.

"Where are they getting them?" Kennedy wanted to know.

"From you," said Martin. "You're lifting the horizons of negroes." He reminded Kennedy of the rhetoric in his inaugural address: *"My fellow citizens of the world, ask not what America will do for you but what together we can do for the freedom of man."*

If the horizons of African Americans had been lifted to the point of activism, it had been an unintended consequence. Kennedy had expressed the aspiration in the context of the cold war and had little interest in moving more than cautiously in propelling action on the front lines of the civil rights movement. But African Americans, fed up with systemic oppression and economic inequality in the Jim Crow South, had their own idea of what "the freedom of man" meant and were taking matters into their own hands.

Among them was a grandson of slaves, James Howard Meredith. A native of rural Kosciusko, Mississippi, where he grew up on a farm the seventh of ten children, Meredith was a student at Mississippi's all-Black Jackson State University after serving in the Air Force for nine years. As Kennedy spoke the words of his inaugural address against the harsh winter air in Washington, Meredith made a decision: He would challenge racial segregation by attempting to gain admission to the University of Mississippi, "Ole Miss," in Oxford, a bastion of Mississippi's proud segregationist tradition. For Meredith, it wasn't about education. It was about "power," about "enjoying everything any other man enjoys." He was a son of Mississippi. As such, he believed its most distinguished institution of higher learning stood there for him and those like him.

Twice Meredith had applied and twice he had been rejected. Then, aided by the NAACP, he mounted a legal challenge to the school's segregation policy, and was granted admission in the fall of 1962. Gaining a court order from the Fifth Circuit of the U.S. Court of Appeals ensuring his acceptance to the university and actually enrolling, however, were two different things. Intent on protecting the status quo, Mississippi's defiant segregationist governor, Ross Barnett, stood firmly in the way of Meredith's admission—literally at first.

When the twenty-nine-year-old Meredith showed up to register for the university at a Jackson, Mississippi, state government building flanked by two U.S. marshals, the bespectacled sixty-four-year-old Barnett was soon there to greet him. "Where's Meredith?" he asked mockingly as laughter filled the room where Meredith was conspicuously the only African American. Eight minutes later, after telling Meredith that he was denied admission "in order to prevent violence . . . in order for his own protection . . . and in order to maintain and perpetuate the dignity and tranquility of the great and sovereign state of Mississippi," Barnett sent him off with a copy of his gubernatorial proclamation to the same effect. The headline in the next day's *Jackson Daily News* portended the tumultuous days ahead: "Thousands Said Ready to Fight for Mississippi."

For over a week Bobby Kennedy had been talking with Barnett about the situation by phone, trying to orchestrate Meredith's peaceful enrollment, just as he would in the days ahead. Barnett's resistance was no surprise to him or to his brother. The Kennedys understood that Barnett needed to maintain a segregationist pose, resisting integration as a political expedient, just as Barnett knew that he would ultimately have to yield to federal authority.

Negotiations between the two went back and forth, Barnett often dripping with "bless your heart" smarminess that belied his resistance. He asked Bobby if the Kennedys were really prepared for a showdown "over one black boy . . . backed by the NAACP, which is a communist front." An unapologetic, intractable racist, Barnett would never be convinced that "white and Negro should go together." Bobby responded that it wasn't a matter of their personal opinions. John Kennedy looked at it much the same way. When an aide reminded the president of the great risk he was taking by throwing the weight of the presidency around the enrollment of one African American, he responded, "I have no choice. I don't have the power to call off Meredith."

On September 26, Meredith tried enrolling again, this time on the Ole Miss campus in Oxford, accompanied by eight U.S. marshals. Barnett drove 165 miles from Jackson to Oxford in his powder blue Cadillac to once again cut off Meredith's efforts. Instead, state troopers did it for him, forming a blockade that prevented the marshals from advancing on Ole Miss's grounds. For the next several days, negotiations between the attorney general and the Mississippi governor surged through long-distance phone lines. On September 27, the motorcade carrying Meredith and two dozen marshals turned around when Bobby and Barnett couldn't come to terms on how many marshals would draw their guns on Barnett, compelling him to step down and allow Meredith to register. "General," Barnett had said, hoping for an overwhelming show of federal force, "we got a big crowd down here, and if one pulls his gun and we all turn, it would be very embarrassing. Isn't it possible to have them all pull their guns?"

Barnett had arranged for 220 highway patrolmen to be on campus to enlist in Meredith's protection, but the matter of getting Meredith matriculated remained at a standstill. Bobby had been reluctant to get his brother directly involved, but he now believed the situation warranted his direct intervention. On September 29, Barnett received a call from the president.

"What can they do to maintain law and order and prevent the gathering of a mob and the actions taken by a mob? What can they do? Can they stop that?" Kennedy demanded of Barnett.

"Well, they'll do their best to. They'll do everything in their power to stop it," Barnett drawled, before adding, "You don't understand the situation down here."

"The only thing is, Governor," replied Kennedy, "I've got my responsibilities. This is not my order. I just have to carry it out. So, I want to get together and try to do it with you in a way which is most satisfactory and causes the least chance of damage to the people in Mississippi."

Later that afternoon, Barnett dangled a proposition: Meredith could register for classes in Jackson while the administration would give Barnett cover by suggesting that federal authorities had gone around him. Grasping for a resolution to the crisis, Kennedy agreed. What was the alternative? But on the night of Sunday, September 30, 1962, all hell broke loose in Oxford, Mississippi.

The evening prior, Barnett was on hand with a crowd of fifty thousand at a football game in Jackson as the seventh-ranked Ole Miss Rebels took on the Kentucky Wildcats. At halftime, the governor stepped defiantly to a microphone at midfield. "I love Mississippi," he proclaimed, his fist in the air as he stood his ground, whipping the crowd into a frenzy. "I love her people, our customs. I love and respect our heritage." It was a shot over the bow aimed directly at the White House. As for the deal to get Meredith registered, Barnett had taken it off the table.

In response, the Kennedys took the gloves off. Bobby, who had secretly recorded all of the conversations he and the president had with Barnett, called the governor offering proof of the deal that Barnett had made with the administration. The president, Bobby told him, would be making his own speech in which he would disclose that Barnett had reneged on his promise to aid in registering Meredith, and, as a result, he had federalized the National Guard to enlist in Meredith's protection as he registered for classes. Barnett panicked.

"You don't mean to say the president is going to say that tonight?"

"Of course he is," Bobby shot back. "We have it all down."

Bobby was true to his word. On Sunday evening, the president spoke to the nation. "Americans are free to disagree with the law but not to disobey it," he said somberly. "For in a government of laws and not of men, no man, however prominent or powerful, and no mob, however unruly or boisterous, is entitled to defy a court of law." He then addressed the student body of the University of Mississippi:

> You have a new opportunity to show that you are men of patriotism and integrity. For the most effective means of upholding the law is not the State policeman or the marshals or the National Guard. It is you. . . . The eyes of the nation and of all the world are upon you and upon all of us, and the honor of your university and state are in the balance.

The appeal fell on deaf ears. As Kennedy spoke, a mob of between two and four thousand riled students and outside agitators began gathering on campus. They came zealously after a radio address from Barnett in which he announced to Mississippians that he had been forced to admit Meredith, who had been flown to Oxford and moved into Baxter Hall, a campus dormitory. Meanwhile, state senator George Yarbrough ordered the withdrawal of the 220 state highway patrolmen Barnett had committed to enlist in Meredith's protection. It fell to five hundred U.S. marshals, most of them border patrol agents and prison guards who had been newly sworn in to their current duties, to maintain order. They anxiously awaited reinforcement from the National Guard troops, who had yet to be mobilized from Memphis, some eighty miles away.

A riot broke out almost immediately. The horde angrily waved Confederate flags, sang "Glory, glory segregation" to the tune of "The Battle Hymn of the Republic," and chanted "Two, four, one, three: We hate Kennedy." They burned cars and threw rocks and bottles, storming Baxter Hall when they learned it was where Meredith was being housed, as the marshals tried in vain to fend them off with tear gas, which quickly ran out. Gunfire rang out as chaos and confusion reigned over the campus. Assistant U.S. attorney general Nick Katzenbach hunkered down at the Lyceum, an administrative building that had served as a hospital for soldiers during the Civil War, trying to update the White House by phone. Should the marshals fire back in self-defense? he asked. "No," Kennedy ordered, with specific instructions that they were "not to fire under any conditions" unless Meredith's life was threatened. Before daylight, sixteen thousand U.S. Army regulars were brought in by air.

Throughout the night, Kennedy monitored the scene from the West Wing before groggily retiring to bed at 5:30 a.m. after the situation quieted. By then, the devastation in Oxford was becoming clear: Reports came in that a French journalist and a local jukebox repairman had been murdered through gunshots to the head, and over three hundred people were injured, including more than a third of the marshals, twenty-seven from gunshot wounds.

Late in the day an unnerving stillness set over Oxford, which was now occupied by twenty-three thousand troops, dwarfing its population of ten thousand. James Meredith, flanked by a phalanx of six marshals, registered as Ole Miss's newest student before attending his first class, a course on American history.

Indeed, American history's mystic chords had echoed throughout the ordeal. When Kennedy's legal aide Norbert Schlei brought him the presidential proclamation calling for the federalization of the National Guard to protect Meredith, much as Eisenhower had done to protect the "Little Rock Nine" in 1957, Kennedy studied it. Then he rapped his knuckles on the antique table on which he signed the order in a small White House study. "You know, that's

General Grant's table," he told Schlei pointedly, invoking Ulysses Grant, whose battlefield aggressiveness had helped to turn the tide of the Civil War toward the Union. Before Schlei adjourned to inform the press about the proclamation, Kennedy added, "Don't tell them about General Grant's table." Regardless, the reverberations of history a century earlier were plain, as the Old South desperately clung to the vestiges of an antebellum, antediluvian past and was dragged by federal law into a new era. As Martin Luther King, Jr., reprovingly observed, Mississippi's leadership had allowed Ole Miss to "become a battleground for a cause that was lost a hundred years ago."

Yet King wasn't much happier with the Kennedys, whose behind-the-scenes machinations with Barnett and his administration, in his view, "made Negroes feel like pawns in a white politician's game." Yes, Kennedy had called in federal troops to allow for the admission of one Black student, tactically managing another civil rights crisis just as he had with the Freedom Rides a year earlier. But he had left the broader question of equal rights and tearing down the walls of segregation largely unaddressed.

Appealing to Kennedy's own sense of history, King implored him to channel Lincoln by using the hundredth anniversary of the Emancipation Proclamation on January 1, 1963, to put forth "a modern Emancipation Proclamation." "The key to everything is federal commitment," King held, "full, unequivocal, and unrelenting," and he wasn't seeing it from the White House. The president, he believed, had "the understanding and the political skills" to address civil rights, but his "moral passion" was missing. That was hard to argue. What King and others in the movement wanted to know was, would he find it?

"THE GRAVEST ISSUES"

It was a rare morning that John Kennedy didn't scan the newspapers without becoming vexed by something that caught his eye. On the unseasonably warm morning of Tuesday, October 16, 1962, as he read in a bathrobe, pajamas, and slippers, he found it on the front page of the *New York Times* in a story that ran above the fold. "Eisenhower Calls President Weak on Foreign Policy," its headline blasted, "Denounces 'Dreary Record' Challenging Statements by Kennedy on Achievements: He Sees Setback to U.S."

"It is too sad to talk about," the paper reported the former president carping at Kennedy's record at a GOP dinner in Boston, while questioning the "clarity and force" of the administration's UN ambassador and Eisenhower's former rival for the presidency, Adlai Stevenson. He went on to boast of his own time in office. "In those eight years, we lost no inch of ground to tyranny," he said. "No walls were built. No threatening foreign bases were established. One war was ended and incipient wars were blocked."

To some degree, it was payback. Ike was still bruising from the false claims Kennedy had made about the "missile gap" during the campaign. But there was some validity in his assessment. In his two terms in office, Eisenhower had racked up an impressive foreign policy record, including neutralizing the Soviets, who had regarded him warily, while Kennedy hadn't achieved much aside from projecting a dazzling celebrity image abroad.

At 8:45 the same morning, McGeorge Bundy knocked on Kennedy's bedroom door, a batch of grainy black-and-white photographs under his arm. "Mr. President," he said, handing them to Kennedy, "there is now photographic evidence, as you will see, that the Russians have offensive missiles in Cuba." The revelation confirmed the worst of Kennedy's fears: The USSR had been secretly establishing a military beachhead for offensive purposes just ninety miles from American shores. "What are we going to do?" he asked Bundy. It would be the question Kennedy would ask throughout the gut-wrenching thirteen days ahead in what would become the central trial of his presidency and the most dangerous moment in human history. Underlying the question was a momentous enigma: how to stand firm against the threat in Cuba without pushing the Soviets beyond the brink of nuclear war.

If Dwight Eisenhower believed Kennedy to be out of his depth in foreign policy, so did Nikita Khrushchev, who seized the chance to exploit the weakness he perceived in his adversary. As Arthur Schlesinger later wrote, "Moscow had calculated that the United States, with the Bay of Pigs still in the world's recollection, could not convincingly object to Castro's taking defensive precautions against another invasion." Khrushchev believed the buildup would ensure Cuba's survival "right in front of the open jaws of American imperialism."

His concerns over Cuba's future were understandable; after the Bay of Pigs, Khrushchev became aware of the CIA's covert Operation Mongoose, involving a number of schemes to subvert the Castro regime or take the charismatic Cuban dictator out

171

altogether. Operation Mongoose included a program known as ZR Rifle that aimed to use known mobsters to assassinate Castro. Other plots were hatched toward instability and sabotage, including one, seriously entertained though not executed, that involved a CIA air drop of rolls of toilet paper with photos of Khrushchev and Castro on alternating squares designed to "drive Castro mad." Though Operation Mongoose failed to achieve its objective—sometimes haplessly—it reflected the Kennedy administration's desperate persistence around Cuban regime change.

More important for Khrushchev, offensive weapons in Cuba would allow the Soviets a "broader geopolitical strategy." Nuclear warheads and missiles in the Western Hemisphere would keep the U.S. in check militarily, countering the intermediate-range Jupiter missiles that the Eisenhower administration had installed three years earlier near the Soviet border in Italy and Turkey. They could also be used as bargaining chips over Berlin. Then there were political considerations. As Khrushchev's support was slipping at home, the move would allow him to focus on domestic spending rather than the further proliferation of the Soviet nuclear arsenal at a time when, contrary to Kennedy's missile gap assertions, the United States had roughly nine times more nuclear weapons than the USSR.

Along with the Kennedy legend, the Cuban missile crisis has grown to mythological proportions through the years, with the heroic JFK coolly staring down the rash, bellicose adversary who had dared to ship tactical nuclear missiles to America's backyard. But Khrushchev's reasons for the move on Cuba—bolstering Cuba's security in the face of an existential American threat and strategically countering a pronounced disparity in nuclear weaponry including the U.S. offensive missiles in Turkey near the Soviet border—seem, in retrospect, less a reckless gambit and more a calculated risk. As longtime JFK Library historian Sheldon Stern wrote, "Kennedy and his administration, without question, bore a substantial share of the responsibility for the onset of the Cuban missile crisis."

U.S. intelligence had known for some time that the Soviets had been deploying troops and weapons to Cuba. Since mid-July, U.S. spy planes had monitored the buildup. Throughout the balance of the summer, they had identified thirty Soviet ships in Cuban ports carrying two thousand military advisers, surface-to-air missiles, torpedo boats armed with missile capabilities, and MiG-21 fighter jets. Still, there was no conclusive evidence that the effort was of an offensive nature, which would have contradicted the Soviets' public statement the previous month that the shipment of military equipment was "exclusively for defensive purposes." Moreover, U.S. intelligence experts generally believed that the Kremlin would be too rational and Khrushchev too cautious to take such a provocative stand. "Were it to be otherwise," Kennedy warned in a White House statement read by Pierre Salinger to the press corps on September 4, "the gravest issues would arise."

On October 14, after reconnaissance missions had been scrapped since early in the month due to adverse weather conditions, photographs taken from a U-2 spy plane proved that it was indeed "otherwise." The photos showed clearly that a medium-range missile site was being constructed on the western part of the island. If operational, it meant that much of the eastern seaboard would be within firing range, including Washington, D.C., which could be decimated by a nuclear launch in less than fifteen minutes. Subsequent intelligence findings would reveal the audacious scale of the operation; the Soviets had planned to export forty-two thousand troops to the island, along with thirty-six SS-4 medium-range and twenty-four SS-5 intermediate-range ballistic missiles capable of discharging nuclear warheads. Just one of the SS-4 missiles would deliver over seventy times the impact of the atomic bomb the United States dropped on Hiroshima at the close of World War II. But the evidence that Bundy shared with the president on the morning of October 16 alone was enough for Kennedy to realize the scope of the operation and the threat to U.S. security.

"Caroline, have you been eating candy?" Kennedy asked his daughter as she entered the Cabinet Room just before noon on the same morning. "Answer me, yes or no."

A month shy of her fifth birthday, Caroline Kennedy impishly evaded an answer. Scurrying out of the room and on to the White House Rose Garden, she left her father to convene with the thirteen men he had summoned urgently. The bulk of them were those who would help guide Kennedy through the anguishing decisions ahead. The "ExComm," as they would become known—an abbreviation for Executive Committee of the National Security Council—comprised an inner circle whose advice Kennedy had come to value after the baptism by fire that had been his first year in the presidency. They were those whom he trusted not to leak to the press and who had his best interest at heart: Bobby, naturally, and White House insiders McGeorge Bundy and Ted Sorensen; cabinet members Dean Rusk, Robert McNamara, and Douglas Dillon; Max Taylor, appointed by Kennedy just over two weeks earlier as chairman of the Joint Chiefs of Staff, replacing the contemptuous Lyman Lemnitzer; undersecretary of state George Ball; and a handful of other cabinet undersecretaries. Lyndon Johnson was on the edge of the group. Some not present would also come into play, including Adlai Stevenson, CIA director John McCone, and former secretary of state under Harry Truman, Dean Acheson.

Blown-up photos of the Cuban sites stood on easels at the end of the heavy boat-shaped Cabinet Room table. Kennedy sat in the middle with his back to the presidential seal on the wall, Gilbert Stuart's famous unfinished portrait of George Washington, and a bust of Abraham Lincoln staring into the room from its periphery. Under the table, Kennedy secretly activated a recording system that would tape all of the ExComm meetings, material he planned to use in writing a memoir in his post-presidency.

A CIA analyst pointed out nebulous patches on the photos that he identified as the medium-range ballistic missile launch site along with crates that contained the missiles. "How long have we got . . . before [a missile] can be fired?" Kennedy asked. Marshall Carter, the CIA's deputy director, wagered a guess: "Two weeks, maybe one."

Kennedy made it clear that the missiles had to go—there was no question about that—and that the United States must act swiftly and decisively. There was simply no way he could survive politically otherwise. Just days earlier, Bundy had taken to the airwaves to debunk New York Republican senator Kenneth Keating's repeated warnings that the Soviets were building a missile site in Cuba.

"Ken Keating will probably be the next president of the United States," Kennedy quipped grimly to Kenny O'Donnell after Bundy had briefed him on the U-2 photos. When China fell to communism in 1949 during the Truman administration, Kennedy had been a member of Congress as the GOP steadily beat the cold war drum on "Who lost China?" If the Soviets successfully planted offensive weapons in Cuba on Kennedy's watch, the damage to him and the Democratic Party would be devastating.

The president asked the group for "an intensive survey of the dangers and all possible courses of action." He first turned to Rusk, who posed two options: "One, the quick strike; the other, to alert our allies and Mr. Khrushchev that there is an utterly serious crisis in the making here . . . a situation that could well lead to general war; that we have an obligation to do what has to be done but do it in a way that gives everybody a chance to pull away from it."

"[Why] did the Russians set this up?" Kennedy asked.

"Khrushchev knows we have nuclear superiority," Rusk said. "Also, we have missiles nearby in Turkey, places like that." Kennedy asked how many U.S. missiles were in Turkey. "About fifteen," Rusk answered.

The secretary of state suspected that despite the Soviet leadership's assurances that they would place no offensive weapons in the West, Khrushchev had made the decisions due to his "obsession" over Berlin. "For the first time I'm beginning to wonder whether maybe Mr. Khrushchev is entirely rational about Berlin," he said.

Khrushchev's state of mind was key. Throughout the crisis, Kennedy would make the assumption—as would Khrushchev of Kennedy—that his adversary was of sound, rational mind and didn't want war any more than he did, despite Khrushchev's truculent bluster in Vienna. At the same time, Kennedy was conscious of not pushing Khrushchev too hard at the risk of setting him off. This, after all, was the same man who just two years earlier reacted to an anti-Soviet speech at the United Nations by launching into a tirade and hammering his shoe on a general assembly desk.

They all agreed that more U-2 surveillance flights over Cuba were needed to monitor the buildup. They were also of the mind that secrecy around the developments in Cuba was paramount. Lyndon Johnson, whose relationships on Capitol Hill ran deeper than any in the room, acknowledged that the news should be kept from Congress. "I realize it's a breach of faith, but we're not going to get much help out of them," he said. In order to keep the situation under wraps, the group would strive to maintain a business-as-usual air in the days ahead.

The meeting lasted over an hour. Kennedy ended it where he began it. "We're certainly . . . going to take out those missiles," he reiterated. Additional military actions were also on the table, including an invasion of Cuba or a blockade around the island, he said, but the air strike on the missiles seemed an inevitability. None of the options he was considering at that moment included a diplomatic solution. He ordered another ExComm meeting at 6:30 that evening, one of nine meetings to come.

In the early afternoon, the president addressed a group of journalists who had gathered at the State Department for a foreign policy conference. "Our major problem overall," he said, "is the survival of our country . . . without the beginning of the third and perhaps the last war." None of the reporters knew the increased prospect of a nuclear holocaust that arose with the news delivered to him that same day, nor the added burden he would soon assume with the decisions he alone would have to make in the muddled darkness that lay immediately ahead. But perhaps Kennedy himself had it in his mind as he ended the session with a slightly misquoted poem from matador Domingo Ortega that he recited from memory. While many critics crowd the stadium to watch a bullfight, the poem went, the only one to truly understand what it is to be in the arena is "the one who fights the bull."

"BURDEN OF CHOICE"

If Cuba was much on the mind of the president, an October 17 front-page *Washington Post* story revealed that it was also on the minds of the American people. Though Americans had no knowledge of Soviet offensive missiles being sent to the island nation, Republicans, in advance of the midterm election less than a month away, were stirring up anxiety over the Soviets bolstering the defense of Castro's government—and it was working. The *Post* reported that 344 editors across the United States considered Cuba a primary campaign issue. Their contention was borne out by the results of a Gallup Poll revealing that 71 percent of the American public advocated some military action against the Castro regime, a sharp increase from results of a similar poll conducted three months earlier. At the same time, the poll reflected that 51 percent believed that an attack on Cuba would trigger World War III.

That was the balance Kennedy sought to strike as the missile crisis evolved: taking decisive action against the Soviet arms shipments without setting off a catastrophic world war. It meant keeping the military leadership at arm's length, resisting their reflexive jingoism. Kennedy's wariness of the "brass hats," as he called them, was affirmed after a Cabinet Room meeting with the Joint Chiefs of Staff on the morning of October 19. Since learning of the missiles, the administration had received additional photos from U-2 surveillance missions pointing to the construction of five launching pads for intermediate-range missiles, but as the situation had developed, Kennedy and his inner circle had thought more prudently about their military options.

An air strike was still on the table, to be sure. But the group also more seriously considered a naval blockade, preventing Soviet ships from delivering missiles and other supplies to Cuba by shutting them out at sea. Curtis LeMay, the zealous, cigar-chomping Air Force chief of staff, stated the views of the chiefs unequivocally: The only answer was a quick, systematic bombing strike on the missile sites before they became operational. Otherwise, LeMay told Kennedy, "they're going to push on Berlin and push *real hard* because they've got us on the run." Kennedy worried about West Berlin, too, fearing that the Soviets would use the crisis as an excuse to take the city. He asked how the Soviets would respond to the air strikes. "They'll do nothing," LeMay replied with certainty.

The chiefs sensed Kennedy's reluctance. As Earle Wheeler, the Army's chief of staff, told the group afterward, it was apparent that Kennedy was leaning toward "the political action of a blockade." LeMay pushed harder, intimating that the chiefs might make their opposition to a blockade public. "There's one other factor that I didn't mention that's not quite in our field, [which] is the political factor," he said. "I think that a blockade and political talk would be considered by a lot of our friends and neutrals as being a pretty weak response to this. And I'm sure a lot of our own citizens would feel that way, too. In other words, you're in a pretty bad fix at the present time."

Kennedy was not amused. "What did you say?" he asked.

179

"You're in a pretty bad fix," LeMay repeated.

"You're right in there with me," Kennedy said with a laugh, belying his gall.

"Can you imagine LeMay saying a thing like that?" he vented to Kenny O'Donnell after the meeting. The warmongering military leaders, he contended, had "one great advantage in their favor. If we listen to them, and we do what they want us to do, none of us will be alive later to tell them that they were wrong."

As he left the Oval Office, he ran into Bobby, who was walking with Ted Sorensen through a West Wing hallway. "This thing is falling apart," Kennedy told his brother. "You have to pull it together."

It was the kind of cryptic thing one Kennedy brother might say that the other would understand intuitively. Sorensen construed it to mean that the president had ruled out an air strike in favor of a blockade, siding with Bobby, who, initially prone to an aggressive response, had begun to see the bombings as a sneak attack that was immoral and out of step with American values—a "Pearl Harbor in reverse." But the president was keeping all his options open. Earlier the same morning, he had instructed Bundy to "have another look" at bombing and to keep the alternative "alive." He would cling to the notion of air strikes throughout much of the crisis and would not abandon it, as Bundy said later, until "very late in the game."

Later in the morning, in keeping with the effort to maintain the appearance of normalcy, Kennedy took off on a campaign swing in the Midwest, flying to Cleveland before moving on to Springfield, Illinois, to lay a wreath on Lincoln's grave. Then it was on to Chicago in the late afternoon, where, as he entered the Blackstone hotel, he was greeted enthusiastically by a crowd, save for a pro-

would publicly make good on his promise—reliably putting country above party. At a GOP political rally in Pittsburgh on October 25, he declared, "Until this urgent problem is solved . . . every loyal American will without hesitation carry out and conform to any instruction pertaining to it proclaimed by the commander-in-chief."

On Monday evening at seven p.m., Kennedy, steady and solemn, brought his message to the largest audience to that point ever to watch a presidential address. He began by informing them of the "unmistakable evidence" of offensive missile sites being built on the "imprisoned island" of Cuba, "providing nuclear strike capability against the Western Hemisphere." It set a dangerous precedent. The pre–World War II days of the 1930s, he said, provided a "clear lesson: aggressive conduct, if allowed to go unchecked and unchallenged, ultimately leads to war." The Soviet Union, he explained, had consistently denied the activity, including Soviet foreign minister Andrei Gromyko, who just five days earlier had assured Kennedy in an Oval Office meeting that the Soviets would "never be involved" in building up offensive missiles in Cuba. Kennedy then called on Khrushchev to "halt and eliminate this clandestine, reckless, and provocative threat to world peace . . . to abandon this course of world domination and to join in an historic effort to end the perilous arms race and to transform the history of man." Until the missiles were withdrawn and peace was at hand, he warned, the United States would impose "a strict quarantine on all offensive military equipment under shipment to Cuba."

"Let no one doubt that this is a difficult and dangerous effort," he said, concluding his eighteen-minute remarks:

No one can foresee precisely what course it will take or what costs or casualties will be incurred. . . . But the

tester who, alluding to Cuba, hoisted a sign that read "Less profile—More courage."

Meanwhile, ExComm, now officially the National Security Council, met in George Ball's seventh-floor State Department conference room, where they debated the central question: Air strike or blockade? As his brother's closest adviser, Bobby became the de facto leader of the group. "In all those rooms," Bundy said, referring to the places the ExComm would meet over the thirteen days, "RFK was really the senior person."

Bobby led the argument that a sneak bombing attack would be condemned by the international community and strip the United States of its moral authority. The group generally came around to his thinking, though Bundy, heeding the president's directive, continued to keep a strike in the mix of potential responses. A blockade made sense in giving Khrushchev a chance to peacefully back down from the crisis and opening up the possibility of a diplomatic solution. But it also presented problems; it was not a benign alternative to an air strike but a provocative military action that would also be seen by the Soviets as an act of war, albeit one that would allow more time for thoughtful consideration from the other side.

The following morning, Kennedy, sporting a gray fedora, left Chicago at Bobby's urging, begging off the balance of his campaign swing by feigning a cold and slight fever. By early afternoon, he was back in Washington, where the growing speculation that something was amiss was palpable. Faced with the possibility of the story leaking to the press, Kennedy decided to take the issue directly to the American people. He scheduled an Oval Office address for the evening of Monday, October 22, but the *Washington Post* put a crimp on his plans with its page-one story in their Sunday edition that read "Marine Moves in South Linked to Cuban

Crisis." Kennedy was furious. The White House had been successful in quashing a similar story from the *New York Times*, but the *Post* piece came out of the blue.

Kennedy himself called the *Post*'s publisher, Phil Graham, imploring him to refrain from publishing a piece planned for the following morning further exposing the situation in Cuba. Graham reluctantly agreed, instead running a more ambiguous story that spanned the front page, with the headline, "Major U.S. Decision Is Awaited." It nonetheless began ominously: "Official Washington yesterday wrapped itself in one of the tightest cloaks of secrecy ever in peace-time while key policy-makers worked out a major international decision they were forbidden to discuss."

At noon on Monday, October 22, Pierre Salinger added to the growing uncertainty, announcing that the president would speak to the nation at seven that evening on a matter of "the greatest urgency." By then, Kennedy had gravitated firmly toward the idea of a blockade, approving the view that the ExComm had reached, as one aide put it, as "a rolling consensus" after "exhaustive exploration of every possibility." A blockade appealed to Kennedy because it would leave the "burden of choice" to Khrushchev to respond—if a war broke out, it would be because Khrushchev chose to engage—though Kennedy changed the name from "blockade" to "quarantine," which sounded less antagonistic.

Throughout the weekend, the State Department had generated forty-three letters to allied heads of state throughout the world, all signed by the president and delivered by diplomatic courier along with copies of Kennedy's speech. Among them was a letter to Khrushchev in which Kennedy reinforced his policy that the United States would not "tolerate any action" on the Soviet Union's part to "disturb the balance of power" and "would do whatever must be done to protect its own security and that of its allies."

In the early evening, before his speech, Kennedy met privately with twenty congressional leaders of both parties who had been summoned back to Washington, some ferried by Air Force plane or fighter jets. Kennedy briefed them on the situation in Cuba, laying out the U-2 surveillance photos. "We've decided to take action," he told them, explaining his intention of carrying out naval blockade.

The group responded tepidly. Richard Russell, Jr., the powerf chairman of the Senate Armed Services Committee, supported invasion, seeing a war with the Soviets as inevitable. A blocka he believed, would only show weakness. "We're either a first-c power or we're not," he admonished Kennedy. William Fulbr also advocated an invasion, taking Kennedy by surprise, sinc had been full-throated in his opposition to the Bay of Pigs inva just eighteen months earlier. He contended that while seizi Russian ship would be an "act of war," a point Lyndon Joh had made earlier in the month before the situation had escal an invasion of Cuba would "not actually be an affront to Ru

The meeting made plain to Kennedy that gaining the su of Congress would be a slog, and the chance of members m their dissent public was even greater than that of the militar reported directly to Kennedy as their commander in chief had known the job was this tough, I wouldn't have beaten West Virginia," he said afterward to his onetime Democrat for the presidency Hubert Humphrey.

Those who had once occupied his office were more en ing. In briefing calls earlier in the day with the three li presidents—Herbert Hoover, Truman, and Eisenhowe pledged his support. Despite the disparaging comment made about Kennedy in Boston earlier in the month, Eise the most politically relevant of Kennedy's three pred

greatest danger of all would be to do nothing. . . . Our goal is not the victory of might, but the vindication of right—not peace at the expense of freedom, but both peace and freedom, here in this hemisphere and, we hope, around the world. God willing, that goal will be achieved.

The country rallied around Kennedy in the wake of his speech. Over the next few days, nearly fifty thousand telegrams would pour into the White House, supporting him ten to one. A Gallup Poll showed that 84 percent of Americans approved of the blockade versus only 4 percent who were opposed. The press was also favorable, with *Time* calling Kennedy's resolve "one of the most decisive moments of the twentieth century." Noting the "extraordinary gravity" of Kennedy's message, the *New York Times* wrote forebodingly, "A critical moment of the cold war was at hand. . . . The President had decided on a direct confrontation with—and challenge to—the power of the Soviet Union."

The White House and the country were now on a state of high alert. Though, in adherence with international law, the White House would wait until the State Department had issued a formal proclamation before enacting the blockade, the brinkmanship with the Soviet Union had begun. "From then on," Jackie Kennedy recalled later of her and her husband throughout the balance of the crisis, "there was no waking or sleeping. . . . There was no day or night."

THE KNOT

It didn't take long for Nikita Khrushchev to respond to Kennedy's speech. At noon on Tuesday, October 23, the State Department received a letter from him to Kennedy, one of ten the premier and the president exchanged throughout the crisis. "By what right do you do this?" he blustered.

> You, Mr. President, are not declaring a quarantine, but rather are setting forth an ultimatum and threatening that if we do not give in to your demands you will use force. Consider what you are saying! . . . No, Mr. President, I cannot agree to this and . . . I am convinced that in my place you would act the same way. . . . We will then be forced on our part to take the measures we consider necessary and adequate in order to protect our rights.

Kennedy immediately shot back.

I think you will recognize that the steps which started the current chain of events was the action of your Government in secretly furnishing offensive weapons to Cuba. . . . I hope that you will issue immediately the necessary instructions to your ships to observe the terms of the quarantine.

That evening, after receiving unanimous approval from the Organization of American States—a welcome validation of the president's actions and a diplomatic coup for Dean Rusk—Kennedy was given the proclamation ordering the quarantine, which would begin at 10:00 a.m. the following morning. After asking a lighting technician three times what date it was, Kennedy signed it somberly at 7:06 a.m., writing out his full name. There was no going back. At that moment, his biggest fear was that the Soviets would launch a preemptive nuclear strike, but he was resigned to the possibility. As he told Bobby later that night, it was his only choice. "If they get mean on this one in our part of the world, what will they do the next time?" he asked rhetorically.

"Well, there *isn't* any [other] choice," Bobby agreed. "If you hadn't acted, you would have been impeached."

"That's what I think, I would have been impeached," Kennedy said.

As the quarantine went into effect on the morning of Wednesday, October 24, fifty-six American ships—including the USS *Joseph P. Kennedy Jr.*—sailed toward Cuba to form their blockade within a five-hundred-mile radius of the island. At the same hour, ExComm met in the Cabinet Room. CIA chief John McCone, fresh from an inconveniently timed honeymoon, briefed the group on the latest developments. Two of the Soviet ships they were tracking, he told the group, were accompanied by a submarine moving toward the American ships. It may have been the darkest hour of the crisis for Kennedy, as the realities of a potential engagement with the Soviet fleet were setting in.

"At what point are we going to attack [a submarine]?" Kennedy asked in the hope that it could be averted. "I'd much rather attack a merchant ship." McNamara advised against it, claiming that to defer an attack on the submarine would be "extremely dangerous."

"We could easily lose an American ship by that means," he said. "This is what we must be prepared for and this is what we must expect."

As the conversation continued, Bobby caught the blue-gray-eyed gaze of his brother across the Cabinet Room table. He could see the tension in his face and in his balled-up fist. As he later recounted to Schlesinger:

> The danger and concern that we all felt hung like a cloud over us. . . . These few minutes were the time of greatest worry by the President. . . . Was the world on the brink of a holocaust and had we done something wrong? Isn't there some way we can avoid having our first exchange be with a Russian submarine—almost anything but that, he said. . . . I felt we were on the edge of a precipice and it was as if there were no way off.

Some relief came with news delivered to McCone a half hour into the meeting. Intelligence reports indicated that twelve of twenty-five Soviet ships heading for Cuba had "stopped dead in the water" and were turning back. Rusk said, "We're eyeball to eyeball and I think the other guy just blinked." The Russians had relented for the moment, but the crisis was far from over.

The following day, October 25, Adlai Stevenson brought the issue to the United Nations, where he prosecuted his case against the USSR in an emergency meeting of the UN Security Council. It wasn't an easy sell—even to allies. In the eyes of many in Western Europe, America was heedlessly rattling nuclear sabers over offensive missiles near its shores when they had been living with Soviet weapons in neighboring countries for years. For that matter, since 1959, so had the USSR. Charles de Gaulle claimed that being allied with the United States at that moment meant, in effect, "annihilation without representation." Keeping allied powers on the country's side and other nations at least neutral was pivotal to Kennedy's overall strategy.

Stevenson, intellectual and urbane, was hardly the confrontational type. Kennedy didn't have much faith in him. Describing the State Department, which he believed to be lightweight and ineffectual, JFK once said, "They're sort of like Adlai." But as the world watched the session on television, Stevenson rose to the occasion. Confronting his Soviet counterpart, Valerian Zorin, he demanded, "Do you, Ambassador Zorin, deny that the USSR has placed and is placing medium and intermediate range missiles and sites in Cuba? Yes or no—don't wait for the translation—yes or no?"

Zorin scornfully dodged the question. "I am not in an American courtroom, sir," he argued, "and therefore I do not wish to answer a question that is put to me in the fashion in which a prosecutor puts questions. In due course, sir, you will have your reply."

Stevenson continued to press for an answer, insisting that Zorin was "in a courtroom of world opinion right now." Once again, Zorin stonewalled, repeating that Stevenson would have his answer "in due course." Stevenson pounced. "I am prepared to wait for my answer until hell freezes over," he snapped. Then he exposed the Kremlin's deception, presenting evidence of the missiles by placing a series of twenty-six poster-sized photos from the U-2 spy planes on easels.

His had been a powerful performance. "Terrific," Kennedy said as he watched from the Oval Office. "I didn't know Adlai had it in him."

As the face-off played out in the Atlantic, Americans braced for the worst. Though the prospect of a nuclear war had hung over the country since the Soviet Union had developed atomic bombs a dozen years earlier, prompting the building of backyard bomb shelters and routine "duck and cover" drills in schools, tensions between the superpowers had never risen so high. The public made a run on canned goods, gasoline, and other basic supplies as anxiety heightened.

"I don't think America had ever faced such a real threat of destruction as at this moment," Khrushchev would later write in his memoirs. U.S. Strategic Air Command readiness stood at DEF-CON 2, just short of war. In Buenos Aires, evangelist Billy Graham gave a sermon on "The End of the World" for a congregation of ten thousand.

Speaking at a dinner in New York, Martin Luther King, Jr.'s evolving dream was one of peace. "In these critical days," he said, "we need broad understanding and a faith in the future, so that the dream of peace may become a reality." *Time*'s Hugh Sidey, after a sobering conversation with Kennedy in the Oval Office, followed by a stress-relieving skinny dip in the White House pool at Kennedy's prodding, left wondering, like many around the world, if he and his own family would see another tomorrow.

The first family was no different. On Saturday, October 20, before leaving Chicago prematurely from his Midwest campaign swing to get back to Washington, Kennedy called Jackie at Glen Ora, where she had just arrived with the children for the weekend. Without telling her why, he asked her to return to the White House. She could hear in his voice that something was wrong and would learn about the crisis when the two reunited later in the day. In the ensuing days of the ordeal, she would later say, she felt closer to her husband than she ever had. She never left the White House nor even saw the children so that she could make herself available to him night and day, walking with him on the South Lawn when he needed a break, sleeping when he slept. When it was suggested that she and the children might be flown to Camp David if a nuclear strike seemed imminent, she insisted on remaining by his side. "Please don't send me anywhere," she asked him. "I just want to be with you, and I want to die with you and the children do, too—[rather] than live without you."

Through it all, Kennedy remained cool, holding everyone, as one aide said, "under tight control." Ted Sorensen recalled, "He insisted on knowing all his options and what [solutions] were possible. He did not do anything rash. He did not panic or overreact—did not yield to the military. He was calm—never lost his sense of humor, perspective, modesty." Sorensen experienced the humor firsthand; during the height of the ordeal, Kennedy turned to him and joked, "I hope you realize there's not enough room for everyone in the White House bomb shelter."

On Friday evening, October 26, Kennedy received a long cable from Khrushchev. Far from belligerent, the premier seemed level-headed, reasonable. "Everyone needs peace," he stated, pledging that the USSR would withdraw their missiles from Cuba with a commitment that the United States wouldn't invade the island, and that if U.S. ships retreated, the Russian ships, too, would back off. Likening the crisis to a rope in which Kennedy had "tied the knot of war," he wrote that the more the two sides pulled, "the tighter the knot will get tied." If, on the other hand, the two sides gave the rope slack, the knot would loosen and could be untied. "We are ready for this," Khrushchev assured him. Kennedy and ExComm were encouraged by the letter's conciliatory tone.

Then, another unexpected turn, this one unwelcome. On the afternoon of what would become known as "Black Saturday," October 27, as work continued unabated on the missile sites in Cuba, the president learned during a meeting with the ExComm that antiaircraft guns were firing at U-2 spy planes surveilling the island. McNamara recommended that the United States "attack back." Kennedy wasn't so sure. "Let's wait and see whether they fire on us tomorrow . . . then we can meet here and decide," he said.

He didn't have to wait long. Minutes later, McNamara got word that a U-2 plane had been shot down by a Soviet surface-to-air missile, killing its pilot. "It looked as if it might be slipping out of control," said one of Kennedy's aides of the moment. "There was a feeling we were moving toward [war]." The president and his men were exhausted, reeling from day to day with little sleep as they groped for a peaceful solution that seemed increasingly unlikely.

Circumstances went from bad to worse. At 1:41 p.m., McNamara was informed that a U-2 plane conducting atmospheric testing over Alaska was missing over the Soviet Union. According to Air Force general David Burchinal, upon hearing the news, McNamara blurted, "This means war with the Soviet Union!" He called the president with the news several minutes later. Subsequent reports would indicate that the plane had mistakenly drifted into Soviet airspace, where Soviet MiGs tried to intercept it, unable to shoot it down. The White House caught its breath forty-five minutes later when it was reported that, after ten hours and twenty-five minutes, the longest recorded U-2 flight, the plane had evaded capture and had landed safely in northwest Alaska—but just barely.

Tensions mounted again that evening. At ten p.m. came another letter from Khrushchev, this one read by a broadcaster to the Soviet people on Radio Moscow. If the premier had just a day earlier offered a means of untying the "knot of war," he now inexplicably pulled it tighter. The tone of the five-page letter was different—more strident. So were the terms it proposed. The Soviet Union would take its missiles out of Cuba only if the United States did so in Turkey, Khrushchev demanded. He continued:

> You have placed destructive missile weapons, which you call offensive, in Turkey, literally next to us. How then can recognition of our equal military capacities be reconciled with such unequal relations between our great states? This is irreconcilable.

Or *was* it Khrushchev? The ExComm debated the meaning of the different letters. Why the change in tenor? Had there been a power struggle in the Kremlin? Was Khrushchev still in power? Regardless, the ante had been upped. The next crucial question for the group arose: How should the president respond?

Eventually, the group came up with a solution: Respond to the first letter, disregard the second. Kennedy, though, was keeping his options open. That included the prospect of removing the Jupiter missiles in Turkey as part of the deal. Earlier in the day in a meeting with the ExComm, he had expressed his willingness to put the Jupiter missiles on the bargaining table, recalling that a year earlier he had advocated their removal due to their obsolescence. The Cuban missiles added 50 percent capacity to the Soviet nuclear arsenal; why not make the trade? Kennedy was warming to the idea. "We can't very well invade Cuba . . . when we could have gotten [the missiles] out by making a deal on the same missiles in Turkey," he said. "If that's part of the record, I don't see how we'll have a good war."

The idea of a missile swap wasn't new. As early as October 23, it was discussed at the White House as a means of averting a crisis. Though Bobby's back channel, Georgi Bolshakov, had broken his trust by denying less than two weeks earlier that the Soviets had been shipping offensive missiles to Cuba, Bobby floated the notion to him using Charlie Bartlett and *New York Daily News* reporter Frank Holeman as go-betweens.

Afterward, Bolshakov cabled the Soviet foreign office in Moscow: "R. Kennedy and his circle consider it possible to discuss the following trade: The U.S. would liquidate its missile bases in Turkey and Italy, and the U.S.S.R. would do the same in Cuba." But he added a catch: "The conditions of such a trade can only be discussed in a time of quiet and not when there is a threat of war." Keeping the removal of the Jupiter missiles out of the immediate deal was crucial in ensuring that nuclear blackmail did not become a tactic for the USSR or other nuclear powers in the future. Still, it put the Jupiter missiles on the table, which, along with an opinion piece by influential syndicated columnist Walter Lippmann that Khrushchev had read and perceived as signaling the possibility of a missile trade, may have accounted for the terms in Khrushchev's second letter.

As Kennedy prepared for a full-scale invasion of Cuba, approving the call-up of twenty-four air squadrons and three hundred troop carriers, he sent Bobby to see Anatoly Dobrynin, one of three secret meetings Bobby would have with the Soviet ambassador during the crisis. The attorney general brought Dobrynin a message from the president that the United States needed assurances that work was halted on the missile bases and the nuclear warheads returned to the Soviet Union. Otherwise the U.S. would have no alternative but to take military action early the following week. If, on the other hand, the Soviets removed the missiles and returned them to the USSR with UN oversight, the U.S. would pledge not to invade Cuba.

The ambassador inquired about a missile swap with those in Turkey. Bobby set him straight, insisting there would be "no quid pro quo." "However," he recalled saying, "President Kennedy had been anxious to remove those missiles from Turkey and Italy for a long period of time. He had ordered their removal some time ago, and it was our judgment that, within a short time after this crisis was over, those missiles would be gone." He expressed the president's desire for peace but said "time is running out"; they would need an answer the following day. Then he left Dobrynin and returned with little hope to the White House, where he and his brother waited for the other side to play its hand.

"Black Saturday" turned to a brighter Sunday. The crisis receded on the gentle, Indian summer Sunday morning of October 28. In his fifth and final letter of the crisis, broadcast on Radio Moscow like his previous letter, Khrushchev committed to the discontinuation of the missile sites and a return of the missiles to the Soviet Union under the verification of the United Nations in exchange for the United States' pledge not to invade Cuba. Kennedy accepted Khrushchev's "statesmanlike decision" in a White House statement released to the press. The knot of war had been loosened; peace was at hand. Not included in the settlement was Bobby's implicit verbal commitment to remove the Jupiter missiles from Turkey and Italy, a pledge the Kennedy administration secretly made good on in the following year. Khrushchev had publicly accepted the terms in the first letter; but in effect it was the terms in his second letter that carried the day—though for years the public wouldn't know about the removal of the missiles in Turkey and Italy as part of the deal.

Just as Kennedy had struggled with the "brass hats" during the course of the crisis, resisting their persistent calls for war, so had Khrushchev. His own military higher-ups had strongly opposed removing the missiles from Cuba, looking at him, as he recalled, like "a traitor" when he asked for their guarantee that if the missiles remained in place there was no chance of a nuclear war. At that point, Khrushchev thought, "To hell with these maniacs. If I can get the United States to assure me that it will not attempt to overthrow the Cuban government, I will remove the missiles." But it would cost him politically.

In briefing all of the former presidents separately by phone, Kennedy told Eisenhower that Khrushchev had taken "a step down" as a result of the crisis as his western ambitions sank into the Atlantic. His global humiliation would result over time in his loss of favor with Castro, the Chinese, and his own Politburo, which would eventually oust him from power in 1964. Still, Kennedy expected his combative Russian foe to resurge, anticipating that he would have to go "toe to toe on Berlin" with him as early as the following month. Wisely, Kennedy resisted crowing over his triumph in Cuba, which may have put additional political pressure on Khrushchev and aroused further tension.

During the summit in Vienna the previous year, when Khrushchev's bellicose tone made the prospect of nuclear war between the superpowers seem more likely, Kennedy had jotted a note to himself summoning the words of Abraham Lincoln as a civil war with the Confederacy seemed inevitable: "I know that there is a God and I see a storm coming. If he has a place for me I am ready."

As the thirteen agonizing days of crisis began fading into history on the evening of October 28, Kennedy once again conjured the sixteenth president, this time jokingly. Referring to Lincoln's fateful evening out after the Civil War was finally behind him, he told Bobby, "This is the night I should go to the theater." The allusion to Lincoln was somehow apt. At that moment, as the biggest storm in his presidency had passed, Kennedy stood in the pantheon of presidents.

Echoing the sentiments of myriad pundits after the dark clouds of October lifted, *New Yorker* political journalist Richard Rovere wrote that Kennedy's was "perhaps the greatest personal diplomatic victory of any president in our history." Along with the hard-won respect of his Soviet rivals came Kennedy's increased stature on the world stage, on which he now strode without peer, his gravitas newly in tandem with his celebrity luster.

On the eve of his inaugural, Kennedy had emerged from his second transition meeting with Eisenhower mystified by his "equanimity" as he carried out the colossal burdens of the job. Now, twenty-one months later, his triumph over the crisis—bigger than any faced by Eisenhower during his time in the White House—owed to his own restraint, dispassion, and cool head. Khrushchev acknowledged as much in his memoirs. "In the final analysis," he wrote, "[Kennedy] showed himself to be sober-minded and determined to avoid war. He didn't let himself become frightened, nor did he become reckless. He didn't overestimate America's might, and he left himself a way out of the crisis." At that most perilous hour, Kennedy's equanimity made all the difference.

"THE ANTITHESIS OF
A POLITICIAN"

There was political battle to be waged in the fall of 1962. No sooner had the Cuban missile crisis passed than the midterm election in early November beckoned, with Kennedy turning his attention from his duties as the nation's commander in chief to those as his party's standard-bearer. With the election certain to be a referendum on the Kennedy administration, he had been committed since the previous summer to working as hard as any president in history to ensure the success of the Democratic Party, going out into the hustings with the aim of widening the majorities it already boasted in Congress and state capitals throughout the nation. To that end, his campaigning across America would take him more than nineteen thousand miles, more than Eisenhower had racked up in midterm stumping in 1954 and 1958 combined.

"Two years ago I said that it was time to get the country moving again," he said to a rain-soaked crowd in West Virginia. "In the last two years we have made a start, but just a start. But we have begun to act, for no Congress in the last generation has passed as much affirmative and constructive legislation as the present Congress."

When he sought the presidency, Kennedy, despite a perfect record of six straight election victories and fourteen years in the halls of Congress, he saw himself as "the antithesis of a politician." In a January 1960 interview, he claimed he wasn't the "hail-fellow-well-met" his maternal grandfather, John "Honey Fitz" Fitzgerald, had been. When Kennedy first ran for Congress, vying for the same seat Fitzgerald had once held, he lived with him and his grandmother in Boston's Bellevue Hotel. He could see firsthand that he possessed none of the political skills that came instinctively to Honey Fitz. His brother Joe was the politician for his generation of Kennedys, he thought, not him. Rather he was, in his own view, "an introvert." As he explained it, "I'd rather read a book on a plane than talk to the fellow next to me, and my grandfather wanted to talk to everybody else."

Yet in the postwar age, as the country's issues became more serious, he saw the prototypical gregarious, back-slapping politician as "on the way out." Voters had become "rather cold in judgment"; they were looking for competence, not a glad-hander to kiss their babies.

"I think you have to be able to communicate a sense of conviction and intelligence and . . . some integrity," he observed. "Those three qualities are really it." If so, Kennedy exuded them, along with a star appeal that was undeniable. In midterm election rallies, he electrified ardent crowds, his hands thrust in his suit coat pockets—"What the hell am I supposed to do with them?" he wondered when asked about the habit—flashing a mild smile, and casting a distant "Nice to see you" reserve. John Kennedy had *become* the political standard.

Still, even with Kennedy's magnetism and an approval rating that had spiked thirteen points to 74 percent in the wake of the Cuban missile crisis, the odds were against him. Traditionally, the midterm elections had been a stumbling block for incumbent presidents, with the president's party averaging losses of forty-four seats in the House and five in the Senate. In the twentieth century, only FDR, during the Depression in 1934, had broken the cycle by adding seats. Plus, polls indicated that nearly 50 percent more Republican voters believed they had a reason to vote than Democrats, an ominous delta in a midterm election, with voter turnout routinely lower. Regardless, Kennedy was determined to put in the work to buck the midterm slumps of his predecessors.

His motivation was more than just wanting gains for his party. That was part of it, to be sure, but despite the majorities in both houses of Congress and his boasts on the stump of their "affirmative and constructive" activity, the Eighty-Seventh Congress had been a fickle ally to the thirty-fifth president. Kennedy was rankled by his failure to put the New Frontier's stamp on the country, with Congress opposed to the major bills of his domestic agenda, including many southern members of his own party, who were just as inclined to resist progressive legislative measures as their conservative Republican colleagues.

Far more than when he was among its members, he now had an appreciation for the "collective power" and "bloc action" of the legislative branch as it worked against him in the executive branch. His future success hinged on appealing to moderate Republicans and expanding the Democratic majority with liberal members while maintaining party unity by ensuring that the party's southern members—tantamount to distant cousins in the Democratic family by 1962—remained in the fold.

A particular frustration for Kennedy was his thwarted attempt to pass a bill creating a medical program benefiting the elderly, later to become Medicare under Lyndon Johnson. "This bill serves the public interest," he said at a televised rally to rev up public support in May. "We are behind every country, pretty nearly, in Europe, in this matter of medical care for our citizens." The American Medical Association saw it differently, demonizing the program as "socialized medicine" that, among other evils, would prevent recipients from choosing their own doctors.

Ronald Reagan, a mid-career B-movie actor yet to run for political office, also got into the act, lending his voice to an AMA recording that doctors' wives would play at their homes during social gatherings as part of an initiative called Operation Coffee Cup. From record-player speakers Reagan sounded the warning that "one of the traditional methods of imposing statism or socialism on a people has been by way of medicine." The AMA's efforts were enough to daunt Republican and Democratic lawmakers alike, crushing any hope Kennedy had of getting the bill through, just as they had Harry Truman before him.

Likewise, a sweeping education bill, which would have poured federal money into elementary and secondary schools throughout the country, fell short due to Kennedy's refusal to allow for aid to parochial schools, which he believed would invite controversy due to his Catholicism. He was also looking toward 1964, where his reelection prospects would ride principally on the health of the economy, hoping for a compliant Congress to pass a tax cut to stimulate economic activity.

On the eve of the election, November 5, 1962, Kennedy flew to Boston, where he kept a cramped one-bedroom apartment at 122 Bowdoin Street that had been his voting place of record since he got into elective politics, and paid a visit to his grandmother, the ninety-seven-year-old widow of Honey Fitz. The following morning, he voted in the basement of a Beacon Hill police station, joining the fifty-three million Americans who would cast their ballots that day, just short of two-thirds of the electorate. Kennedy emerged from the voting booth in less than a minute before heading off for Hyannis Port to await the election's results.

When he awoke on the Cape the next morning, the news was good. Far from the deep losses of previous off-year elections, the Democrats had gained four seats—and one Kennedy—in the Senate, bringing northern and midwestern liberals into the upper chamber: Birch Bayh from Indiana, George McGovern from South Dakota, Gaylord Nelson from Wisconsin, and Kennedy's thirty-one-year-old brother, Ted, from Massachusetts. House Democrats, meanwhile, had lost just four seats, retaining 259 seats versus the GOP's 175. The gubernatorial tally ended up even, with the thirty-five contests nationwide producing no net gain for either party. Kennedy described himself as "heartened" by the election's results.

The icing on the cake may have been the Kennedy antagonists who had fallen to defeat, including four members of the arch-conservative John Birch Society who failed to win reelection to Congress, and a deflated Richard Nixon, who was overtaken in the California governor's race by incumbent Pat Brown by more than a quarter of a million votes. After the results came in, Nixon tried to shrug it off. "Losing California after losing the presidency," he said privately, "well, it's like being bitten by a mosquito after being bitten by a rattlesnake." But it stung far more than he let on. His bitterness leaked out as he addressed the media. Calling it his "last" press conference, he petulantly told the reporters he thought to be licking their chops at his political demise, "Just think how much you're going to be missing. You won't have Nixon to kick around anymore." Then, alluding to Kennedy's controversial cancellation of his subscription to the *New York Herald Tribune* during the steel crisis, he couldn't resist giving his former presidential rival a last jab, adding, "Unlike some people, I've never cancelled a subscription to a paper, and also I never will." The following week *Time* sounded the message that "barring a miracle [Nixon's] political career ended last week."

The day after the election, on November 7, Eleanor Roosevelt succumbed to tuberculosis at age seventy-eight. In a statement, Kennedy called her "one of the great ladies of the century" whom he considered "an inspiration and a friend." The friendship was largely unrequited. To the end, Kennedy's considerable charms eluded her. Shortly before her death she wrote the president, "I listened . . . to your last press conference and decided that it did not take the place of fireside chats. . . . I wish you could . . . deepen and strengthen your voice on radio and T.V. It would give you more warmth and personality." But it didn't appear to hurt the naturally cool and introverted JFK, whose twentieth-century midterm results were topped only by Mrs. Roosevelt's husband's twenty-eight years earlier. As Democratic National Committee chairman John Bailey proclaimed after the numbers came in, Kennedy had "received a midterm vote of confidence which will affect our country's destiny as greatly as did FDR's midterm victory in 1934."

Indeed, JFK, as he himself surmised at the dawn of the new decade, seemed to "fit the times." On the same day it reported on Mrs. Roosevelt's passing, the *New York Times* wrote, "The outcome of the election demonstrated support for President Kennedy's Cuban policies and warded off a Republican threat to his legislative strength. The President emerged with greater prestige—and political strength." The old guard was fading; the new guard had come, and it was thriving.

"GRACE UNDER PRESSURE"

Eleanor Roosevelt's opinion notwithstanding, JFK did what *Time* called "an updated, visual version of FDR's folksy fireside chats," offering a mid-December televised interview to news anchors of the three networks—ABC, CBS, and NBC. Sitting in the Oval Office in his rocking chair, the president reflected on the tempestuous year as it neared its end. When asked how he saw the job two years in versus his perception prior to taking the office, Kennedy offered a humble reply: "I would say the problems are more difficult than I imagined them to be. The responsibilities placed on the United States are greater than I imagined them to be and there are greater limitations upon our ability to bring about a favorable result than I imagined there would be. . . . There is such a difference between those who advise, or speak, or legislate and the man . . . who [says] 'This shall be the policy of the United States.'"

Regardless, Kennedy had grown comfortable in the role. One could hear it in his collected voice, his willingness to concede mistakes, his grasp of the issues before him. Despite the year's tumult, he harbored "a great deal of hope" as the New Year approached. He said that in the last two decades, the United States, composed of just 6 percent of the world's population, had beat back threats from Nazi Germany and the communist states—and "if it were not for us the Communists would be dominant in the world today." He went on to say there was "reason to be rather pleased with ourselves this Christmas."

The rocking chair in which Kennedy sat for the interview, under which wooden blocks had been placed to prevent him from swaying out of range of the television cameras, had become a symbol of the Kennedy presidency. It had been recommended as a remedy for his chronic back pain by Kennedy's personal physician, Janet Travell. Jackie Kennedy bought more than a dozen of the rockers from the P & P Chair Company of Asheboro, North Carolina, upholstered separately with white fabric, and placed them throughout her husband's orbit—in Hyannis Port, Palm Beach, Glen Ora, and Camp David, and on Air Force One, in addition to the Oval Office—where they awaited her husband as a balm. It was incongruous somehow, the energetic young president and a chair associated with whiling away the hours in front porch idleness.

He was the embodiment of vigor to the extent of parody— "viggah" in Kennedy-speak—making physical fitness one of the goals of his administration. Determined to maintain an athletic physique himself, he fixated on his weight, laboring to remain in the 170-pound range, even traveling with a bathroom scale to keep himself in check. He challenged U.S. Marines to a fifty-mile hike in twenty hours, causing a groundswell across the country; established the President's Council on Physical Fitness; and told *Look* magazine, "Whether it is the astronaut exploring the boundaries of space, or the overworked civil servant laboring into the night to keep a government program going, the effectiveness and creativity of the individual must rest, in large measure, on his physical fitness and vitality."

Americans were aware of Kennedy's back problem, a condition they were led to believe originated as part of his war experience on *PT-109*, adding to his heroic mystique. (In actuality, his back vertebrae likely started deteriorating due to steroids he was taking for intestinal issues beginning in the late 1930s.) "How's your aching back?" a reporter asked him in August 1962. "Depends on the weather—political and otherwise," JFK said.

And yet the public had no idea of how sickly the president was. Pain and illness were a constant factor in Kennedy's presidency, as silent and ever present as his Secret Service detail. Throughout his life, it had always been there casting its shadow. Jackie once asked him, *If you could have one wish, what would it be?* "I wish I had more good times," he replied, an answer she found bewildering. In her mind, he was a "glamorous figure" whose charmed life had been full of "gay trips to Europe, girls, dances, everything." Upon reflection, though, she realized "what he meant was that he had been in pain so much."

She recalled the "pathetic" sight of him struggling up the stairs of a plane or hobbling to a podium on crutches, then standing there as if it never happened, "in control of everything." It was not unlike Franklin Roosevelt, whose handicap was all but invisible to a public that saw not a man crippled by polio but his vital, ebullient force. FDR was aided by the press, which was complicit in ignoring his condition. In JFK's case, it was because he, his family, his aides, and his doctors had hidden his illnesses and medical remedies from the press, knowing that Americans would raise understandable concerns if made fully aware of the extent of his maladies.

In 1959, Arthur Schlesinger asked Kennedy if he had Addison's disease. "No one who has the real Addison's disease should run for the presidency," he replied, "but I do not have it." Schlesinger said later that Kennedy drew "a distinction between true Addison's and broadly construed Addison's," though Schlesinger didn't know exactly why Kennedy believed his case wasn't "true." After winning the presidency, the president-elect firmly denied having the disease when asked about the rumor by a reporter and judged himself to be in "excellent" health. He was backed up by the opinion of Travell, who boasted that he had "astounding vitality" and would continue the pattern of lying about Kennedy's condition after becoming his White House physician.

Behind the scenes, the vitality was hardly in evidence. In order to prevent back movement that might cause pain, Kennedy wore a corseted brace around his torso from his waist to his chest, held in place by an Ace bandage, stiffening his posture and rendering him unable to pick up his children. To endure news conferences and interviews like the one he gave the networks in December, Kennedy received seven to eight injections of procaine for his back. "I don't care if it's horse piss," he said of the multiple shots, "it works."

It was part of a staggering regimen of medicines administered to the president routinely throughout the course of his time in office, the extent of which was revealed in 2002, when historian Robert Dallek was given access by the John F. Kennedy Library Foundation to Kennedy's secret medical files. Kennedy enlisted a legion of medical professionals to tend to his rash of illnesses and persistent pain—an allergist, an endocrinologist, a gastroenterologist, an orthopedist, and a urologist, as well as other doctors, including Travell and Max Jacobson, known as "Dr. Feelgood" for the "pep pills" he prescribed like aspirin to celebrities. On any given day, Kennedy was given myriad drugs. For pain: codeine, Demerol, or methadone. For anxiety: meprobamate, Librium, or Stelazine. For sleep: barbiturates. For infection prevention: injections of a blood derivative, gamma globulin. Plus there was thyroid hormone and Ritalin.

During times of extreme stress, his medications were ramped up. In the midst of the Cuban missile crisis, he was taking painkillers, antispasmodics for colitis, antibiotics for a urinary tract infection, antihistamines for allergies, and steroids for his Addison's disease. But, as Dallek wrote, "Judging from the tape recordings made of conversations during [the Cuban missile crisis], the medications were no impediment to [lucidity] during these long days; on the contrary, Kennedy would have been significantly less effective without them, and might even have been unable to function." To be sure, the medications seemed to have little adverse effect on Kennedy aside from grogginess and fatigue, though in December 1962, Jackie grew concerned that her husband was "depressed" due to the antihistamines he was taking for food allergies. The answer was to prescribe the antipsychotic drug Stelazine for two days.

Aside from his rigid carriage due to the back brace, Kennedy exhibited few physical manifestations of illness, though in retrospect one can see how the cortisone shots he got regularly had expanded his once angular, chiseled face. "That's not my face," he would say with some distress as he looked in the mirror, pulling at his cheeks. "Vain as always," Ben Bradlee said of Kennedy, "it bugged him if he appeared a little jowly at press conferences, which he often did."

Jackie recalled her husband paraphrasing Somerset Maugham: "Suffering doesn't ennoble, it embitters." Yet Kennedy never seemed resentful over the pain or illnesses he suffered. A habitual Sunday churchgoer who knelt nightly for a quick prayer as routinely as brushing his teeth, Kennedy, Jackie imagined, must have thought God was "unjust" and may have wondered "'Why does this all happen to me?'" But, she added, "he never said that."

Schlesinger, echoing the views of others close to Kennedy, said,

"He never uttered a word of self-pity or complaint." Somehow, he had found a way to overcome it. Harold Macmillan wrote after a meeting with Kennedy in late 1961, "He is very restless owing to his back. . . . It is really rather sad to see a young man so afflicted, but he is very brave and does not show it." Upon learning the depth of his brother's medical history in 2002, Ted Kennedy said, "While I was not aware of the exact details of my brother's medical condition, I did see the great courage he exhibited throughout his life in triumphing over illness and pain."

In *Profiles in Courage*, John Kennedy called courage "that most admirable of human virtues." An admirer of Ernest Hemingway, Kennedy was drawn to the author's definition of courage as "grace under pressure." He included it in the book's introduction with attribution to the author, even going so far as to write Hemingway to validate the quote. (Though Hemingway declined to respond, Kennedy's editor confirmed that Hemingway had used the phrase in a 1929 *New Yorker* interview with Dorothy Parker.)

While keeping his medical conditions and treatment from the public is a stain on his presidency—the public has a right to know the full details of its chief executive's health as a matter of security—there was something undeniably noble and courageous in how Kennedy stoically shouldered debilitating pain and illness, never letting on that it was a constant torment as he carried out the exacting duties of his job. In an era in which vulnerability was often perceived as a weakness, Kennedy kept any feelings he had to himself, consistent with the "Kennedys don't cry" admonition his parents sounded throughout his childhood like a family mantra.

Indeed, the higher purpose of the office he held may have helped to sustain him. The fragility of his health had long given him an appreciation for life's fleeting nature. He had spent his forty-some years trying to outrun mortality, racing toward some greater ambition and loftier height, and now he stood at the peak—"the seat of all power" and "the place to be . . . if you want to get anything done"—where, after a rough start, he could grow and make his mark. As Dave Powers said, "He loved being where the action was. He was always at his best under pressure. He became more determined with each disappointment." The presidency, more than anything else, had given John Kennedy's tenuous life meaning.

IV

THE PEAK

On the last day of his life, JFK is greeted by a crowd outside the
Hotel Texas in Fort Worth, November 22, 1963.
Cecil Stoughton, White House Photographs, JFK Library

BIRMINGHAM

Toward the end of 1963, Martin Luther King, Jr., settled into a cross-continental evening flight from Atlanta to Los Angeles, his head nestled against a small white airline pillow. Soon into its westward route, the plane hit a patch of turbulence, lurching violently. In the dim cabin light, King turned to a reporter from *Time* sitting next to him. "I guess that's Birmingham down below," he said.

The new front line for the escalating campaign for civil rights, Birmingham, Alabama, had hit King and the soldiers of the non-violent civil rights movement he led with all it had in 1963. In its way, the movement hit back harder. "In 1963, there arose a great Negro disappointment and disillusionment and discontent," King explained to *Time*. "It was the year of Birmingham, when the civil rights issue was impressed on the nation in a way that nothing else before had been able to do. It was the most decisive year in the Negro's fight for equality. Never before had there been such a coalition of conscience on this issue."

Earlier in the year, in the first days of spring, King and his SCLC, in partnership with the Alabama Christian Movement for

Human Rights (ACMHR), had begun a direct-action campaign in Birmingham. Alabama's newly elected governor, George Wallace, had stated his administration's policy categorically in his gubernatorial inauguration speech in mid-January. Outside the state's capitol, over which the Confederate flag, not the American flag, proudly flew, in the place where Jefferson Davis stood as he was sworn in as the president of the Confederacy, Wallace pledged, "Segregation now, segregation tomorrow, segregation forever."

No one needed to tell the ruling class of Birmingham. The state's largest city, with a population of just over 340,000, 40 percent of which was Black, Birmingham had a long, baleful history of racism, including a series of dynamite explosions perpetrated with impunity to keep African Americans in their place in a post–World War II Jim Crow society. It explained the city's notorious nickname: Bombingham. King called it "the most thoroughly segregated city in the country." The city had banned a book featuring black and white rabbits and rejected a minor league baseball franchise due to its integration. The Birmingham campaign, according to ACMHR's president, Fred Shuttlesworth, would be "a moral witness to give our community a chance to survive." But its success was by no means assured. The SCLC's previous effort in Albany, Georgia, failed to generate much media attention or forward progress for the movement. King called 1962 "a year that civil rights was displaced as the dominant issue in domestic politics." Shuttlesworth acknowledged that they "needed a victory," promising King that Birmingham would "shake the country." But it was by no means assured.

Called "Project C" for confrontation, the campaign began on April 3, a day after a mayoral runoff election that saw the defeat of the virulently racist commissioner of public safety, Eugene "Bull" Connor, to the more moderate, less menacing Albert Boutwell, who agreed to meet with any African American leader who wished to talk with him—except Martin Luther King, Jr. In the pre-Easter buying season, second only to Christmas in retail riches, the campaign coalesced Birmingham's African Americans around store boycotts, sit-ins at segregated public places, and protest demonstrations at city hall. Participants were resolved to go to jail—"a badge of honor," civil rights leaders called it. King was at the forefront, espousing Gandhian nonviolence as the best means of activism, committed to going to jail himself. And if King was there, so was the press, a key to the campaign's objective in exposing Americans to the atrocity of systemic racism—though the presence of newsmen in Birmingham wasn't necessarily about the campaign's righteousness but of a more macabre nature. "Go where Mahatma goes," one major newspaper ordered its southern correspondent, referring to King. "He might get killed."

Not all of Birmingham's Black population was supportive of the effort. A. G. Gaston, a successful African American businessman who offered his A. G. Gaston Motel to King and his retinue at a reduced rate, argued that what Black people needed was a "Martin Luther King of economics." "It doesn't do any good to arrive at first-class citizenship," he argued, "if you arrive broke." He believed the answer was quiet negotiation and compromise with Birmingham's leadership, not stoking tensions at a time when small advances were being made in the city and throughout the South. The *New York Times, Washington Post,* and *Time,* which titled its article on Project C, "A Poorly Timed Protest," held similar views.

John Kennedy saw it the same way, moving ever cautiously on civil rights, which threatened to compromise his broader domestic agenda and alienate him from southern Democrats, increasing the risk of losing southern support for his reelection in 1964. Foreign policy continued to be Kennedy's principal focus, and he saw the exposure of racism as jeopardizing moral authority abroad as the U.S. battled against cold war communist forces for hearts and minds.

Moreover, the Kennedys regarded King warily. While they were inclined to work with Beltway insiders like the heads of the National Urban League, the Brotherhood of Sleeping Car Porters, and the NAACP—Whitney Young, A. Philip Randolph, and Roy Wilkins, respectively—they saw King as a provocateur operating outside the system. The FBI's view of King was far worse, due largely to King's ties to white New York–based lawyer Stanley Levison, an adviser and benefactor to King, whose past deep support for the Communist Party and Soviet leader Joseph Stalin gave J. Edgar Hoover fits. In May, while the campaign in Birmingham was raging, Kennedy invited civil rights leaders to the White House but pointedly excluded King, telling Bobby, "King is so hot that it's like Marx coming to the White House."

Nonetheless, a report Kennedy solicited from his brother on civil rights reinforced his belief that his administration was on the right track. Submitted to Kennedy on January 24, 1963, Bobby's report called 1962 a "year of great progress on civil rights," including Kennedy finally making good on his campaign promise to desegregate public housing with "a stroke of a pen," an order he signed on November 20. But Bobby warned of the challenges that remained "not only in the South . . . but throughout the country."

Kennedy's wariness on the issue of race was evident the following month at a White House reception he hosted around Lincoln's birthday and the centennial of his Emancipation Proclamation. Celebrities and the major leaders of the movement were in attendance, though King sent his regrets. As he saw entertainer Sammy Davis, Jr., and his white wife, Swedish actress May Britt, Kennedy bristled. "Get them out of here," he ordered out of fear of photographers capturing the interracial couple, causing political damage. When aides approached Jackie in the residence with the hope that she might go downstairs and have a private meeting with Davis and Britt in order to allow photographers to go into the reception without spotting them, she was appalled by the suggestion, declining to go downstairs at all. The event began without the first couple in attendance as Kennedy tried to smooth things over with his wife. Eventually, she agreed to go down briefly for formal group photographs, before immediately retiring back to the residence.

Later in February, Kennedy sent a "Special Message on Civil Rights" to Capitol Hill in which he asserted that "more progress" on civil rights had been made during his administration "than in any comparable period of history," and proposing the continuation of the U.S. Commission on Civil Rights and a largely toothless voting rights bill. The bill got little attention and even less traction in Congress. Part of it, as Bobby said, was that there was "no public outcry." But even more so, it was because Kennedy was in no hurry to put the full weight of the presidency on the line for civil rights. As Roy Wilkins, the head of the NAACP, said, "They were putting a toe in the water, but they weren't diving in." Birmingham and the "moral witness" it bore would change that.

In the early morning hours of April 11, 1963, as he sat in a haze of cigarette smoke with his lieutenants and stakeholders in room thirty of the A. G. Gaston Motel, the spacious suite they used as their "war room," Martin Luther King, Jr., had a decision to make. The previous day, Birmingham's sheriff served him a state-court injunction that banned King and other leaders of the campaign from demonstrating, effectively rendering their effort impotent.

Violating it would mean jail. Despite the debate in the room—never before had King defied a court injunction—there was little doubt in King's mind over the course they would take. Jail it was.

After rallying followers at a mass meeting at the 16th Street Baptist Church, one of sixty-five consecutive night gatherings the church would hold, King discovered that the bail money he and others had raised by appealing to supporters of the movement to spring civil rights protesters from jail had dried up. King met with twenty-four advisers who discussed what to do next. Should King go out and raise funds, breaking the momentum of "the battle of Birmingham," or continue to lead the effort and go to jail with no certainty as to when he and others would be bailed out? King listened in "the deepest quiet" he had ever felt. Once again, he chose jail. "I don't know what will happen," he said. "I don't know where the money will come from. But I have to make a faith act."

On Good Friday, April 12, King and his friend and SCLC co-founder Ralph Abernathy dressed for jail in light blue cotton shirts and blue jeans, marched with a group of sixty from the 16th Street Baptist Church toward city hall, as thousands of Blacks cheered them on, clapping and singing. After four and a half blocks, they met a horde of policemen led by Bull Connor waiting for them at a barricade, a tableau of foreboding blue. King and Abernathy stood before them, then knelt and prayed before being grabbed by the seats of their pants by motorcycle cops. The two were tossed into a paddy wagon with the other marchers and carted off to the Birmingham jail.

King was thrown into solitary confinement, held in a narrow, dark cell—no mattress or blanket—where, denied contact with any outsiders, he faced "a nightmare of despair." Recalling how Kennedy had stepped up for her husband when he was jailed in

Georgia in 1960, Coretta Scott King called Bobby Kennedy to see if the White House could help. On Monday, April 15, the president called to let her know that her husband would be phoning her shortly. By then, due to the influence of the White House, conditions for King had changed.

Though he remained in solitary confinement, his jailers had given him a mattress and blanket, and allowed him to shower and briefly visit daily with his lawyers, who had smuggled in a pen and a copy of the *Birmingham News,* dated April 12, the day King had been jailed. The newspaper included an open letter written by a group of eight local clergymen—all white—condemning King and the protests he had catalyzed, which they contended had inflamed tensions in the community. Civil rights, they claimed, should be pursued at a legal level in the courts, "not in the streets."

In the murkiness of his small cell, King scrawled a response, writing in the newspaper's margins, then on scraps of toilet paper and sheets from a legal pad. Page by page, the lawyers furtively carried out the letter, which was typed up by King's aides at the Gaston Motel. The product became the "Letter from Birmingham Jail," an impassioned seven-thousand-word challenge to the eight clergymen and those like them who "paternally believe [they] can set a timetable for another man's freedom."

> Frankly, I have yet to engage in a direct action campaign that was "well timed" in the view of those who have not suffered unduly from the disease of segregation. For years now I have heard the word "wait." It rings in the ear of every Negro with piercing familiarity. This "wait" has almost always meant "never." . . . We must come to see with the distinguished jurists of yesterday that "justice too long delayed is justice denied."

First published as a pamphlet by the American Friends Service Committee, a Quaker group committed to nonviolence, the letter was picked up by various publications as King's powerful rebuke spread virally, eventually making its way to the White House.

King and Abernathy were released from jail on April 20, after A. G. Gaston posted their $5,000 bail. By then thousands of dollars had poured into SCLC's coffers. Project C had continued while King and Abernathy had been imprisoned. Now, with King back in circulation, the momentum grew. In early May, student protesters, some as young as six, became part of the campaign's swelling ranks. A group of more than nine hundred students descended on Birmingham on May 2, attempting to integrate lunch counters, department stores, and white churches; more than seven hundred were arrested and jailed. Many Americans, including Bobby Kennedy, were outraged that children were being used as soldiers on the front line.

The following day Bull Connor once again awaited the young demonstrators menacingly, this time determined to rein them in before they left the Black section of Birmingham, where they had begun their march. Weaponizing vicious German shepherds and fire hoses that jettisoned seven hundred pounds of pressure, Connor gleefully shouted, "Look at those niggers run," as the marchers scattered to protect themselves. It was a turning point. The press, including all the major television and newspaper outlets, took it all in, training cameras on the chaos and violence. "Don't worry about your children who are in jail," King told followers at a church rally that evening. "The eyes of the world are on Birmingham."

John Lewis was among those who watched the savagery play out on television. "Like the rest of America," he wrote, "[I] was absolutely stunned by what I saw. Snarling German shepherds loosed on teenaged boys and girls, the animals' teeth tearing at slacks and shirts. Jet streams of water strong enough to peel the bark off a tree aimed at twelve-year-old kids, sending their bodies hurtling down the streets like rag dolls in a windstorm. . . . It looked like battle footage from a war." Indicting Kennedy indirectly, Radio Moscow, broadcasting around the world, said, "We have the impression that American authorities both cannot and do not wish to stop outrages by racists."

In fact, John Kennedy was as appalled as much of America. The following day's *New York Times*, with its lead photo of a German shepherd lunging ferociously into the chest of a young Black man as a police officer pulled him toward the dog, grabbed him almost as forcefully. It made him "sick," Kennedy told a meeting of leaders of Americans for Democratic Action. "I am not asking for patience," he said. "I can understand why the Negroes of Birmingham are so tired of being asked to be patient." Still, he wasn't prepared to act, contending privately and publicly that there was nothing much he could do, and continuing to believe that it was more of a legal issue than a moral one.

If in the weeks ahead Kennedy came to see civil rights as a moral cause, it came in large measure because of his brother's evolving view. In late April, Bobby went down to Alabama to size up the five-foot-seven George Wallace in Montgomery, where he received a venomous reception. As he ascended the steps of the state capitol, the attorney general was greeted by white demonstrators who held up signs like "Koon Kissin' Kennedys." After trying to shake the hand of a state trooper, he was met by a nightstick that was jabbed into his stomach. It was as though he had entered a hostile foreign country.

But a deeper impression was made on him in New York City during a June 7 meeting he had with a number of Black intellectuals and celebrities who had gathered at his invitation—though the response he received was nearly as antagonistic as it had been in Montgomery. The group had been assembled by thirty-eight-year-old novelist James Baldwin, whose celebrated *New Yorker* piece titled "Letter from a Region in My Mind" claimed, "The Negroes of this country may never be able to rise to power, but they are very well placed indeed to precipitate chaos and ring down the curtain on the American dream." John Kennedy was among those who were taken by Baldwin's powerful essay, and later by a May 17 *Time* cover story on Baldwin called "The Root of the Negro Problem." He encouraged Bobby to draw Baldwin out on the matter; Baldwin and the "rowdy" group he put together at Bobby's urging didn't hold back.

The gathering, in the Kennedy family's spacious Central Park South apartment, began civilly enough before Jerome Smith, a young Freedom Rider who had been arrested and hospitalized for the beatings he sustained, lit into Bobby about the plight of African Americans. He "put it like it was," recalled actress and singer Lena Horne, "the plain, basic suffering of being a negro," becoming so worked up in his diatribe that he blurted out he wanted to vomit just being in the same room with Bobby Kennedy. At least, that's what Bobby heard. What Smith was trying to convey was that having to make a plea to the attorney general for rights that should intrinsically be his as an American citizen made him *feel* like vomiting. Nonetheless, the assault hit Bobby between the eyes. As he turned to ignore Smith, the anger in the room hissed louder. Bobby sat down reeling, trying to collect himself.

The Irish were persecuted, too, he told the group. His grandfather had landed on American shores the object of prejudice; now, two generations later, his great grandson was president. As Baldwin took in the attorney general's words, his scorn for Kennedy's insularity was as palpable as his shock at his "naïveté." His family had been in America far longer, Baldwin countered, and they were still clinging to society's lowest rung.

Though the meeting lasted three hours, it stayed with Bobby in the days to come. "After Baldwin," said Nicholas Katzenbach, Bobby's deputy attorney general, "he was in absolute shock. Bobby expected to be an honorary Black. . . . He thought he knew so much—and he didn't." Initially, Bobby seethed—he excoriated Baldwin to aides, deriding him for his homosexuality—but as his anger cooled, his mind began to change, turning to empathy. In his way, Bobby Kennedy knew what it was to grow up feeling less-than, and he talked more and more about how he would feel if his children had been on the other side of Jim Crow segregation. If he had been born Black in America, he told an aide several days after the New York meeting, acknowledging his privilege, his feelings wouldn't have differed much from those of Baldwin.

In mid-May, John Kennedy got his own view of George Wallace during a visit to Muscle Shoals, where he delivered a speech and was accompanied by the Alabama governor afterward on a helicopter ride to the U.S. Army's Redstone Arsenal in Huntsville, thirty-five minutes away. Just days earlier in Birmingham, bombs had been set off at the A. G. Gaston Motel and at the home of King's younger brother, A. D. King, though no one was hurt. Birmingham, Kennedy warned Wallace, was "getting an almost impossible reputation throughout the country and the world." Just as impossible, Kennedy realized, was getting Wallace to do something about it. He had long ago concluded that Wallace and other southern defenders of segregation were "hopeless," incapable of change. Martin Luther King, Jr., and Fred Shuttlesworth, Wallace informed Kennedy, were driving "around town in a big Cadillac, smoking expensive cigars," competing over who could "go to bed with the most nigger women, and white and red women, too."

Five years earlier, after being defeated in a gubernatorial run by an opponent who more effectively exploited race to his own political ends, Wallace vowed never to be "outniggered" again. If his demagoguery was in doubt, Wallace made it as clear as his diminutive profile in the doorway of the Foster Auditorium on the campus of the University of Alabama in Tuscaloosa on June 11, 1963. After the university was bound by an Alabama district judge to admit two African Americans, James Hood and Vivian Malone, to attend summer sessions, which would mark the dawn of its integration, Wallace responded that he would "be present to bar the entrance of any Negro who attempts to enroll." Defying Kennedy's directive not to get in the way, Wallace remained true to his word, blocking Hood and Malone from registering for classes by standing in the door of the auditorium.

Conscious of the chaos around the integration of Ole Miss the previous year, the White House prepared for a standoff. Earlier that day, Kennedy had federalized the Alabama National Guard, mobilizing a hundred troops to be on hand with Justice Department officials on the university's campus, ready for the worst. Another 1,600 troops were put on standby, along with four hundred regular Army troops. A crisis was averted when Wallace, after reading a statement refusing to "willingly submit to illegal usurpation of power by the Central Government," stepped aside, allowing Nicholas Katzenbach to escort the students safely into the auditorium.

"I want to go on television tonight," Kennedy said after watching the coverage. For some time, he had talked about doing a major address on the necessity of meaningful civil rights reform, but the bulk of his advisers counseled against it, claiming it was too soon. Bobby was the lone exception. "He urged it, he felt it, he understood it, and he prevailed," said Burke Marshall. "I don't think there was anyone in the cabinet—except the president himself—who felt that way on the issues, and the president got it from his brother." John Lewis saw Bobby's influence as being the main factor in JFK's pivot on civil rights. Kennedy was "cautious, truly cautious on civil rights," Lewis said. "What I truly believe [is that] Robert Kennedy . . . became such an influential influence-maker in that administration and had such a close relationship with his brother, that he was able to help educate his brother and bring him along."

Tasked with writing the speech on short notice, Ted Sorensen was unable to complete a draft by the time Kennedy was to go on air at eight p.m. Bobby urged his brother to augment the speech by talking extemporaneously. The eighteen-minute address, in which Kennedy would announce his administration's bill proposing the most sweeping civil rights reform in America's history to that point—ending segregation in education, guaranteeing equal access to public facilities, and protecting voting rights—came largely from his heart. America was confronted, Kennedy said, "with a moral issue."

> It is as old as the scriptures and is as clear as the American Constitution. The heart of the question is whether all Americans are to be afforded equal rights and equal opportunities. . . . If an American, because his skin is dark . . . cannot enjoy the full and free life which all of us want, then who among us would be content to have the color of his skin changed and stand in his place? Who among us would then be content with the counsels of patience and delay?

One hundred years of delay have passed since President Lincoln freed the slaves, yet their heirs, their grandsons, are not fully free. . . . And this Nation, for all its hopes and all its boasts, will not be fully free until all its citizens are free. . . .

Now the time has come for this Nation to fulfill its promise. The events in Birmingham and elsewhere have so increased the cries for equality that no city or State or legislative body can prudently choose to ignore them.

It would become one of Kennedy's most important and enduring speeches. British prime minister Clement Attlee said in 1945 of his predecessor Winston Churchill's oratorical splendor during World War II, "Words at great moments of history are deeds." While Kennedy had yet to put into place any landmark policy changes on civil rights, his speech carried special significance. King and other civil rights leaders who had been waiting for Kennedy's "moral passion," heard it that evening. "Can you believe that white man not only stepped up to the plate," King said privately, "he hit it over the fence!" Roy Wilkins, the NAACP's executive secretary, called it, "a compassionate appeal, man-to-man, heart-to-heart. . . . That was his peak. That was perhaps his greatest pronouncement." Finally, Wilkins thought, Kennedy had "brought passion" to the issue of civil rights.

But any illusions that Kennedy's appeal had put civil rights on higher ground in the South were short-lived. Just after midnight, in the driveway of his Jackson, Mississippi, home, Medgar Evers, a World War II veteran of D-Day and the NAACP's Mississippi field director, was murdered with a gunshot to the back. He was carrying T-shirts that read "Jim Crow Must Go."

LYNDON

At Washington's annual Gridiron Club dinner in 1958, amid much speculation that he would seek the Democratic nomination for the presidency in two years' time, John Kennedy related a wry story about himself and his probable rivals. "I dreamed about 1960 the other night, and I told Stuart Symington and Lyndon Johnson about it yesterday," he said. "I told them how the Lord came into my bedroom, anointed my head, and said, 'John Kennedy, I hereby anoint you President of the United States.'" Symington responded bemusedly: "That's strange, Jack, because I had a similar dream last night in which the Lord anointed me President of the United States." Johnson heard out both of his Senate colleagues. "That's very interesting, gentlemen," he said, "because I, too, had a similar dream last night—and I don't remember anointing either one of you."

There was more than a little truth in it. In 1958, Senate majority leader Lyndon Baines Johnson stood astride Washington as the almighty master of the legislative process, wielding as much power in the job as anyone who had preceded him. Under the Capitol dome at least, LBJ *was* God.

So it was more than a little surprising that a chastened LBJ, roundly defeated by Kennedy in the 1960 Democratic primaries and outmaneuvered by the Kennedy campaign at the Democratic National Convention in Los Angeles, accepted his rival's invitation to be his running mate. No one, as the narrative goes, was more surprised than those in the Kennedy family.

Was the invitation offered as a political formality for the sake of party unity, currying the favor of the powerful southern wing of the party that had been its dominant influence since the Great Depression? Or was it a serious proposal, allowing for geographic balance that would prove to be a crucial factor in the ticket's razor-thin victory? The matter has long been a source of speculation. Some members of the Kennedy family propagated the former version of the story, including Bobby, who claimed that his brother, taken aback by Johnson's acceptance, asked Bobby afterward, "Now what do we do?" Jackie reinforced that view in an interview with Arthur Schlesinger in early 1964. "I think everyone was disappointed because of all the people [considered], they liked Lyndon Johnson the least," she recalled. "But I know Jack had to do it . . . to annul him as majority leader because here this man with this enormous ego would have been just enraged and blocking Jack in every way. . . . Everyone was even amazed that he accepted." Those recollections, given in the wake of JFK's assassination as Johnson ascended to the presidency accidentally, might be taken with a grain of salt, given, as they were, by two who saw Johnson as a crass pretender to the throne, unworthy of taking up Kennedy's mantle and possibly getting in the way of Bobby's own political rise.

But there is reason to believe that the offer was sincere. Johnson passed the most important test for a running mate—he was, in Kennedy's mind, the most capable of handling the duties of the presidency. Before embarking on his campaign for his party's presidential nomination, Kennedy considered his rivals over a steak lunch in his Senate office with *Saturday Evening Post* columnist Stewart Alsop. "I know all the other candidates pretty well," he told Alsop, "and frankly I think I'm as able to handle the presidency as any of them, even abler—except Lyndon, and he doesn't have a chance." Ted Sorensen said that Kennedy saw LBJ as "a man of enormous ambition, vanity and appetites, but also Washington political skills—skills that JFK knew he could not match" along with a "mental toughness" that the White House required.

The notion of Johnson as Kennedy's running mate also had the advocacy and full support of one crucial member of the family: Joe Kennedy. As Ted Kennedy recalled, "I remember [LBJ's] name being discussed by the President [JFK] and my father the day, or the evening, or two evenings, before the actual balloting, the nomination. . . . My father was sympathetic to that possibility. There were other names that were being considered. . . . [But] I've always believed the personal preference for [LBJ] had been my father's."

It was consistent with the advice he had given Jack four years earlier. Joe had counseled his son to reject the prospect of becoming the running mate of anyone, with "one exception." According to Ted, he felt "the only one that President Kennedy [*sic*] should serve as the vice president would be then-Senator Johnson." Johnson also sensed the admiration that Joe had for him. "I have the feeling that Joe Kennedy felt his boy had no chance to be president except for what I did as majority leader," he said. In fact, the Kennedy patriarch expressed his willingness to fund an LBJ-JFK ticket in 1956, an offer Johnson turned down.

Still, prior to getting the offer to join the 1960 ticket, Johnson hadn't done himself any favors with the Kennedy family. In a last-ditch effort to capture the presidential nomination himself, Johnson had spread the rumor throughout the convention in Los Angeles that Kennedy had Addison's disease. Additionally, he reminded delegates that Kennedy had failed to vote to censure Joseph McCarthy in 1954, and that Joe Kennedy, who supported the appeasement of Nazi Germany, "thought Hitler was right." But Joe understood political hardball as well as any. Maybe in part because of that, he believed the Senate majority leader would make the best running mate for his son.

So did *Washington Post* editor Phil Graham, who saw Johnson's potential as a national leader. A friend of Kennedy and Johnson, Graham lobbied both men on the notion of Johnson, nine years Kennedy's senior, rounding out the ticket. Though in January Kennedy said his pick of vice presidents would be Maine senator Edmund Muskie, Graham and syndicated columnist Joe Alsop were pleasantly surprised to see Kennedy warming to the idea of Johnson as his running mate.

After making the decision, it was Kennedy who had to do the lobbying. Sam Rayburn, the powerful Speaker of the House and a mentor and friend of Johnson, stood in the way of Johnson going on the ticket, counseling Johnson against it. Kennedy implored the speaker, "We can carry . . . no southern state unless we have something that will appeal to them. Do you want Nixon to be president?" Afterward, Rayburn changed his tune, urging Johnson to take the offer.

"How come you say this morning I ought to [accept] when last night you said I shouldn't?" Johnson asked.

"Because I'm a sadder and wiser and smarter man this morning than I was last night," Rayburn explained. "Nixon will ruin this country in eight years. And [if you don't accept the nomination] we're just as sure to have [Nixon as president] as God made little green apples."

But soon after Johnson accepted, Kennedy got cold feet. As influential liberal members of the party rose up against his pick, including Walter Reuther, the powerful head of the United Auto Workers, and Michigan governor Mennen Williams, he began to reconsider. Their resistance mirrored that of members of the Kennedy camp, including Bobby, who saw Johnson as a boorish southerner and a bad fit.

Acting as his brother's go-between, Bobby went to Johnson's suite at Los Angeles's Biltmore Hotel three times to seek his withdrawal. The story of what transpired varies. According to Bobby, in the last of those meetings, Johnson wept, saying, "I want to be vice president and if the president [*sic*] will have me, I'll join him in making a fight for it."

Johnson remembered things differently. After Bobby told him the liberals would "raise hell," he recalled saying, "The only question is—is [the ticket] good for the country, and is it good for the Democratic Party?" John Connally, Johnson's campaign manager, remembered telling Bobby, "Look, let's don't kid ourselves. [John] Kennedy could control this convention, Walter Reuther notwithstanding. . . . If there is some reason John Kennedy wants Lyndon Johnson off the ticket, he has to call him."

What's not in dispute is that the call never came. If Bobby's view of Johnson hadn't changed, his brother's did. The offer of the vice presidential nomination stuck. JFK and LBJ emerged from the convention as running mates, strange bedfellows inherent in the messy business of politics, who would ride on to a thin victory that would have been far less probable if not for the regional balance Johnson brought to the ticket.

Why had Johnson accepted the job? Former congresswoman Clare Boothe Luce posed the question on the night of Kennedy's dazzling inaugural. "Clare, I looked it up: one out of every four presidents has died in office," Johnson replied, his Texas accent twanging like a steel guitar. "I'm a gamblin' man, darlin', and this is the only chance I got." As glib as his answer was, it was more likely that Johnson saw his power as majority leader diminishing with either a Kennedy or Nixon presidency; the former would reduce him to being a water carrier for Kennedy, and the latter would have him dealing with a Republican president unlikely to play ball on bipartisan domestic initiatives to the extent that Eisenhower had.

Far less surprising than Johnson accepting the vice presidential nomination was that Johnson hated the job. John Adams, the nation's first vice president, called the role "the most insignificant office that ever the invention of man contrived or his imagination conceived." Johnson's fellow Texan John Nance Garner, who had served as the first of FDR's three vice presidents, put it more bluntly, likening it to "a bucket of warm piss," while Truman, FDR's last VP, said it was as "useful as a cow's fifth teat." LBJ described it just as earthily, offering two barnyard analogies. "The vice president is generally like a Texas steer," he maintained. "He's lost his social standing in the society in which he resides. He's like a stuck pig in a screwing match."

Holed up in a deluxe six-room suite on the second floor of the Old Executive Office Building next to the White House, Johnson felt isolated and irrelevant. John Kennedy knew it as much as anyone. One of Johnson's press secretaries, Liz Carpenter, recognizing her boss's plight, told Charlie Bartlett, "I wish you'd ask the president to call Lyndon once in a while because he's awfully lonely up here. . . . Maybe the president could call once in a while and ask for his advice on some of these problems." When Bartlett mentioned it to Kennedy, he replied, "Gosh, Charlie, I really mean to do that. . . . I feel so sorry for Lyndon up there. That's a terrible job for anybody."

But especially so for Johnson, who, like Kennedy, had entered into politics as a congressman at age twenty-nine, bustling with ambition. As a young representative, he'd quickly earned the admiration of Franklin Roosevelt, who believed that he could ascend to the presidency, calling him "the kind of uninhibited young pro" he would have liked to have been as a young man—and might have been if he "hadn't gone to Harvard."

Indeed, Lyndon Johnson, a product of hardscrabble small-town life in the Texas Hill Country, went to Southwest Texas State Teachers College, a fact that he was as conscious of as the Ivy Leaguers who surrounded him in the Kennedy White House. The chip on his shoulder was often as unmistakable as his southern drawl, made bigger by the ridicule of Kennedy acolytes who lampooned him with the nickname "Uncle Cornpone"—this despite John Kennedy's threat that anyone treating him less than they would treat him in the same position would be fired. Their contempt gnawed at Johnson. It was, as Lady Bird Johnson said, "like a pebble in [his] shoe." The proud Texan scorned them in return as "Harvards," a code word for effete, privileged intellectuals who talked more than they delivered, in contrast to him, an up-from-the-bootstraps achiever with a hard-earned reputation for getting things done.

Kennedy, who admired those qualities in Johnson, was more sympathetic, knowing how difficult it must have been for him as second fiddle. "I spent years of my life when I could not get consideration of a bill until I went around and begged Lyndon Johnson to let it go ahead," he told Arthur Schlesinger of his days in the Senate. Upon landing the White House, he insisted that Lyndon and Lady Bird Johnson be extended every courtesy, ordering his chief of protocol, Angier Biddle Duke, to "watch over [the Johnsons] and make sure they're not ignored." While Biddle ensured their inclusion in White House social events, the Johnsons were often ignored nonetheless, lost in the blinding social whirlwind that surrounded the Kennedys. Johnson conceded that he never "saw any indication of anything but friendship and respect" from Kennedy. "[President Kennedy] and I were not like brothers," he said. "We were not constant companions. [But] I don't recall that we ever had any element of bitterness or deep feeling enter into any of our discussions."

To say the least, any goodwill the Kennedy clan may have had for Johnson was not shared by Bobby. While John Kennedy was prone to see the good in the shades of gray of the complicated LBJ, described by author Stephen Harrigan as "a tormented personality powered by a furious twin engine of nobility and venality," RFK, who saw the world in black-and-white terms, saw only the bad. A Kennedy friend said Bobby was "a harder personality than his brother. Bobby can make enemies." He found one in Lyndon Johnson.

"I can't stand the bastard," Bobby said of Johnson to Richard Goodwin, "but he's the most formidable human being I've ever met." Bobby was bound to loathe the over-the-top Johnson, who was his opposite in almost every respect. Johnson blew hot; Bobby ran cold. Part of Johnson's prodigious persuasive power was his flesh-pressing physicality; he used every inch of his six-foot-three frame to bend his subjects to his will in what was known throughout Washington as "the Johnson Treatment." It was anathema to the diminutive Bobby, who at the time approached the world with cross-armed detachment.

"It was southwestern exaggeration against Yankee understatement," Arthur Schlesinger observed. A moral absolutist, Bobby despised Johnson's mendacity, claiming that he "lies all the time . . . in every conversation I have with him, he lies." At a May 29, 1963, meeting Johnson chaired for Kennedy's Committee on Equal Employment Opportunity, Bobby openly humiliated Johnson by angrily challenging as "phony" the statistics on workforce improvement among African Americans that Johnson had presented.

"Bob just tore in," one attendee of the meeting commented. "It was a pretty brutal performance"—and one not easily shrugged off by Johnson. A Lyndon Johnson voodoo doll gifted to Bobby by a friend at a Hickory Hill gathering in late 1963 produced peals of laughter, none more than from Bobby himself.

For his part, Johnson saw Bobby as the worst of the "Harvards," a "little shit-ass" lightweight who would never be in the White House but for barefaced nepotism. "Bobby elbowed me out," he complained later, making him feel like an unwelcome guest at a party to which he had been invited. In a February 1963 article, "The Vice-Presidency: Seen, Not Heard," *Time* wrote of Johnson as a once "towering figure":

> "Power is where power goes," Johnson confidently told a friend before taking office as Vice President. He was wrong—power has slipped from his grasp. [He is] chairman of the President's Committee on Equal Employment Opportunity, the National Aeronautics and Space Council and the Peace Corps National Advisory Council. He sits in on meetings of the Cabinet and is a member of the National Security Council. But all of this together adds up to only a fraction of his old power and

influence. He is free to speak up but nobody, really, has to heed him anymore.

From the beginning of the Kennedy administration, due in large measure to Bobby's contempt, Johnson was an outsider who simply didn't fit into the New Frontier.

By the spring of 1963, after muddling through the vice presidency for nearly two and a half years, Lyndon Johnson was unable to hide his melancholy. George Reedy, one of his press secretaries, observed, "He just looked lugubrious. He reminded me of one of those Tennessee bloodhounds . . . with the drooping ears." When an invitation came to speak at Gettysburg on Memorial Day, a month before the one hundredth anniversary of the bloodiest battle of the Civil War, Johnson dismissed it out of hand. His personal assistant, Juanita Roberts, didn't let it go at that. She saw its possibilities, a chance for her boss, "the distinguished son of distinguished Confederates," to make a statement around the centennial of a pivotal turning point in American history.

As the twentieth-century fight for civil rights raged, Johnson soon saw its potential, too. Though he had climbed the political ranks early in his career by toeing the line on segregation—it would have been nearly impossible to be a viable candidate in Texas otherwise—he had gained enough power in the Senate by the midfifties that he began to go his own way on civil rights. In 1956, he refused to sign the Southern Manifesto, supported by a fifth of those in Congress resolving to defy the Supreme Court decision *Brown v. Board of Education* banning segregation in schools, and a year later as Senate majority leader championed the symbolic though largely impotent Civil Rights Act of 1957—the first civil rights bill passed since Reconstruction. Privately, he was just as committed. Shortly after assuming the vice presidency, he wrote on the deed to a Washington house he and Lady Bird had planned to purchase, pertaining to common zoning ordinances restricting neighborhoods from racial integration, "The above does not apply to racial covenants. I will not accept them."

His convictions ran deep. At the age of twenty-one, he had taught marginalized Mexican American students in the dusty small town of Cotulla, Texas, seeing in their eyes the sting of poverty and racial injustice. It had a searing effect on his conscience. So, apparently, had the letter Martin Luther King, Jr., had written from his jail cell in Birmingham, imploring long-awaited change. In a meeting with the vice president, King had been impressed by Johnson's "emotional and intellectual involvement" in the civil rights movement's quest for equality and social justice. Likewise, it seemed, Johnson had been stirred by King's resistance to putting it off any longer. The speech he delivered in Gettysburg on May 30, nearly two weeks before Kennedy's speech asserting "a moral crisis," echoed King's call from Birmingham.

> One hundred years ago, the slave was freed. One hundred years later, the Negro remains in bondage to the color of his skin. The Negro today asks justice. We do not answer him—we do not answer those who lie beneath this soil— when we reply to the Negro by asking, "Patience." . . .
>
> The Negro says, "Now." Others say, "Never." But the voice of responsible Americans—the voice of those who died here and the great man who spoke here—their voices say, "Together." There is no other way.

Until justice is blind to color, until all education is unaware of race, until opportunity is unconcerned with the color of men's skins, emancipation will be a proclamation, but emancipation will not be a fact.

It was the tallest Lyndon Johnson would stand in the thankless role he had taken on as vice president. But more important, it foreshadowed the towering mark he would make, standing on the shoulders of the late John F. Kennedy, in impatiently delivering meaningful civil rights reform by steamrolling the Civil Rights Act of 1964 into law thirteen months later.

"TO TURN THE WORLD
AWAY FROM WAR"

While Kennedy had come to see civil rights differently by the spring of 1963, his view on the cold war had evolved as well. To be sure, he had always seen the utter futility of war. After the Vienna summit with Khrushchev two years earlier, when the possibility of a war with the Soviets seemed more likely, he became emotional in a private conversation with Bobby. "The thought of women and children perishing in a nuclear war," he said, as his eyes filled with tears, "I can't adjust to that."

As tensions with the Soviet Union subsided in the wake of the Cuban missile crisis, Kennedy used his heightened stature as a world leader to do something about it, shifting his cold war strategy away from building up arms around mutually assured destruction in an ideological deadlock and toward peaceful coexistence, advocating a treaty that would prohibit the United States and the USSR from conducting nuclear tests and deter other foreign powers from developing nuclear weapons. "It is insane that two men, sitting on opposite sides of the world," he said in a White House meeting, "should be able to decide to bring an end to civilization."

But it can—if it is sufficiently effective in its enforcement and if it is sufficiently in the interest of its signers—offer far more security and far fewer risks than an unabated, uncontrolled, unpredictable arms race.

With his twenty-seven-minute speech, Kennedy changed the cold war paradigm of looking at the leadership of the Soviet Union as geopolitical adversaries to viewing them as potential partners toward a lasting peace. Though the remarks would gain significance in the years after they were delivered, they got little media attention at the time. Importantly, though, the Kremlin had heard Kennedy loud and clear, allowing the speech to be published in the Soviet newspaper *Pravda* and broadcast in Russian in its entirety, save for one censored paragraph, on Voice of America radio. The address, surmised Arthur Schlesinger, gave Khrushchev "both personal reassurance and a weapon he could use against China" to show Kennedy's good intentions. Khrushchev later called the speech "courageous." While "pushing back on communism," he said, Kennedy had acknowledged "the inevitability and necessity of coexistence of states with different social systems."

On June 22, less than two weeks after the American University address, Kennedy set off on his second presidential trip to Europe, with ports of call in West Germany, Ireland, France, and England. This time he went alone, leaving Jackie, in her third trimester of pregnancy with their third child, at Camp David, where she escaped the Washington heat in the Cacoctin Mountains with Caroline and John Jr. Kennedy's visit to West Germany, the first leg of the trip, was highly anticipated. Upon arrival in Cologne, he was greeted by Konrad Adenauer, who had been mayor of the city before the Nazis ousted him in 1934 and, since 1946, had served as West Germany's first chancellor.

As the president and chancellor were chauffeured in a sleek black Mercedes, they were cheered by droves of German citizens who flooded the streets of Cologne, waving American flags and chanting, "Ken-ah-dee, Ken-ah-dee." Surveying the crowd, Adenauer told Kennedy they had come out because they knew their future was linked to America's, but added, "It is mild here compared to what it means to those in Berlin."

Adenauer was right about Berlin. On the morning of June 26, he and Kennedy arrived in the divided city, where wildly cheering crowds packed the streets as many as twenty deep. Pierre Salinger called it "the greatest reception the president had received anywhere." Estimates had it that 60 percent of Berlin's population of 3.2 million had come out to see the American president.

Just before noon, as he neared the Brandenburg Gate, Kennedy set his eyes on the Berlin Wall for the first time. "No one is ever prepared for the Wall," wrote Schlesinger of the wretched scar that bifurcated East from West, now made up mainly of huge concrete slabs. "It shocked and appalled the President." Kennedy had hoped to peer into East Berlin from the top of the gate, but the East German government saw to it otherwise, putting up large red banners on the gate's five arches to obstruct his view. But he got his chance as his motorcade moved on to Checkpoint Charlie, the American crossing point between East and West. Ascending the stairs of one of the guard towers, he asked to be alone. Atop he could see three hundred yards into the neighboring city, shrouded in gray, its streets desolate and lifeless, in stark contrast to the profuse, jubilant display of humanity that flooded West Berlin. In the distance, well beyond the hundred-yard area in the foreground that the East German government had designated a forbidden zone, he saw several women open a window and wave their handkerchiefs at him. He asked Major General James Polk, the American commander of the city, if it was dangerous for them to do so. The general replied that it was, moving Kennedy deeply.

As many as 450,000 West Berliners crammed into the plaza outside city hall where Kennedy was to speak. Prior to his arrival, Kennedy showed Polk a copy of the remarks his speechwriting team had prepared for him. "This is terrible," Polk said. Kennedy agreed. Taking matters into his own hands and stirred by the emotions of the day, Kennedy crafted his own speech in the temporary solace of the office of West Berlin's mayor, Willy Brandt, just before taking the stage. Aided by a translator, Kennedy wrote out the words *Ish bin ein Bearleener*—a phonetic translation of the German words for "*I am a Berliner.*"

Minutes later, Kennedy appeared before the mass of Germans, who roared their approval, "clapping, waving, crying as if it were the second coming," noted Schlesinger. The frenzy was almost disquieting. "If I told them to tear down the Berlin Wall, they'd do it," Kennedy remarked to his military aide Godfrey McHugh. It was cause for alarm for the eighty-seven-year-old Adenauer, who had been jailed by the Nazis as an enemy of the state in 1944. "Does this mean Germany can one day have another Hitler?" he asked Dean Rusk.

The crowd quieted a bit as Kennedy took the podium.

> Two thousand years ago, the proudest boast was "civis Romanus sum." Today, in the world of freedom, the proudest boast is "Ich bin ein Berliner." . . .
>
> There are many people in the world who really don't understand, or say they don't, what is the great issue between the free world and the communist world. Let them come to Berlin. There are some who say that communism is the wave of the future. Let them come to

Berlin. . . . And there are even a few who say that it is true that communism is an evil system, but it permits us to make economic progress. *Lass' sie nach Berlin kommen.* Let them come to Berlin. . . .

All free men, wherever they may live, are citizens of Berlin, and, therefore, as a free man, I take pride in the words "Ich bin ein Berliner."

The crowd roared its approval as Kennedy spoke the last words. As Thomas Putnam, the former director of the JFK Library, wrote, "Other than *ask not*, they were the most famous words he ever spoke . . . [a] defiant defense of democracy and self-government [that] stand out as a high point of his presidency." It was a personal high point for Kennedy as well. "We'll never have another day like this as long as we live," he told Ted Sorensen before the sun set on Germany and they flew off on Air Force One to Ireland, which would turn out to be as much a homecoming for Kennedy as it would a state visit.

With his televised address on civil rights and his speeches at American University and in Berlin—all executed in June within a sixteen-day span—Kennedy achieved an oratorical hitting streak that no other president has matched. The civil rights and American University orations reframed the most pivotal domestic and foreign policy issues, respectively, paving the way toward progressive policy changes; the Berlin speech manifested American leadership in the international cause of freedom as the United States continued to battle ambitious communist states abroad for hearts and minds.

Good things awaited Kennedy the following month, too. Seizing a moment of détente with the Soviets, he dispatched Averell Harriman to Moscow in early July. In just twelve days, Harriman negotiated a U.S.-Soviet agreement on the prohibition of nuclear testing in the atmosphere, underground, and in space. The president announced the agreement with televised remarks on the evening of July 26. "So, let us try to turn the world away from war," he said. "Now, for the first time in many years, the path of peace may be open." After the Senate approved the Limited Nuclear Test Ban Treaty in late September by a vote of 80 to 19, Kennedy signed it on October 7, 1963, nearly a year to the day after the beginning of the Cuban missile crisis, when the world stood on the precipice of nuclear holocaust. The treaty would become Kennedy's proudest accomplishment, a vital step toward the elusive realization of his fondest hope: keeping the peace.

SEPTEMBER SONG

Though fortune had smiled generously on John Kennedy throughout his forty-six years, tragedy always patiently lay in wait. Wednesday, August 7, 1963, arrived on a melancholy note. The date marked the twentieth anniversary of his wartime rescue after his PT boat was cut in half by a Japanese destroyer. Two members of Kennedy's crew had died as a result of the crash, and the chapter stood as a reminder, along with the passing of two of his eight siblings and his bouts with near-fatal illness, of the tenuous hold of life.

Another came the same day. At 11:43 a.m., Evelyn Lincoln, Kennedy's secretary, hastily approached the president in the West Wing with the news that his wife had gone into premature labor in Hyannis Port, five and a half weeks before she was due to have the baby by Caesarean section in Washington. Kennedy was soon rushed aboard Air Force One, headed to Otis Air Force Base on Cape Cod, where a suite had been prepared for the first lady in its modest hospital. The president's second son was born while he was en route, at 12:52 p.m., but it only added to the urgency of his arrival. Patrick Bouvier Kennedy—weighing under five pounds—entered the world laboring for breath.

As Kennedy rushed to New England, his mixed record as a husband and father surely must have weighed on his mind. Spousal fidelity had never been a strong suit, but his dalliances were only part of the issue. In 1956, hearing three days after the fact that Jackie had given premature birth to a stillborn daughter, Arabella, Kennedy was in Capri, carelessly enjoying a European holiday cruise on the Tyrrhenian Sea, where he intended to stay. It fell to Bobby to tend to the situation back home, comforting Jackie and arranging for the burial of the infant. Only the admonishment of Florida's George Smathers, Kennedy's fellow senator, compelled him to return stateside. In a transatlantic call, Smathers berated him, "You'd better haul your ass back to your wife if you want to run for president."

In November 1960, Jackie again went into labor prematurely in Washington, as Kennedy, now the president-elect planning his administration at his father's Palm Beach estate, hurried back to her in a cold sweat on the DC-6 plane reserved for the press. "I'm never there when she needs me," he was overheard nervously muttering to himself.

Kennedy arrived at Otis Air Force Base Hospital to find Patrick barely clinging to life. The infant, doctors told him, was struggling with hyaline membrane disease, the most common form of death for infants born prematurely; his chances of survival were 40 to 50 percent, but the first forty-eight hours would be critical. Kennedy was able to briefly see his son, who was then flown by helicopter to Children's Hospital in Boston and placed in a steel hyperbaric chamber designed to keep his lungs open. After a brief visit with Jackie, Kennedy told his mother-in-law, Janet Auchincloss, "Nothing must happen to Patrick, because I just can't bear to think of the effect it will have on Jackie." He then flew to Children's

Hospital, where he consulted with doctors, asking repeatedly if his child would be mentally retarded before letting it go when one replied, "Mr. President, we're trying to save the baby's life."

"He is only 4 pounds, 10 and a half ounces, but Wednesday he held the heartstrings of the world in his little red fists," wrote the *Boston Globe* of the day of Patrick's birth. Early Friday morning, the president was awakened in a hospital room at 2:00 a.m. by a member of his Secret Service team as the newborn's health began to fade. Patrick was wheeled into the corridor where Kennedy, sitting in a wooden chair and dressed in a surgical cap and gown, kept vigil. As the baby's heart stopped beating at 4:19 a.m., his father held his small fingers in his own. "He put up quite a fight," he said in a whisper. "He was a beautiful boy." Kennedy then retreated to the quiet privacy of a hospital boiler room, where he sobbed over the loss.

That morning, Kennedy returned to Cape Cod with the somber task of informing his wife of their son's death. He fell to his knees, his arms around her, as tears streamed down his face. It was only the third time Jackie had seen her husband cry. "There's one thing I couldn't stand. If I lost you . . ." she comforted him. "I know . . . I know," he said.

Stoicism marked both of the Kennedys after the death of their son. As they prepared to reenter public life, Kennedy told his wife, "We must not create an atmosphere of sadness in the White House, because this would not be good for anyone. Not for the country, and not for the work we have to do." It informed her fortitude not only in the wake of her son's death but in the unimaginable days ahead in late November.

The loss further bound the public to the president and first lady, just as it deepened their relationship, drawing them closer than they had ever been. Janet Auchincloss saw it in her daughter and son-in-law on September 12, when the couple celebrated their tenth wedding anniversary at an intimate candlelit dinner party at the Auchinclosses' Hammersmith Farm in Newport, where they had been married ten Septembers earlier.

"They'd certainly been through as much as people can go through together in ten years," Auchincloss said a year later. "Tragedy and joy, and their children's births and deaths, and then Jack's illnesses, Jackie's . . . Caesarean operations, and then the campaigning, and occupying the highest office in the world. . . . And I felt that all their strains and stresses which any sensitive people have in a marriage, had eased to a point where they were terribly close to each other. I almost can't think of any married couple I've ever known that had a greater understanding of each other." Journalist Theodore White, who had chronicled Kennedy's 1960 presidential victory in his book *The Making of the President*, said, "There had always been this wall between them, but their shared grief tore that wall down. At long last they were truly coming closer together."

For years they had chosen to see the best in each other, gently looking past pronounced flaws—"reciprocal forbearance," Arthur Schlesinger called it. Now there was a tenderness that had settled on their marriage. In a letter to Charlie Bartlett written shortly after her wedding anniversary, Jackie thanked Bartlett for introducing her to Jack a dozen years earlier, crediting her husband for helping her to "re-attach" to her life after Patrick's death and allowing her to see "all the lucky things" they shared together. Kennedy seemed to have a greater appreciation for her, too.

"It was more than an 'understanding,'" a close friend said. "Jack was getting to the point where he really appreciated her—as a political asset and as a person." While his womanizing hadn't stopped, it had slowed. The same friend anonymously recounted Kennedy calling him and saying, "There are two naked women in my room and I'm sitting here reading the *Wall Street Journal.* Does this mean I'm getting old?"

A wistfulness and greater sense of mortality had also befallen Kennedy after his infant son's passing. In early September, the Kennedy family came together at Hyannis Port to celebrate the seventy-fifth birthday of Joe Kennedy, whose stroke nearly two years before had left the once formidable patriarch reliant on a wheelchair and speechless except for the word *no,* which he often repeated as though simply to express himself in the only way he could. The president sat with him for long periods, reporting on the job and kissing him on the head when he left his side. The birthday gathering was a typical Kennedy family occasion—lively, clamorous, and chaotic—as the compound became a hive of activity: sailing, touch football, rooms filled with light chatter and laughter as a litter of Kennedy children ran in and out. On the evening of September 6, the family and close friends gathered around the piano and merrily sang songs as the old man, sitting mutely in a red, white, and blue party hat, proudly watched over the festivities. The blithe mood broke when the president requested "September Song," a sentimental ballad about a man coming to terms with the sunset of his life. As Kennedy sang the words through misty eyes, the room fell silent.

> *Oh, the days dwindle down to a precious few.*
> *September, November*
> *And these few precious days I'll spend with you.*

The song was a JFK favorite, one he often requested. Oleg Cassini, who had heard him sing it on several occasions, said, "It was all part of his elegant fatalism. It expressed what Jack felt about himself, that he wouldn't be around for very long." But in the last months of 1963, it resonated with new poignancy. Though Kennedy was always conscious of life's fragility, a sense of foreboding now hovered around him. While sailing on Nantucket Sound late in the summer with Lem Billings and Charlie Bartlett, the boat silently adrift as the winds on the Atlantic hushed for a moment, Kennedy looked out at the horizon. He was always happiest and most at peace when he was on the water. "How do you think Lyndon would be if I got killed?" he asked.

THE MARCH

The president shifted uncomfortably in his chair. On June 22, eleven days after his television address in which he called civil rights a "moral issue," he, Bobby, and Lyndon Johnson met for two hours with Black leaders in the West Wing. James Farmer, Martin Luther King, Jr., John Lewis, A. Philip Randolph, Roy Wilkins, and Whitney Young—the "Big Six" leaders of the Congress of Racial Equality, the SCLC, the Student Nonviolent Coordinating Committee, the Brotherhood of Sleeping Car Porters, the NAACP, and the National Urban League, respectively—had come to meet with Kennedy, who had hoped to enlist the men in turning down the heat on what one of Kennedy's aides predicted would be "a long, hot summer." As far as Kennedy was concerned, protests were only adding to the fervor. The civil rights bill he had proposed earlier in the month, he reminded them, would be a "serious fight" in the halls of Congress. "The vice president and I know what it will mean if we fail. A good many [domestic] programs I care about may go down the drain as a result of this," he reminded them, while suggesting that the bill would have a better chance of passing if Black protesters stayed off the streets.

Randolph, the elder of the group, listened respectfully. Blacks were "already in the streets," he countered. The regal seventy-four-year-old civil rights and union leader, who had been elected president of the largely Black union of the Brotherhood of Sleeping Car Porters over four decades earlier, had met with his share of presidents through the years. "Mr. President," he said in a rich baritone, "the Black masses are restless, and we are going to march on Washington."

It wasn't the first time Randolph had talked of a protest march on the capital. In 1941, he used the threat of a mass march to compel Franklin Roosevelt to ban discrimination in the defense industries, and again in 1947 to pressure Harry Truman to desegregate the military. This time he was determined to see to fruition a protest march to dramatize the civil rights revolution in America—and it made Kennedy uneasy. "You could tell by the body language," John Lewis recalled, "he didn't necessarily like what he heard."

Kennedy tried to dissuade Randolph, expressing his concern that the march would erupt in violence that would compromise the movement, risking a backlash in Congress and across America. Randolph was unyielding. The march would be "peaceful and nonviolent," he assured Kennedy. Kennedy remained unmoved, holding to the firm belief that the march was ill-timed.

King chimed in: "Frankly, I have yet to see any direct action campaign that didn't seem ill-timed. Some people said Birmingham was ill-timed."

"Including the attorney general," Kennedy joked.

Roy Wilkins added that he and his counterparts would have problems with their constituents if they *didn't* march. Kennedy knew the current was too strong to swim against. "Well, we all have our problems," he said, sighing as he rose from his seat to leave the meeting. "You have your problems. I have my problems." Afterward, the civil rights leaders adjourned to the South Lawn, where they met with the White House press corps. "We had a meaningful and productive meeting with the president," Randolph said, speaking for the group. "We are going to march on Washington."

Indeed, in many ways civil rights had *become* the problem for Kennedy. More than half of Americans believed racial tension to be the most important issue the nation faced. By the summer of 1963, after a spike in his approval ratings in the wake of the Cuban missile crisis, Kennedy's poll numbers had started to erode. Immediately after he had proposed his civil rights bill in June, 36 percent of the American public were of the mind that he was pushing the issue too hard, a number that rose to 41 percent in July, and would leap to 50 percent at the end of August. Not surprisingly, his approval numbers, while inching downward nationally throughout the year, dropped disproportionately in the South, slipping from 60 percent in June to 44 percent in September. "Do you think we did the right thing by sending the [civil rights] legislation up?" he would ask Bobby throughout the summer. "Look at the trouble it's got us in."

As far as Kennedy was concerned, the March on Washington for Jobs and Freedom, as Randolph called it, would add to the trouble, especially given the high profile of the event. In a letter to Kennedy before the march, Randolph promised it would be "the largest outpouring of Americans of all races, colors, and creeds ever to assemble in our Nation's Capital." In addition to the Big Six and other civil rights leaders, a number of celebrities had committed to attend—Sidney Poitier, Josephine Baker, Bob Dylan, Joan Baez, Marlon Brando, Diahann Carroll, Paul Newman, Harry Belafonte, James Baldwin, Charlton Heston, Sammy Davis, Jr., and Ossie

Davis—adding to the allure of the event, which was expected to be watched on live television by millions across the country.

King also represented potential trouble for Kennedy. After the meeting with the Black leaders, Kennedy asked King to take a private walk through the Rose Garden. "I assume you know you're under very close surveillance," he told King, alluding to the FBI's watch over him and the SCLC. The reason was King's relationship with his white New York–based lawyer and close adviser Stanley Levison, who was seen by the bureau, in Kennedy's words to King, as "a conscious agent of the Soviet conspiracy."

Though racist and reactionary, the zealous J. Edgar Hoover wasn't wrong about Levison, who at least since the early fifties had deep ties to the Communist Party as a supporter of Soviet leader Joseph Stalin and a financial benefactor for the Communist Party USA. Who could say whether King's efforts for societal change were really part of a communist plot to subvert the government? Concerned about his civil rights bill's chances, Kennedy, allying with King, warned, "If they shoot you down, they'll shoot us down, too. So, we're asking you to be careful."

On August 27, King and his wife, Coretta, checked into Washington's Willard Hotel, where King met with SCLC aides on the speech he was to deliver at the March on Washington the following day. The preeminent national leader on civil rights, King was slated to give the last address of the event, not just because of his prominence and oratorical might but because some of the others slated to speak wanted to ensure they would get exposure on national television, as crews packed up in the late afternoon to prepare pieces for the evening news. Moreover, just like all the other leaders on the bill, King had been given a time limit for his re-marks: eight minutes.

"There's no way in the world, Martin, that you can say what needs to be said in eight minutes," Walter Fauntroy, one of King's aides, said as King discussed the matter with his lieutenants. "They can't limit you—the spokesman of the movement—to that." King thought otherwise, worrying that if he went on any longer, he would be seen as showboating among his peers. "Look, Martin," Fauntroy said, "let the Lord lead you. You go on and do what the Spirit say do [*sic*]."

The following morning, King awoke to television news reports that attendance for the march was "about 25,000"—far less than anticipated. The march's organizer, Bayard Rustin, was on the Na-tional Mall, the two-plus-mile expanse of lawn between the back of the Capitol and the Lincoln Memorial, where reporters ques-tioned him about the poor turnout. "Gentlemen, everything is going exactly according to plan," he bluffed as he stared down at the empty page of a legal pad.

But any worry that the march would fail to draw the crowds that had been projected dissolved by late morning as the Mall was flooded by Americans from all over the country and every walk of life, three African American faces for every white one. Not only were the numbers not a disappointment, but organizers were stunned by the growing crowd, which would swell to between 200,000 and 300,000—the largest civil rights demonstration in the nation's history. Just under 6,000 police and 4,000 troops mixed among them, standing ready for a breakout of violence or chaos that never came. Throughout the humid late morning and early afternoon, the throng advanced peacefully as a slow-moving tide toward the Lincoln Memorial, where the event kicked off as the massive marble statue of the sixteenth president, the Great Emancipator, looked on impassively.

At the White House, John Kennedy spent the morning in a meeting before retreating to the residence to take in the march's proceedings on television. Marian Anderson sang the national anthem, followed by a steady parade of speakers who came to the rostrum one after another to deliver their remarks: members of the Big Six; Rosa Parks, Diane Nash Bevel, Myrlie Evers, and other "Negro Women Fighters for Freedom"; members of the clergy; AFL-CIO president Walter Reuther; and others. The tempo changed when Mahalia Jackson rose to the podium to sing two spirituals, "I Been 'Buked and I Been Scorned" and "How I Got Over," kicking the gathering into a higher gear.

After a speech by a rabbi from the American Jewish Congress, King, introduced by Randolph as "the moral leader of the nation," took the stage. King's deep, lilting voice fell on the masses before him: "We have come to this hallowed spot to remind America of the fierce urgency of now. This is no time to engage in the luxury of cooling off or to take the tranquilizing drug of gradualism. Now is the time to make real the promises of democracy."

Then, as the Georgia preacher wound down his eight minutes, Mahalia Jackson cried out, "Tell them about the dream, Martin!" Spurred on by Jackson, caught up in the moment, and intoxicated by the crowd, King veered off from his planned remarks, weaving together fragments of speeches he had made in the past to fit the grandeur of the hour. "All of a sudden, this thing came out of me that I had used . . . many times before," he said later, "that thing about 'I have a dream.'"

> I have a dream that my four little children will one day
> live in a nation where they will not be judged by the

color of their skin but by the content of their character.

I have a dream today.

Up until then the event had been precisely what Randolph had envisioned, a demonstrable expression of the movement for racial equality in keeping with America's most sacred creed: "All men are created equal." King's triumphant sixteen-minute oration made it far more, an indelible moment that defined the idealism of the era—much as Kennedy's inaugural address had nearly three years earlier—lifting Americans beyond themselves to aspire to a higher measure as a nation.

At the White House, Kennedy watched King with admiration. "He's damn good," he said. "Damn good!" Later, in the lead story in the *New York Times*, James Reston wrote, "Washington may not have changed a vote today, but it is a little more conscious tonight of the necessity of being ready for freedom. It may not 'look to it' at once, since it is looking to so many things, but it will be a long time before it forgets the melodious and melancholy voice of the Rev. Dr. Martin Luther King, Jr. crying out his dreams to the multitude." Kennedy said publicly that "the cause of 20,000,000 Negroes has been advanced."

After the march, as the crowd dissipated, the Big Six were driven to the White House. In the Cabinet Room, the president approached King and shook his hand, saying simply, "I have a dream," with a nod of approval. John Lewis sensed Kennedy's relief: "It was finally over, without crisis, incident, or explosion." True enough, Kennedy's greatest fear had been assuaged. But more than that, he felt the event was a positive step toward the passage of his civil rights bill. The House and Senate had both recessed just after one p.m. so that those lawmakers who wished to attend could make the event, and Kennedy was pleased when he heard the throngs chanting "Pass the bill! Pass the bill!" as they took their seats.

Still, it would be a heavy lift. In another front-page article, this one titled, "Congress Cordial But Not Swayed," the *New York Times* noted that the march "appeared to have left much of Congress untouched—physically, emotionally, and politically." During the course of Kennedy's seventy-five-minute meeting with the leaders, during which he gave a state-by-state rundown of where Congress stood on the bill, Randolph remarked that it would take "nothing less than a crusade to win approval," adding, "and I think nobody can lead this crusade but you, Mr. President."

But, as his uninspired years in the House and Senate suggested, Kennedy was hardly a crusader in the halls of Congress. Ill-suited to engage in the arm-twisting and horse-trading needed to get a political hot potato like the civil rights bill passed, he showed neither the legislative sway nor the will to push the bill into law. "He could never have passed that bill," Andrew Young said. "I don't think Kennedy was that committed. He wanted to be a good president and had a concept of greatness, but he was really too young." Roy Wilkins saw it that way, too. "Kennedy was not naïve," he noted, "but as a legislator he was very green."

Kennedy's poll numbers on civil rights didn't help. In October 1963, *Newsweek* published a survey further showing civil rights and the racial turmoil that had befallen the country as a liability for Kennedy, concluding, "It has hurt John F. Kennedy, and it may have hurt him badly." Kennedy had known that long before, when he introduced the bill in June. "I may lose the election because of this," he had told the Big Six when they met at the White House on June 22. "I don't care."

The truth was more complicated. Kennedy cared deeply about his reelection, which was partly why he had dragged his feet on civil rights to that point. But he also saw a confluence of historical forces coming to bear in bringing civil rights to the fore, caused, as much as anything, by the revolution waged by King and the movement he led. Reminded in a September 12 press conference of poll data that showed that half of Americans thought he was pushing too fast on civil rights, Kennedy replied, "This is not a matter on which you can take the temperature every week or two weeks or three weeks, depending on what the newspaper headlines must be. I think you must make a judgment about the movement of a great historical event which is taking place in this country."

The moral imperative was made even more plain three days later, on September 15, at 10:22 a.m., when a bomb exploded at Birmingham's iconic 16th Street Baptist Church. The blast occurred just before Sunday morning services were to begin, resulting in the deaths of four girls—three fourteen-year-olds and one eleven-year-old—and injuring more than two hundred others.

By the same token, the Kennedys weren't throwing caution to the wind, either. On October 10, Bobby Kennedy reluctantly gave the FBI the green light to tap King's home phone and later the SCLC's New York office. The bureau would dog King relentlessly in the years ahead. John Lewis maintained that J. Edgar Hoover did everything he could "to destroy the man." King's triumph at the March on Washington had only made him a bigger target in the eyes of the FBI director. The bureau's assistant director, William C. Sullivan, pandering to Hoover, wrote an internal memo calling King's speech powerfully "demagogic," while writing of King, "We must mark him now, if we have not done so before, as the most dangerous Negro of the future in this Nation from the standpoint of communism, the Negro and national security."

A COUP IN VIETNAM

It was a haunting image taken on June 11, 1963, that finally caused the world to take notice that something was going wrong in Vietnam: a Buddhist monk, sitting lotus style in a busy Saigon intersection, engulfed in flames. Sixty-three-year-old Thich Quang Duc, in a saffron robe, had emerged from a blue sedan with two other monks, one of whom doused him with gasoline from a five-gallon canister as Quang Duc sat on a cushion, rubbing a string of wooden holy beads and serenely chanting "*Nam mo amita Buddha*," "Return to eternal Buddha." Then he struck a match, starting the fire that would end his life. Some 350 monks and nuns formed a barrier around him, looking on for ten long minutes as his body turned to charred black and dissolved into the street.

A photograph taken by Associated Press photographer Malcolm Browne would appear on front pages around the world. John Kennedy was talking on the phone with Bobby about the civil rights crisis in Alabama when he caught a glimpse of it on one of the newspapers that he had yet to get to on his nightstand. "Jesus Christ!" he blurted out. Quang Duc's fiery public suicide was part of a protest against the oppressive treatment of Buddhists under the pro-Catholic government of South Vietnam's president Ngo Dinh Diem, a sign of the growing instability that caused the nation and the world to wonder why the United States was supporting the authoritarian regime. The statement Quang Duc left behind spoke to the problem: "Before closing my eyes to Buddha, I have the honor of presenting my words to President Diem, asking him to be kind and tolerant toward his people and to enforce a policy of religious equality."

Discord had been growing for years between the pro-Catholic South Vietnamese government and the Buddhist clergy, seething on May 8 when Buddhists in Hue, a city in the central part of the country, staged a protest that was seized upon by government troops, who killed nine and wounded fourteen others. Unwisely, Diem and his younger brother and closest adviser, Ngo Dinh Nhu, refused to grant equal rights to the Buddhists and make concessions on issues like flying religious flags, despite the fact that over three-quarters of the country's population considered themselves Buddhist. Instead, in the days after the massacre in Hue and Quang Duc's self-immolation, the regime doubled down on repression, raiding Buddhist pagodas, resulting in more bloodshed. The regime's cruelty toward the Buddhist population was further evident when it was reported that Nhu's notorious wife, known as Madame Nhu, mocked Quang Duc's martyrdom, declaring, "I would clap my hands at seeing another monk barbecue show." The outrage grew in the weeks after Quang Duc's suicide as seven additional monks burned themselves to death in protest of Buddhist repression. While none would have the same impact, the acts were mounting reminders of the chronic turmoil and tyranny of South Vietnam under Diem's reign.

The previous year there had been hope in the Kennedy administration that South Vietnam was stabilizing under Diem's leadership and that the United States would be able to begin the withdrawal of its 1,680 military advisers. Now things weren't looking so good. In fact, the situation in Vietnam had been deteriorating since the beginning of the calendar year, when the ARVN, supported by American helicopters, had been overwhelmingly defeated by Vietcong forces in the Mekong Delta—despite the advantages the ARVN boasted in troop size and U.S.-supplemented military equipment. The upset marked a turning point of sorts for the Vietcong, giving the underdog communist guerillas newfound confidence that the war could be won regardless of U.S. support of the ARVN.

But it was the photograph of Quang Duc burning on a Saigon street that brought the issue of American support of Diem to a head. Kennedy was deeply concerned about the matter. The day after the image appeared, he met with Henry Cabot Lodge, Jr., who had agreed to serve as his ambassador in South Vietnam, relieving the pro-Diem Frederick Nolting. The president, Lodge said, "referred to the picture, and to what was in Saigon—the fact that apparently the Diem government was entering a terminal phase." Lodge later told Malcolm Browne that Kennedy had said, "We're going to have to do something about that regime."

If there was any doubt that Kennedy was committed to supporting South Vietnam in its stand against communist aggression, he dispelled it in an interview with CBS's Walter Cronkite in Hyannis Port on September 2. "I don't agree with those who say we should withdraw," he said. "That would be a deep mistake." But he made it clear that it was the South Vietnamese who would have "to win or lose" the war and that winning would require the people's support of the government, which had slipped over the past two months.

A week later he reinforced the importance of staying the course in Vietnam in an interview with Chet Huntley and David Brinkley, the anchors of NBC's *Huntley-Brinkley Report*. When asked by Brinkley if he had any reason to doubt "the so-called domino theory," suggesting that if South Vietnam fell to communism other nations would quickly follow in succession, Kennedy replied firmly, "No, I believe it. . . . If South Vietnam went, it would not only give [China] an improved geographic position for a guerilla assault on [Malaysia], but would also give the impression that the wave of the future in Southeast Asia was China and the communists." His concern, he said, was that Americans would "get impatient and say because they don't like . . . the government in Saigon that we should withdraw," but warned, "that only makes it easy for the communists."

Kennedy's continued support stood in opposition to liberals in Congress who advocated using the deterioration of the Diem government as an excuse for the United States to pull the plug in South Vietnam, and to Western European leaders, including Charles de Gaulle, who advocated allied nations coming together to reunify Vietnam under a coalition government that was neither communist nor under the thumb of Western nations. Asked if the administration had been late in recognizing "the nature" of the Diem government, Kennedy told Brinkley, "We don't want to carry on a direct assault upon the government; we have to deal with the government that is there."

But while the Diem government was there for the moment, it was precarious at best. Kennedy's threat to cut off aid unless there were "important changes and improvements" in the relationship between their governments, including the ouster of Nhu, who was blamed for much of the turmoil, was patently rejected by the defiant Diem, as relations between his government and the United States began to fray. Concerns about Diem's administration grew further as rumors from Saigon reached Washington suggesting that Nhu, who was characterized by a high-ranking state department official as "basically anti-American," had sought negotiations with the North Vietnamese. In an August 26 meeting with the national security team, Dean Rusk warned that if Diem didn't change his internal policies, "we're on the road to disaster."

The spectacular unraveling of the Diem regime came in the months ahead. Before taking on the ambassadorship in September, Lodge was told by a prominent Vietnamese that unless Diem, Nhu, and Madame Nhu left Vietnam, "there was no power on earth" that could prevent their assassination. Lodge quickly came to believe that as long as Diem was in place the relationship between the United States and the South Vietnamese government was irreparable, the war was unwinnable, and a coup d'état against the South Vietnamese president was inevitable.

As it happened, plans to take Diem out were being hatched by disaffected ARVN generals as Lodge took his post. In late August, members of the military secretly reached out to the United States to gain support for a plot to overthrow him. Though their plans came apart amid disorganization and uncertainty among the conspirators, another plot, led by General Duong Van Minh, known as "Big Minh," was brought to Lodge in October.

Washington was split on supporting the coup. In the end, Kennedy declined to back deposing Diem, but instructed Lodge "not to thwart" it, a position Lodge advocated. But as with the Bay of Pigs, the president wanted the United States to be in a position to deny direct involvement in the overthrow, which, if unsuccessful, could result in another foreign policy black eye for the administration. McGeorge Bundy signaled as much in a cable to Lodge on

October 25, writing, "We would like to have the option of judging and warning on any plan with poor prospects of success."

In his response on October 29, Lodge expressed his view that regardless of the coup's success or failure, the United States would be blamed, "however unjustifiably," while reminding Bundy that since the conspirators had promised only to give Lodge four hours' advance notice, there was little chance for the United States to "significantly influence [the] course of events."

The same day, Diem, aware of the plot, reached out to Lodge to ask what measures the United States would take to protect him. Lodge offered a feeble reply. "I do not feel well enough informed to tell you," he replied. "It's 4:30 a.m. in Washington and the U.S. government cannot possibly have a view." Making matters worse for Diem, Lodge retracted his offer to help him and his brother escape the country when the State Department sounded alarms that aiding Diem would give the impression that the coup was "American inspired and manipulated."

Back in Washington, Kennedy and his advisers continued to debate the merits of backing the coup. Expressing his reservations, Bobby Kennedy cautioned that they would be "putting the future of the country and really Southeast Asia in the hands of someone we don't know." If it succeeded, the United States "would get the blame for it," and if it failed, Diem would tell the U.S. "to get the hell out of the country." But the debate ended up becoming an academic exercise as the clock ran out on their decision and the coup was at hand.

The end for Diem and Nhu came on November 2. After fleeing the presidential palace through a secret passageway and hiding out in a private home in a Saigon suburb, they sought refuge in a Catholic church in Cholon, where they were apprehended. They were murdered in the back of an armored personnel carrier by bayonet and gunshot upon Minh's order. The U.S. Embassy was given only four minutes of warning by the junta, which then cut off telephone service to the American military advisory group.

The gruesome assassinations shook Kennedy, who learned of Diem's and Nhu's demise during a meeting with his National Security Council. Maxwell Taylor recalled the president leaping to his feet and rushing from the room "with a look of shock and dismay on his face," and Schlesinger, who saw the president shortly afterward, said he "had not seen him so depressed since the Bay of Pigs." Conscious of history's judgment, Kennedy made a three-and-a-half-minute recording for posterity two days later, on November 4, in which he explained his position on the coup as his children, six-year-old Caroline and three-year-old John Jr., blithely ran in and out of the Oval Office:

> I feel that we must bear a good deal of responsibility for it. . . . Politically the situation was deteriorating, militarily it had not had its effect. There was a feeling, however, that it would. . . . The question now is whether the generals can stay together and build a stable government or whether Saigon will begin [to] turn on this government as repressive and undemocratic in the not too distant future.

The entire matter of Vietnam, however, would soon fall to Kennedy's successor.

Would JFK have stayed the course in Vietnam? Part of the lore of Camelot suggests that he would have had the judgment and foresight to withdraw from Vietnam before it turned into the quagmire that it would become under Lyndon Johnson, who steadily escalated the war during the course of his presidency as he sought an honorable peace that eluded him.

The speculation arose years after Kennedy's death with a claim from Senate majority leader Mike Mansfield in 1969 that Kennedy had pledged in late 1963 to pull U.S. troops from Vietnam after his reelection. An early skeptic of the war, Mansfield had warned Kennedy that the United States would be drawn "inexorably" into a lost cause in Vietnam; he claimed that Kennedy had come around to his point of view and resolved to withdraw all American troops by 1965. The story gained greater traction in 1970 when it was promulgated by Kenny O'Donnell in an article for *Life* magazine. After meeting with Mansfield, Kennedy reportedly told O'Donnell of his plans, predicting, "I'll be damned as a communist appeaser," but adding, "I don't care . . . but I can't do it until I'm reelected. So we had better make damned sure I *am* reelected."

An October 4, 1963, memorandum from Maxwell Taylor, declassified in 1997, revealed the Pentagon's plans to draw down military personnel in South Vietnam by one thousand by the end of 1963, which ultimately happened, with all planning to be "directed toward preparing Republic of Vietnam forces for the withdrawal of all United States special assistance units and personnel by the end of calendar year 1965." Still, it is unclear whether Kennedy asked for the report or it was ordered by McNamara, as McNamara claimed later. If Kennedy ordered it, was it a means of compelling Diem to comply with U.S. demands to reform his government, or a façade to show the success of the effort in Vietnam as the 1964 election neared? Or was it a bona fide policy decision departing from his earlier position?

A big hole in the conjecture that Kennedy would have pulled

out of the war is the fact that Bobby Kennedy, his most trusted adviser, disputed the notion. Asked in 1964 if his brother had any such plans, Bobby replied flatly, "No," asserting that it was the Kennedy administration's aim to win the war. Likewise, none of the other top advisers on Kennedy's national security team recalled any conversation with Kennedy in which he signaled an imminent change in policy. Many—including McNamara, Rusk, and Bundy—would go on to serve Johnson as president, advocating the escalation of the war, which by and large continued to have the support of Congress and the American people until 1967.

To be sure, in what would be his sixty-fourth and final press conference on November 14, Kennedy stated that his objective in South Vietnam was "to bring Americans home, permit the South Vietnamese to maintain themselves as a free and independent country, and permit democratic forces within the country to operate." But clearly the former was linked to the latter. When asked about the possibility of foreign aid being cut in Congress, Kennedy said, "I can't believe that the Congress of the United States [would] be so unwise unless we are going to retreat from the world, give up in South Vietnam," pointing out that "if there are failures" in Vietnam, it was he who would "bear the blame." It was consistent with the position he had taken on Vietnam since the beginning of his administration after the cold war bravado of his inauguration pledge to "pay any price . . . to assure the survival and success of liberty."

In his interview with Huntley and Brinkley on September 9, Kennedy had asserted that the communist takeover in China was "the most damaging event, certainly, that has occurred to us perhaps in this century." He was keenly aware of the damage the "Who lost China?" accusations by Republicans in the early fifties had done to Harry Truman and to the Democratic Party as a whole. And as abhorrent as the idea of a prolonged war may have been for Kennedy, it is difficult to imagine him bucking his own policy when the consequences of losing ground to communism in Southeast Asia were so high. Two and a half years earlier, after declining to engage the United States militarily in Laos, he had said, "If we have to fight, let's fight in Vietnam." As Bundy put it, "How does a president explain a 'defeat' [to communism in Vietnam] without a commitment of U.S. ground troops?"

Then again, as commander in chief, Kennedy had consistently averted military conflict as manifest in his handling of Laos, Berlin, and Cuba. If he *had* planned to withdraw U.S. troops early in his second term, he would surely have held his cards close to the vest due to the inevitable political fallout from conservatives and his instinctive distrust of the military brass.

But in the end, speculation about what Kennedy would have done in Vietnam is a fool's errand. Kennedy's decision process was fluid; he kept his options open, never bound to ideology or doctrine but inclined toward circumspection, pragmatism, and peaceful resolution. Who knows what he would have done as the situation in Vietnam evolved? What we know indisputably is that the war in Vietnam—a continuation of a policy of support that had been in place since the Truman administration—would eventually become a losing proposition that would tragically lead to the deaths of 58,000 American troops, between 200,000 and 250,000 South Vietnamese, 1.1 million North Vietnamese and Vietcong soldiers, and as many as 2 million Vietnamese civilians.

DALLAS

Occasionally, John Kennedy would consider what he would do after his presidency. "Oh, probably sell real estate," he once joked when asked about it. "That's the only thing I'm equipped to do." Perhaps half-kiddingly, he suggested to Ben Bradlee that the two of them should buy the *Washington Post*. In more serious moments he mentioned becoming the president of Harvard or running for the Senate. Jackie suspected that she and her husband would have lived between Cambridge and New York, and that he would have occupied his time in the immediate years after leaving office by writing a book, planning his presidential library, and traveling the world, playing the role of "President of the West," an international celebrity and sage voice on the issues of the day.

After two terms, JFK would have been a relatively youthful fifty-one years old, making him the youngest former president since Theodore Roosevelt stepped down in 1909 at age fifty—only to find himself restively pining away for the office he had willingly given up. Hungering to get back into the arena, TR made an unsuccessful bid for the presidency in 1912. Perhaps anticipating the same kind of middle-aged restlessness and longing for lost power from her husband, Jackie told him she wished "they made a rule that would keep you here forever."

"Oh, no," Kennedy said, "eight years is enough of this place."

But it was clear to anyone around him that he loved every second of the job, and he intended to keep it until his two terms were up—and *that* would require earning reelection the following year. To that end, in the late afternoon of November 13, just under a year before Americans would go to the polls, Kennedy convened Bobby, brother-in-law Steve Smith, Kenny O'Donnell, Ted Sorensen, Larry O'Brien, DNC chairman John Bailey, party treasurer Richard Maguire, and director of the Census Bureau and political strategist Richard Scammon to begin formally taking aim at the challenges that lay ahead in the 1964 election. For over three hours the group met in the Cabinet Room. As they discussed Kennedy's prospects, a general feeling of optimism pervaded.

There was reason to be bullish. The economy was humming along, with the gross national product up $100 billion over 1960, Eisenhower's last year in office. The Soviets, humbled by the Cuban missile crisis a year earlier, remained in check as the superpowers enjoyed a period of détente, while in Houston NASA was developing a Saturn I rocket that, if successfully launched, would be the most powerful to date, paving the way for the United States to leapfrog past the USSR in the space race. Plus, Kennedy's approval rating stood at a hardy 59 percent, with national polls reflecting that he was the most admired man in the world, ahead of beloved figures like Eisenhower, Churchill, and renowned evangelist Billy Graham.

At age forty-six, flecks of gray in his thick sheaf of chestnut hair, Kennedy stood astride the world stage nonpareil. "Let's face it, after these many months into his office, JFK is no ordinary chief magistrate," gushed William Styron in an *Esquire* profile published in September 1963, "but the glamorous and gorgeous avatar of American power at the magic moment of its absolute twentieth-century ascendancy. The entire world, including even the Russians, has gone a little gaga over this youthful demigod and his bewitching consort, and [this] writer has to confess that he is perhaps a touch gaga himself."

Just as encouraging were Gallup Polls that matched up Kennedy against prospective Republican rivals Barry Goldwater, Nelson Rockefeller, and George Romney that, in each case, gave Kennedy a double-digit edge. Of the three, Kennedy had feared Rockefeller the most. He believed that had the New York governor entered the primaries in 1960, he would have gotten the GOP nomination and beaten him in the general election. But by 1963, Rockefeller had divorced his wife and married a younger woman, also a divorcée, diminishing his popular appeal on moral grounds.

George Romney, the governor of Michigan, was also seen as a threat. The devout, clean-living Mormon hadn't yet announced his intentions to run for the presidency as he waited for a sign from God. Bobby believed conservatives and moderates alike might fall for "that God and country stuff."

Given his druthers, Kennedy would have chosen Goldwater as his Republican challenger. The preeminent conservative of the day, the senator from Arizona was seen by many, including moderates in his own party, to be an extremist who lacked the temperament to be president in the nuclear age. The impression was reinforced by statements that were considered outrageous by the standards of the early 1960s, including Goldwater's suggestion to drop "a low-yield atomic bomb on the Chinese supply lines in North Vietnam," as well as lobbing "one into the men's room of the Kremlin." They helped to explain a March 1963 poll that had Kennedy winning over Goldwater by a margin of 67 to 27 percent, with 74 percent expecting that Kennedy would be reelected. For Kennedy, a face-off with Goldwater would have been too good to be true.

Still, regardless of his opponent, Kennedy's reelection would by no means be a fait accompli. Kennedy himself was keenly aware of the capricious nature of politics and talked repeatedly about how "tough" the campaign would be. He had seen a steady rise in his disapproval rating, which now stood near 30 percent, with the increase correlating directly with his push on the controversial civil rights bill. In November, he acknowledged the decline in his popularity as a consequence of his stand. "Change always disturbs," he said, "and therefore, I was surprised that there wasn't greater opposition." But it irked him that the civil rights bill, along with a tax relief bill he had proposed to stave off a possible recession the following year, had stalled in Congress with no immediate prospects for resuscitation. "The fact of the matter is that both of these bills should be passed," he groused. The president's legislative impotence—Medicare and other bills had also been stymied—became another cause for worry as the Kennedy team looked toward 1964. But all things considered, Kennedy was riding high.

Absent from Kennedy's reelection strategy session, perhaps conspicuously, was Lyndon Johnson. By the fall of 1963, rumors swirled across Washington that Kennedy would drop LBJ from the ticket—speculation that was quickly struck down by the president himself. Sensitive to how Johnson might respond as the gossip inevitably made its way to him, Kennedy told Johnson's aide Bobby Baker, "I know he's unhappy in the vice presidency. It's . . . the worst fucking job I can imagine. . . . What I want you to do is tell Lyndon that I appreciate him as vice president. I know he's got a tough role and I'm sympathetic." Alluding to the hearsay and invoking the words of FDR, Kennedy instructed Baker to assure Johnson that he had "nothing to fear but fear itself." When

Charlie Bartlett brought up the rumor during a skinny-dip in the White House pool, Kennedy impatiently snapped, "Why would I do a thing like that? That would be absolutely crazy. It would tear up the relationship and hurt me in Texas. That would be the most foolish thing I could do."

Indeed, Texas was on Kennedy's mind in November as the White House planned a two-day, five-city presidential visit throughout the state the week before Thanksgiving. Conventional wisdom has it that Kennedy wanted the trip to mend political fences. As civil rights had come to the fore, heavily Democratic Texas had experienced a split in the party ranks, with Texas governor John Connally heading up the conservative wing, and the liberal faction led by Senator Ralph Yarborough. Though Yarborough's progressivism was closely aligned with Johnson's, they, too, had a fractious relationship due to the vice president's association with Connally, a close friend and former aide. The story goes that Kennedy had hoped to use the trip to bring the two sides together in the interest of party harmony. Both Johnson and Connally would later dispute that notion. "Hell," Johnson said, "if he wanted to bring us together, he could have done that in Washington."

In fact, the trip was mostly about money. As he geared up for 1964, Kennedy saw an opportunity to lean on Johnson and Connally to put the arm on wealthy Texas Democrats, many of whom opposed Kennedy, to support an Austin fundraiser that would add a million dollars to the campaign war chest—a huge sum at the time—and would jump-start the reelection effort. Getting Texans to step up would also be a loyalty test for Johnson, especially as rumors that he would be dropped from the ticket hung in the air.

Connally opposed the trip due to the president's declining popularity in the state, which had seen a drop in Kennedy's approval rating from 76 percent to 50 percent since the beginning of the year due largely to Kennedy's stand on civil rights. Instead, Connally recommended that the president come in the beginning of the next calendar year in order to let things settle a bit. But when the Kennedy camp pushed for the trip in the fall of 1963, Connally pressed them to make it not just the fundraiser in Austin but a two-day swing through the biggest cities in the state, which the Kennedy-Johnson ticket had won in 1960 by a scant two percentage points. Kennedy got his fundraiser, Connally got the president's commitment to a visit that would include stops in Houston and San Antonio on one day and Fort Worth, Dallas, and Austin the next.

On the morning of Friday, November 22, John Kennedy was awakened in Suite 850 of the Hotel Texas in Fort Worth with a gentle rap on the door from George Thomas, who had traveled to Texas with him and the first lady. Thomas informed him that it was raining outside, but as Kennedy made his way to the window, he would find that it hadn't discouraged locals from turning out to greet him.

The trip to Texas marked the first public outing for Jackie with her husband since losing Patrick three and a half months earlier. As ever, she proved to be a big draw, though she declined to participate in the first event of the day, a hastily arranged speech in the parking lot outside the hotel. Originally slated for 8:45 a.m., the event was rescheduled to midmorning, then pulled back to 8:45 again due to the president's concerns that those in the audience would be late to work. "There are no faint hearts in Fort Worth," he said to some three thousand who braved the drizzle, "and I appreciate your being here this morning. Mrs. Kennedy is organizing herself. It takes longer, but, of course, she looks better than we do when she does it."

When the first lady appeared for a breakfast with the heavily

Republican Fort Worth Chamber of Commerce later that morning—dressed in a light pink wool Chanel suit with navy blue trim, a matching pillbox hat, and white gloves—she did not disappoint. "Two years ago, I introduced myself in Paris by saying that I was the man who had accompanied Mrs. Kennedy to Paris," Kennedy said to the delight of the audience, his pride in his wife palpable. "I am getting somewhat the same sensation as I travel around Texas. Nobody wonders what Lyndon and I wear." Reporters surveying those who had come out to see President and Mrs. Kennedy throughout the state would find that at least half, women and men alike, had come to see her.

It was to be a busy day for the Kennedys, as well as for Lyndon and Lady Bird Johnson and Connally and his wife, Nellie, who acted as hosts, accompanying the first couple throughout their trip. After breakfast they would take a short hop to Dallas, where the Kennedys would travel by motorcade to the Trade Mart for a luncheon. Then it would be on to Austin for the fundraising dinner arranged by Connally before spending the night at the vice president's LBJ Ranch seventy miles away in the heart of Texas Hill Country.

There was some trepidation about the first stop. Dallas was not known for its civility—at least to those considered liberals by local fringe Republicans. A month before Kennedy's visit, Adlai Stevenson had given an address at the city's Memorial Auditorium and was accosted afterward by jeering anti-UN extremists. A woman hit him over the head with a placard that read "Down with the U.N.," and a young man spat on him as he walked to his car—then, for good measure, spat on the cop who moved in to arrest him. "Dallas has been disgraced," the *Dallas Morning News* wrote in a page-one editorial the following day. "There is no other way to view the storm-trooper actions of last night's frightening attack on Adlai Stevenson." Lyndon and Lady Bird Johnson were met with similar invective three years earlier. Just prior to the election in 1960, they were besieged outside the Adolphus Hotel by protesters carrying signs that read "Lyndon Go Home" and "Let's Ground Lady Bird." As they crossed the street, they, too, were spat upon.

On the day of his visit, the John Birch Society welcomed Kennedy with an ad in the *Dallas Morning News* accusing him and Bobby of being "soft on Communists, fellow-travelers and ultra-leftists." Kennedy ran across it as he examined the newspapers that morning. "We're heading into nut country today," he told his wife as they prepared for the day. "But, Jackie, if somebody wants to shoot me from a window with a rifle, nobody can stop it, so why worry about it?"

But the visit to Dallas looked promising before it even started; autumn rain clouds turned to boundless blue sky during the Kennedys' thirteen-minute flight to Love Field, where Air Force One touched down at 11:38 a.m. As the first couple disembarked, Lyndon and Lady Bird Johnson awaited them along with a few thousand well-wishers pressed along the fence line beyond the tarmac. The Kennedys spent a few minutes greeting some of them, one of whom presented Jackie a bouquet of a dozen red roses, before they slipped into the plush back seat of the presidential limousine—a 1961 Lincoln Continental, midnight blue gleaming in the North Texas sunshine—that would carry them and John and Nellie Connally to the Trade Mart. The fortuitous change in weather prompted Kennedy to order that the limousine's clear plastic bubble top be removed and its bulletproof windows rolled down.

A hundred and fifty thousand people lined up along the ten-mile motorcade route, swelling to as many as twenty or thirty deep, as the car neared downtown, "absorbed," as one Texas reporter wrote, "in the power and glory of the moment; in this their touch with the fabulous." The first couple glided before them, smiling and waving as they passed, enjoying it all. The crowd was a snapshot of America in its time, mostly white with pockets of Black and brown; housewives and young working women in office garb; men in business suits, others in open collars and hard hats; handfuls of students; small children on the shoulders of their fathers or holding the hands of their mothers with one hand as they held tiny American flags in the other. As the car approached, cheers rose and patches of confetti rained from buildings. "You can't say that Dallas isn't friendly to you today," Nellie Connally said to the president at 12:30 p.m. as the car rounded the curve of Main Street to move toward the highway overpass.

Then came the crackle of gunfire. Three shots in quick succession echoed from the dull red-brick Texas School Book Depository Building across Dealey Plaza. Kennedy was propelled forward by a bullet that hit above his right shoulder, passing through his lower neck, his balled-up fists rushing reflexively toward the wound. He sprung back upright before he was thrust forward again by another shot to the back of his head, which fell to Jackie Kennedy's lap as his body collapsed. "Jack!" the first lady cried out, "Oh, no! No!" Fear and disorder reigned in an instant. Horrified onlookers watched the car race off to Parkland Hospital, just over three miles away.

It arrived at 12:35. Kennedy was stripped of his jacket, shirt, and T-shirt and rushed into Trauma Room One. Malcolm Perry, the thirty-four-year-old doctor on duty, was summoned from lunch in the hospital's main dining room with an emergency page, arriving in short order. Kennedy wasn't breathing. Blood from the gunshot wounds on the back of his head and neck gushed to the floor. Perry ordered a nurse to get three of the other Parkland doctors right away. He gave Kennedy a tracheotomy, then a blood transfusion. Doctors and nurses burst in and out of the small, gray-tile room. The hospital's chief neurosurgeon in residency, William Kemp Clark, entered. Before aiding the other doctors, he approached the first lady, who stood silently to the side, her husband's blood caked on her pink skirt.

"Would you like to leave, ma'am?" he asked her gently. "We can make you more comfortable outside."

"No," she said. Motionless, she remained by his side to the last, her eyes never leaving his. She didn't cry as the doctors fought to save his life, forcefully pumping his chest to bring breath back into his limp body. She didn't cry as they stopped after ten minutes and pulled a white sheet over his head at 1:00 p.m. Central Standard Time, half an hour after the shots were fired, nor when a seventy-year-old priest was brought in to give the patient his last rites, rubbing holy oil in the shape of a cross on his forehead. She held her emotions at bay as she stood placidly before him for the last time and took his wedding ring from his finger, replacing it with hers and whispering into his ear words long left to eternity.

Reports soon went out on the news wires: John Fitzgerald Kennedy was dead.

Left unsaid were the words the thirty-fifth president had planned to use to conclude the speech he was to give in Austin that same evening:

> Let us stand together with renewed confidence in our cause—united in our heritage of the past and our hopes for the future—and determined that this land we love shall lead all mankind into new frontiers of peace and abundance.

"LET US CONTINUE"

Late on the evening of Tuesday, November 26, 1963, Lyndon Johnson sat at a table with aides at the Elms, his home in Northwest Washington, where the Johnson family would continue to live before moving into the White House on December 7. Four days after the assassination of John Kennedy, grief continued to shroud the nation.

On the afternoon of November 22, Johnson had stood somberly between his wife and his predecessor's widow in the cramped, stiflingly hot main cabin of Air Force One with his right hand raised, reciting the oath of office as the thirty-sixth president. On the late morning and early afternoon of Monday, November 25, he walked in the procession behind Jacqueline Kennedy, who marched nobly in a black veil flanked by her two brothers-in-law, the attorney general and the junior senator from Massachusetts, in mourning coats, as President Kennedy's horse-drawn caisson brought his casket down Pennsylvania Avenue to the White House before being transported by motorcade to Arlington Memorial Cemetery, where Kennedy would be laid to rest.

Now, Johnson grouped with members of his staff and outside

ACKNOWLEDGMENTS

In 2003, as I prepared to write my first book, my friend the late Hugh Sidey, *Time* magazine's legendary president-watcher, sent me a letter giving me fair warning about the path I was about to pursue. "The journey you map out is fascinating," he advised, "but tedious, lonely, and terribly complex."

As wise as Hugh was, my journey has turned out different. I've had the good fortune to find that writing books, while largely a solitary experience, is far less isolating than I expected due to my ability to talk and compare notes with friends and colleagues who share my passion for the presidency and American history in general. Among them are Ken Adelman, John Avlon, Peter Baker, Melody Barnes, Michael Beschloss, H. W. Brands, Douglas Brinkley, Ken Burns, Elizabeth Crook, Robert Dallek, Marty Dobrow, Jeffrey Engel, Frank Gannon, Stephen Harrigan, Margaret Hoover, David Hume Kennerly, Jon Meacham, Tim Naftali, Lynn Novick, Robert Schenkkan, Marc Selverstone, Richard Norton Smith, Julia Sweig, Larry Tye, Randall Woods, Lawrence Wright, and Doris Kearns Goodwin, who generously gave me access to the previously unseen papers of her husband, Richard Goodwin, relating to President Kennedy. At the University of Texas at Austin they include Don Carleton, Jamie Galbraith, Will Inboden, Bob Inman, Peniel Joseph, Bill McRaven, Victoria DeFrancesco Soto, Jeremi Suri, Paul Stekler, and the director of the LBJ Library and my teaching partner, Mark Lawrence. And at ABC News: Desiree Adib, Marc Burstein, Chris Donovan, Matthew Dowd, Terri Lichstein, Terry Moran, Martha Raddatz, George Stephanopoulos, and Justin Weaver.

There have been many others who have generously allowed me to probe them on John F. Kennedy and his times through official interviews or offhanded conversations, including Ben Barnes, Sid Davis, Angie Dickinson, Lloyd Hand, Luci Baines Johnson, Henry Kissinger, Bill Moyers, Dan Rather, Lynda Johnson Robb, Bob Schieffer, Larry Temple, Andrew Young, and the late Julian Bond, John Glenn, John Lewis, Julian Reed, Cokie Roberts, Ted Sorensen, Harris Wofford, and, of course, Hugh Sidey.

As John Kennedy knew, no one is better suited to offer perspective on the presidency than those who have held the office. They provide a unique vantage point. I count myself as enormously fortunate to have learned about the presidency through interviews over the years with Barack Obama, George W. Bush, Bill Clinton, George H. W. Bush, Jimmy Carter, and Gerald Ford. I have great respect for each of them—and am obliged to them for the time they have graciously given me.

Incomparable Grace is my second book with my agent, Jim Hornfischer. Sadly, Jim passed away well before his time, prior to its publication. He was a good man, and I am grateful for his support and friendship.

My talented editor, Brent Howard, was enormously helpful in shaping this project, as were Dutton's Grace Layer, Sarah Thegeby,

Acknowledgments

Katie Taylor, Steven Meditz, LeeAnn Pemberton, Tiffany Estreicher, Nancy Resnick, Susan Schwartz, and Ryan Richardson.

Our presidential libraries, operated under the auspices of the National Archives and under the leadership of David Ferriero, archivist of the United States, and Susan Donius, executive for presidential libraries, are national treasures. The John F. Kennedy Presidential Library and Museum was an invaluable resource, including input and assistance I received from Alan Price, Tom Putnam, and Karen Adler Abramson and her team of adept archivists, as well as from the John F. Kennedy Library Foundation's Rachel Flor and Steven Rothstein. So was the LBJ Presidential Library, where I am indebted to longtime colleagues Claudia Anderson, Alexis Castro, Jennifer Cuddeback, Sarah Cunningham, Jenna De Graffenried, Allen Fischer, Brian McNerney, Liza Talbot, and John Wilson.

At the LBJ Foundation, thank you to trustees Stacey Abrams, Robert Allbritton, Ben Barnes, John Beckworth, Julián Castro, Elizabeth Christian, Nicole Covert, Rodney Ellis, Wayne Gibbens, Lloyd Hand, Bill Hobby, Kay Bailey Hutchison, Luci Baines Johnson, Tom Johnson, Jim Jones, Ron Kirk, Vilma Martinez, Cappy McGarr, Lyndon Olson, Catherine Robb, Lynda Johnson Robb, Larry Temple, Casey Wasserman, and Tonya Williams, as well as to the foundation's staff: Sally Allen, Deborah Arronge, Adam Brodkin, Sherry Brown, Jay Godwin, Courtney Hughes, Russ Hull, Balmore Lazo, Sarah McCracken, Chris Stenftenagel, Samantha Stone, Rebecca Szeto, and Anne Wheeler.

The iconic Jacques Lowe photographs of JFK, RFK, and Jacqueline Kennedy within these pages were provided courtesy of the Dolph Briscoe Center for American History at the University of Texas at Austin, one of the nation's leading centers for historical study and the permanent home of the Jacques Lowe Photographic Archive, comprising thousands of prints, contact sheets, negatives, papers, and publications. Lowe was given exclusive access to the Kennedys during the years leading up to JFK's election and the first year of his presidency. Thank you to the Estate of Jacques Lowe and my friend Don Carleton, the Briscoe Center's executive director, for their permission to use the photos.

For reasons big and small, my thanks to Bahar Atvur, Allison Bacon, Craig Barron, Jean Becker, Talmage Boston, John Bredar, John Bryant, Bryan Cranston, Amy Erben, Randy Erben, Bill Gurney, Beth Gibbens, Mary Herman, Tim Herman, Steve Huestis, David Hume Kennerly, Steve Lakis, Beth Laski, Lauren Leader, Maddie LeBlanc, Thom Little, Maggie Lodge, Michael Matuza, Anita McBride, Stewart McLaurin, Kathi Perea, Jim Popkin, Robin Goldman Popkin, Walter Robb, Lee Rosenbaum, Bob Santelli, Nick Segal, Glenn Singleton, Hal Stein, Ashley Temple, Lawrence Temple, Louann Temple, Patsy Thomasson, Jeff van den Noort, Diane Walter, and Leslie Wingo—and to members of our blended family, Susie and Glenn Crafford and their children Elizabeth, Meredith, and James; Jim and Nancy Krombach; Richard and Kim Storm; Skip and Sandy Wood; and our beloved children Isabel, Charlie, Mateo, and Tallie.

Mostly, I am indebted to my wife, Amy, my greatest love, dearest friend, and most ardent supporter.

—MKU
Austin, Texas

NOTES

PROLOGUE

2   **"The Soviet hope is that Mr. Kennedy will buckle":** Ian Shapira, "'He Just Beat the Hell Out of Me': When JFK Met Khrushchev, the President Felt Strong-Armed," *Washington Post*, July 7, 2017.

2   **The curtains in the U.S. Embassy had been:** Reeves, *President Kennedy*, 172.

2   **the normally upbeat Kennedy:** Stacks, *Scotty*, 4.

2   **"How was it?":** Ibid.

2   **"Not the usual bullshit":** Ibid., 4–5.

2   **"President Kennedy, if not pleased, has had":** James B. Reston, "Vienna Talks End," *New York Times*, June 5, 1961.

3   **"the chess game of power":** Sidey, *Portraits of the Presidents*, 62.

3   **"The Boy Wonder Versus the Grandmaster":** Victor Weisz, *New Statesman*, 1961 (specific date unknown).

3   **"was one that attracted the people who wanted":** *Tricky Dick*, CNN Original Series, CNN, 2018.

4   **"His whole demeanor and personality":** John Lewis, Oral History, March 19, 2004, JFK #1, John F. Kennedy Presidential Library, Boston, Massachusetts, JFKLibrary.org.

4   **Yet Americans proved willing to forgive:** David Coleman, "JFK's Approval Ratings, 1961–1963," History in Pieces, historyinpieces.com.

5   **"very young and not strong enough":** Dallek, *John F. Kennedy: An Unfinished Life*, 37.

5   **He envisioned striding the world stage:** Sidey, *Portraits of the Presidents*, 62.

5   **"[Khrushchev] thought that anyone who was so young":** Kempe, *Berlin 1961*, 256–57.

TRANSITION

10 **"Little Boy Blue":** Reeves, *President Kennedy*, 22.

10 **"that old asshole":** Ibid.

10 **"a cold bastard":** Dan Merica and Kevin Liptak, "200 Days In: Obama Still on Trump's Mind," CNN.com, August 11, 2017.

10 **"How did I manage":** Dallek, *Unfinished Life*, 299.

11 **"The margin is thin":** Theodore H. White, "In Search of History," *Time*, July 3, 1978.

11 **"greatest disappointments":** Hugh Sidey, "The Presidency," *Time*, October 21, 1961.

11 **"All I've done for the last eight years":** John Eisenhower, *Strictly Personal*, 285.

11 **With an outgoing approval rating of 60 percent:** "Presidential Approval Ratings," Gallup Historical Statistics and Trends, Gallup.com.

13 **"race, creed, color, or national origin":** "The African American Odyssey: A Quest for Full Citizenship," *The Depression, the New Deal, and World War II*, Library of Congress, loc.gov.

14 **There was also the matter:** Kimberly Amadeo, "History of Recessions in the United States," The Balance, GDP Growth and Recessions, thebalance.com, updated August 14, 2019.

14 **"No man in universal history":** Sidey, *John F. Kennedy, President*, 32.

14 **"the harmony of the transition . . . strengthening our hand":** Office of the Historian, "The Laos Crisis, 1960–1963," U.S. State Department, State.gov.

15 **"Watch this":** Duffy and Gibbs, *Presidents Club*, 122.

15 **"I've just shown my friend here":** Sidey, *John F. Kennedy, President*, 32.

15 **"If Laos should fall":** Reeves, *President Kennedy*, 31.

15 **"the cork in the bottle":** Ibid.

15 **"I would have but I did not feel":** Ibid.

16 **Kennedy got the impression:** Ibid., 32.

16 **"inner satisfaction":** O'Brien, *John F. Kennedy*, 513.

16 **"Should we support guerrilla operations":** Schlesinger, *Thousand Days*, 164.

16 **"To the utmost . . . the effort be continued and accelerated":** Ibid.

16 **"You have an invulnerable asset":** Duffy and Gibbs, *Presidents Club*, 123.

17 **So it now was for Eisenhower:** John Eisenhower, *Strictly Personal*, 285.

17 **"surprising force":** Alan Brinkley, *John F. Kennedy*, 58.

17 **"How can he stare disaster in the face":** Sidey, *John F. Kennedy, President*, 22.

"LET US BEGIN"

18 **"absolutely hopeless":** O'Brien, *John F. Kennedy*, 514.

18 **"general and truly monumental":** Kevin Ambrose and Jason Samenow, "How a Surprise Snowstorm Almost Spoiled Kennedy's Inauguration 60 Years Ago," *Washington Post*, January 19, 2021.

18 **On the National Mall, stretching between:** Sidey, *John F. Kennedy, President*, 31.

18 **Thousands of city workers, employing some seven:** O'Brien, *John F. Kennedy*, 515.

18 **At the White House, stranded Eisenhower staffers:** Ibid.

18 **It wasn't much different across town:** Ibid.

19 **Merman, powerless to get back to her hotel:** "The Lost Inaugural Gala for JFK: Never-Before-Seen Performances," Music Dish, PBS, Thirteen .org, February 18, 2020.

19 **"Have you ever seen":** Reeves, *President Kennedy*, 35.

19 **"charisma" and "drop dead" good looks:** Author interview with Angie Dickinson, March 22, 2021.

20 **It was 3:48 a.m.:** Parmet, *JFK*, 82.

20 **The bacon was a concession by the pope:** Reeves, *President Kennedy*, 34.

20 **"I want to say that the American Revolution":** Sidey, "Introduction and Commentary," in Lowe, *Remembering Jack*, 284.

20 **"never used two or three words":** Waldman, *My Fellow Americans*, 161.

21 **"We prize our individualism":** Richard J. Tofel, "JFK's Inaugural Speech, 50 Years Later," *Daily Beast*, January 9, 2011.

21 **"It's more effective that way":** National Archives and Records Administration, *Kennedy's Inaugural Address of 1961*, 2.

22 **Showcasing the "Jackie look":** Haley M. Rivero, "The Jackie Look," *White House History Quarterly* 52:35–36.

22 **On the short drive:** Sidey, *John F. Kennedy, President*, 33.

23 **"master of words":** O'Brien, *John F. Kennedy*, 514.

23 **"I'll just have to get through":** Rubin, *Songs of Ourselves*, 166.

23 **"Let the word go forth":** JFK Library, "Inaugural Address, January 20, 1961," JFKLibrary.org.

24 **Invoking the martyred Lincoln:** Safire, *Lend Me Your Ears*, 891.

25 **The line is thought to be borrowed:** Clarke, *Ask Not*, 78–79.

25 **"This is the call of the New Frontier":** Papers of Richard Goodwin, provided by Doris Kearns Goodwin, Concord, Massachusetts.

25 **"Jack, you were wonderful":** O'Brien, *John F. Kennedy*, 518.

25 **Nearly three-quarters:** Dallek, *Unfinished Life*, 327.

25 **"set the standard by which presidential":** Safire, *Lend Me Your Ears*, 891.

25 **"from all shades":** "The Nation: We Shall Pay Any Price," *Time*, January 27, 1961.

25 **"fine, very fine":** Dallek, *Unfinished Life*, 326.

26 **"It was just what the people":** Ibid.

26 **"better than anything Franklin Roosevelt":** Sidey, *John F. Kennedy, President*, 34.

26 **"inspiring . . . very compact message,"** Dallek, *Unfinished Life*, 326.

26 **A Gallup Poll taken the following month:** Greenstein, *Leadership in the Modern Presidency*, 120.

26 **"free—as only private citizens":** Ambrose, *Eisenhower*, 540.

26 **"The part that starts":** Boller, *Presidential Anecdotes*, 331.

26 **"struck by the thought":** Todd Purdum, "From That Day Forth," *Vanity Fair*, January 17, 2011.

26 **The new administration moved on:** "Dazzling Military Might Goes on Parade for New President," *Terre Haute Tribune*, January 21, 1961.

27 **"Here goes":** Sidey, "Introduction and Commentary," in Lowe, *Remembering Jack*, 284.

THE SECOND SON

28 **The most conspicuous was the brood's:** O'Brien, *John F. Kennedy*, 342.

29 **"greatest joke in the world":** Beschloss, *Kennedy and Roosevelt*, 157.

29 **"You are about the most bowlegged":** Collier and Horowitz, *Kennedys*, 81.

30 **"If I can get the permission":** Ibid.

30 **"no way":** Ibid.

33 **Joe's carefully honed public image:** Cari Beauchamp, "Two Sons, One Destiny," *Vanity Fair*, January 4, 2012.

33 **"You're a great mother":** Ibid.

33 **In adherence to the parenting precepts:** Moore, *American President*, 438.

33 **"institutionalized living, children in a cellblock":** Collier and Horowitz, *Kennedys*, 61.

33 **Deeply devoted to her faith:** Ibid., 58.

34 **"We want winners":** Ibid.

34 **"For the Kennedys it's either the castle":** Newfield, *Robert Kennedy*, 42.

34 **"give a tinker's damn":** Sidey, *John F. Kennedy, President*, 38.

34 **"Listening to the Kennedy brothers talk":** Smith, *Grace and Power*.

34 **"I can hardly remember a mealtime":** Schlesinger, *Robert Kennedy and His Times*, 79.

35 **"it takes one to know one":** Hill and Hill, *Encyclopedia of Federal Agencies and Commissions*, 417.

36 **In a bike race around their Brookline block:** "Life of John F. Kennedy: Growing Up in the Kennedy Family," JFKLibrary.org.

36 **"Joe just kind of overshadowed":** Collier and Horowitz, *Kennedys*, 62.

36 **"scholarship and sportsmanship":** Beauchamp, "Two Sons, One Destiny."

36 **"If a mosquito bit Jack Kennedy":** Collier and Horowitz, *Kennedys*, 61.

36 **His prospects were grim enough:** Beauchamp, "Two Sons, One Destiny."

36 **A spate of illnesses followed:** Ibid.

37 **"had few days when he wasn't in pain":** Ibid.

37 **"His natural gift of an individual":** Moore, *American President*, 438.

37 **"Don't let me lose confidence":** Ibid.

37 **"be sure it wouldn't have started":** Beauchamp, "Two Sons, One Destiny."

39 **"involuntary," adding, "They sank my boat":** Duncan, *John F. Kennedy*, 34.

39 **"it would be good for Joe"**: Beauchamp, "Two Sons, One Destiny."

39 **"All my plans were tied up"**: Dallek, *Camelot's Court*, 2.

40 **"The burden now falls"**: Beauchamp, "Two Sons, One Destiny."

40 **"There is always an inequity"**: "News Conference 28, 3 March 1962," JFKLibrary.org.

41 **"The point is"**: Levingston, *Kennedy and King*, chap. 3 (digital version).

RISING STAR

42 **"being drafted"**: Dallek, *Unfinished Life*, 6.

42 **"My father wanted his oldest son"**: Ibid.

42 **"dealing with some dead man's estate"**: Interview with Ben Bradlee and James M. Cannon for *Newsweek*, January 5, 1960, JFKLibrary.org.

42 **"satisfactions" in politics would be "far greater"**: Ibid.

43 **he recalled his father remarking that he was "hopeless"**: Ibid.

43 **"worked harder"**: Ibid.

43 **"deserved to win"**: Ted Widmer, "Kennedy After Dark: A Dinner Party About Politics and Power," *Smithsonian Magazine*, October 2012.

44 **"We did our best"**: O'Brien, *John F. Kennedy*, 320.

44 **"There was no question in my mind"**: Lem Billings, Oral History, July 7, 1964, JFK #5, JFKLibrary.org.

44 *Profiles in Courage,* **written with hefty contributions**: Craig Fuhrman, "I Would Rather Win a Pulitzer Than Be President," *Politico Magazine*, February 11, 2020.

45 **"I would rather win a Pulitzer than be president"**: Ibid.

45 **"the strong Democratic winds"**: O'Brien, *John F. Kennedy*, 424.

45 **"He might find it interesting to play"**: Bradlee and Cannon interview for *Newsweek*, JFKLibrary.org.

46 **"We're going to get this thing"**: O'Brien, *John F. Kennedy*, 427.

46 **"Wait a minute now. There are others"**: Ibid.

46 **"Dear Jack, don't buy a single vote"**: Jeff Nussbaum, "Voters Like Pols Who Can Laugh at Themselves," *Washington Post*, March 4, 2016.

46 **Humphrey, who had helped to fund his own campaign**: Marc J. Silverstone, "John F. Kennedy: Campaigns and Elections," UVA Miller Center, millercenter.org.

46 **"an independent retailer competing with a chain"**: Beschloss, *American Heritage Illustrated History of the Presidents*, 420.

47 **"insufficient"**: "Statement of John F. Kennedy, Los Angeles, California, July 4, 1960: Response to Former President Harry S. Truman's Remarks on Kennedy's Candidacy," JFKLibrary.org.

47 **"should have been ruled out"**: Ibid.

47 **"The New Frontier . . . is not a set of promises"**: "50 Years Ago John F. Kennedy of Massachusetts Wins Presidential Nomination at Democratic National Convention," JFKLibrary.org.

48 **In the first debate, which aired on September 26**: Silverstone, "John F. Kennedy: Campaigns and Elections."

48 **After the debate, he saw a 3 percent**: Ibid.

48 **The popular notion that Kennedy won:** Ibid.
48 **"I am not the Catholic candidate for president":** JFK Library, "Address to the Greater Houston Ministerial Association," JFKLibrary.org.
48 **Fifty-four percent of Protestant voters:** Dallek, *Unfinished Life*, 296.
49 **in Chicago's Cook County, 121 votes:** Mark K. Updegrove, "What Nixon Could Teach Trump About Losing," *New York Times*, October 21, 2016.
49 **"We won but they stole it from us":** David Greenberg, "Was Nixon Robbed?" Slate.com, October 16, 2000.
49 **"shirk from its duty":** Updegrove, "What Nixon Could Teach Trump About Losing."
49 **"I never had Addison's disease":** Reeves, *President Kennedy*, 24.
50 **"Jesus Christ, this one wants this":** Dallek, *Unfinished Life*, 100.
50 **"they're still counting votes":** Ibid.
50 **"Sure, it's a big job":** Sidey, *John F. Kennedy, President*, 10.
50 **"feel any different":** Ibid., 17.
51 **"You worry about [campaign] financing":** Collier and Horowitz, *Kennedys*, 246.
51 **"He's having the time of his life":** Ibid., 247.
51 **"Jack doesn't belong anymore":** Sidey, *John F. Kennedy, President*, 17–19.

"THE CENTER OF THE ACTION"
52 **"I suppose anybody in politics":** Kennedy, *Letters of John F. Kennedy*, 123.
52 **"blue as indigo":** McCullough, *Truman*, 974.
52 **But, eventually, as he got:** Ibid.
53 **"Isn't it nice that [Kennedy] would want":** O'Brien, *John F. Kennedy*, 521.
53 **"little attention to organization charts":** Alan Brinkley, *John F. Kennedy*, 59.
53 **"strong president":** Schlesinger, *Thousand Days*, 121.
53 **"a fluid presidency":** Ibid.
53 **"their productivity was in inverse proportion":** Greenstein, *Leadership in the Modern Presidency*, 115.
54 **he read at a manic pace of 1,200 words:** Myrna Oliver, "Evelyn Wood; Pioneer in Speed Reading," *Los Angeles Times*, August 31, 1995.
54 **"25 questions about it, intelligent questions":** Sidey, "The President's Voracious Reading Habits," *Life*, March 17, 1961.
54 **"The tempo of this administration":** Sidey, *John F. Kennedy, President*, 39.
54 **"not appoint any relative":** Dallek, *Unfinished Life*, 317.
54 **"just as tough as a boot heel":** Schlesinger, *Robert Kennedy and His Times*, 107.
54 **"I have now watched you":** Dallek, *Unfinished Life*, 316.

55   "I want Bobby there [as attorney general]": Reeves, *President Kennedy*, 29.

55   Initially, Bobby wasn't sold: Ibid.

55   "kick our balls off": Thomas, *Robert Kennedy*, 110.

55   "I made up my mind": Dallek, *Unfinished Life*, 318.

55   "I need someone I can completely": Collier and Horowitz, *Kennedys*, 256.

55   "damn hair": Dallek, *Unfinished Life*, 318.

56   "So that's it, General, grab your balls": Ibid.

56   "a travesty of justice": O'Brien, *John F. Kennedy*, 507.

56   "I don't know why people": Thomas, *Robert Kennedy*, 110.

56   "Shriver knew the kind of man": Stossel, *Sarge*, 176.

57   "absurd": Tim Weiner, "Robert McNamara, Architect of a Futile War, Dies at 93," *New York Times*, July 6, 2006.

57   "unqualified": Ibid.

57   "Look, Bob," he said, "I don't think there's any school": Ibid.

57   "waste of time": Alan Brinkley, *John F. Kennedy*, 60.

57   McNamara, whom Kennedy considered the smartest: Weiner, "Robert McNamara."

57   "wove together represented almost": Parmet, *JFK*, 88.

57   "an odd mixture of idealism and cynicism": Ibid.

57   "intellectual alter ego": Tim Weiner, "Theodore C. Sorensen, 82, Kennedy Counselor, Dies," *New York Times*, October 31, 2010.

58   "Arthur will probably write": Douglas Martin, "Arthur Schlesinger, Historian of Power, Dies at 89," *New York Times*, March 1, 2007.

58   Schlesinger would serve as a liaison: Ibid.

58   "persecution thing": Jacqueline Kennedy, *Historic Conversations*, 76.

58   Kennedy was always more "at ease": O'Brien, *John F. Kennedy*, 511.

58   "a handy old piece of furniture": Pitts, *Jack and Lem*, 1.

59   "The Presidency itself would show": Schlesinger, *Thousand Days*, 117.

59   "At this point we are like the Harlem": Collier and Horowitz, *Kennedys*, 266–67.

60   "the new, and untried President": Parmet, *JFK*, 98.

60   By mid-February, his approval rating: Ibid.

60   get things done: Louis Harris, "The Harris Survey: JFK Rated Most Attractive of Recent Presidents," April 15, 1985, theharrispoll.com.

61   "What have you done for the women": "Thank You, Mr. President: The Press Conferences of JFK," YouTube.com, posted March 10, 2013.

61   "When we don't have to go through": O'Brien, *John F. Kennedy*, 817.

61   All told, Kennedy would hold: Andrew Glass, "JFK Holds First Televised Conference, Jan. 25, 1961," *Politico*, January 25, 2018.

62   "You won't be able to go to the men's room": Sidey, *John F. Kennedy, President*, 37.

63   "I remember [Kennedy] in a mood": Todd Purdum, "From That Day Forth," *Vanity Fair*, February 2011.

63   As he had with other early guests: Sidey, *John F. Kennedy, President,* 37.
63   "strange dreams": Purdum, "From That Day Forth."
63   "No," Kennedy replied. "I just jumped in": Ibid.

"HOW COULD WE HAVE BEEN SO STUPID?"

67   On one of his first days: Reeves, *President Kennedy,* 44.
67   "I'm awake," Kennedy replied: Ibid., 85.
68   "The Soviet Union announced today": Ibid.
68   Earlier in the day, at 6:07: Chris Gebhardt, "Anniversaries: 50 Years of Human Spaceflight," NASASpaceFlight.com, April 12, 2001.
68   "keep him busy": Sidey, *John F. Kennedy, President,* 30.
68   "What American wants to go to bed": "Space: Under Whose Moon?," *Time,* May 31, 1963.
69   "Do we have a chance": Lyndon B. Johnson, Office of the Vice President, "Memorandum for the President," LBJ Presidential Library, Austin, Texas, August 28, 1961.
69   "impressive scientific accomplishment": "News Conference 9, April 12, 1961," JFKLibrary.org.
69   "Has a decision been reached": Ibid.
69   "First, I want to say that there will": Ibid.
69   The CIA estimated that roughly: O'Brien, *John F. Kennedy,* 524.
69   Cuba's population of just over seven million: "Population Cuba 1961," countryecomony.com.
70   "To the utmost": Schlesinger, *Thousand Days,* 164.
70   "without exception, they have the utmost": Alan Brinkley, *John F. Kennedy,* 66.
70   "this damned invasion": Schlesinger, *Thousand Days,* 246–47.
70   "I try to think of it as little": Ibid.
70   "Kennedy Asks Aid for Cuban": Peter Kihss, "Kennedy Asks Aid for Cuban Rebels to Defeat Castro," *New York Times,* October 21, 1960.
71   "revolution redeemed": Sidey, *John F. Kennedy, President,* 107.
71   A year earlier, he and Jackie had hosted: Thomas Maier, "JFK Loved James Bond: How Ian Fleming Influenced the CIA," *Salon,* April 8, 2019.
71   A key meeting came on the evening: Reeves, *President Kennedy,* 80.
72   Moreover, Lemnitzer just plain didn't trust: Bradlee, *Good Life,* 219.
72   "steadily losing popularity": Reeves, *President Kennedy,* 80.
72   "If one has faith in the human": Ibid., 81.
72   "Gentlemen, we better sleep on it": Ibid., 82.
73   "play down the magnitude": O'Brien, *John F. Kennedy,* 363.
73   The primitive B-26 bombers the CIA dispatched: "The Bay of Pigs," JFKLibrary.org.
73   few insurgents materialized to aid: Ibid.
74   "pulling out the rug": Talbot, "Warrior for Peace."
74   "constantly blamed himself": Taubman, *Khrushchev,* 493.
74   "the worst experience": Bradlee, *Good Life,* 219.

74 "He started to cry, just with me": Jacqueline Kennedy, *Historic Conversations*, 185–86.

75 "rare in the history of the Republic": Alan Brinkley, *John F. Kennedy*, 73.

75 "it is clear that the expedition": Leaming, *Mrs. Kennedy*, 97.

75 "He realized he didn't have": Author interview with Ted Sorensen, New York, January 31, 2008.

75 "Before the invasion the revolution": Perrottet, *Cuba Libre!*, 335.

75 "There is an old saying": "News Conference 10, April 21, 1961," JFKLibrary.org.

75 His approval rating soared to 83 percent: "50th Anniversary of the Bay of Pigs Invasion," JFKLibrary.org.

76 "It's just like Eisenhower": Alan Brinkley, *John F. Kennedy*, 70.

76 "No one knows how rough": Ambrose, *Eisenhower: Soldier and President*, 638–39.

76 "Mr. President, that is exactly": Ibid.

76 "I'm all in favor": Sidey, *John F. Kennedy, President*, 120.

77 "It was the only endorsement": Ibid.

77 "I want to know how": Hugh Sidey, "The Lessons John F. Kennedy Learned from the Bay of Pigs," *Time*, April 16, 2001.

77 "We're not going to plunge": Talbot, "Warrior for Peace."

"YOU WILL NEVER MAKE IT THROUGH ALABAMA"

78 "the belly of the segregated beast": Lewis, *Walking with the Wind*, 128.

79 "to create a crisis so that": Marian Smith Holmes, "The Freedom Riders, Then and Now," *Smithsonian Magazine*, February 2009.

79 "You will never make it": Lewis, *Walking with the Wind*, 140.

79 "Well, boys, here they are": Arsenault, *Freedom Riders*, 143.

80 President Kennedy learned of the attacks: Reeves, *President Kennedy*, 122.

80 "Can't you get your goddamned friends": George F. Will, "A Man in a Hurry—1963," *Washington Post*, November 20, 2003.

80 "I did not lie awake at night": Gitlin, *Sixties*, 136.

81 "the roughest" experience of King's life: Author interview with Andrew Young, November 25, 2020.

81 "called a negro woman when her husband": Ibid.

81 "a suitcase full of votes": Patterson, *Grand Expectations*, 440.

81 "a stroke of a pen": Lewis, *Walking with the Wind*, 124.

81 He would go on to pick up: Patterson, *Grand Expectations*, 440.

82 "He didn't mention race or civil rights": Lewis, *Walking with the Wind*, 124.

82 "Where's the PEN, Mr. President?": Ibid.

82 "Ink for Jack" drive: O'Brien, *John F. Kennedy*, 600.

82 "Knock, knock," Kennedy said: Ibid., 601.

82 64 percent were opposed: Dallek, *Unfinished Life*, 384.

83 **"Domestic policy can only defeat us"**: Stern, *Averting "The Final Failure,"* 35.

83 **"It really is true that foreign affairs"**: Ian Shircore, "The Wounded Kennedy—and the People Who Gave Him Strength," *Spectator*, November 23, 2013.

83 **"He got constantly more committed"**: Burke Marshall, Oral History, January 19–20, 1970, JFKLibrary.org.

84 **Soon after his arrival, Seigenthaler**: Matt Schudel, "John Seigenthaler, Crusading Newspaper Editor and Kennedy Insider, Dies at 86," *Washington Post*, July 11, 2014.

84 **King grudgingly admired the Kennedys**: Thomas, *Robert Kennedy*, 127.

84 **Like the Kennedys, too, King**: Ibid., 128.

85 **"He really knew almost nothing on race"**: Author interview with Andrew Young, November 25, 2020.

85 **It was telling that while**: Lewis, *Walking with the Wind*, 124.

85 **"I think our country has done"**: Oates, *Let the Trumpet Sound*, 173.

85 **"honkers"**: Thomas, *Robert Kennedy*, 131.

85 **"It took guts for the first"**: Ibid.

86 **First Baptist was surrounded**: Schudel, "John Seigenthaler."

86 **They set a parishioner's car**: Oates, *Let the Trumpet Sound*, 175.

86 **King worried that the mob**: Ibid., 174.

86 **"If they don't get here immediately"**: Thomas, *Robert Kennedy*, 130.

86 **Ostensibly disengaged, he tracked**: Reeves, *President Kennedy*, 130.

87 **"Have him call me"**: Sidey, *John F. Kennedy, President*, 141.

87 **That was enough for Bobby**: Reeves, *President Kennedy*, 131.

87 **"You betrayed us"**: Ibid.

88 **"Wait means 'Never'"**: Dallek, *Unfinished Life*, 385.

88 **"a source of deepest concern"**: Alan Brinkley, *John F. Kennedy*, 101.

88 **"Doesn't he know I've done more"**: Dallek, *Unfinished Life*, 387.

88 **"The Kennedys wanted"**: PBS, "Eyes on the Prize: America's Civil Rights Movement, 1954–1985," *American Experience*, January 1987.

89 **As his brother prepared**: Thomas, *Robert Kennedy*, 131.

89 **"continuing international publicity"**: Ibid.

SHOWDOWN IN VIENNA

90 **"mud on his shoes"**: Thomas, *Robert Kennedy*, 131.

90 **"I don't understand Kennedy"**: Dallek, *Camelot's Court*, 22.

90 **"would never amount to a good president"**: William Taubman, *Khrushchev*, 485.

90 **"little boys in short pants"**: Ibid.

91 **Shortly after the failed foray**: McGeorge Bundy to JFK, memoranda, May 16–31, 1961, National Security Files, JFKLibrary.org.

91 **"We would have troops in Laos"**: Moore, *American President*, 450.

91 **"If we have to fight in Southeast Asia"**: Moyar, *Triumph Forsaken*, 129.

91 **"There are just so many concessions"**: Lawrence, *Vietnam War*, 71.

91   **By the end of April:** Moyar, *Triumph Forsaken*, 129.

92   **On his way back:** Smith, *Grace and Power*, 164–65.

92   **"good mood":** Goduti, *Kennedy's Kitchen Cabinet and the Pursuit of Peace*, 45.

93   **"Cuban mistake":** Taubman, *Khrushchev*, 493.

93   **"Getting involved in a fight":** O'Donnell and Powers, *Johnny, We Hardly Knew Ye*, chap. 11 (digital version).

93   **"dramatic accomplishments in space":** LBJ to JFK, memo, April 28, 1961, Famous Names file, "John F. Kennedy," LBJ Presidential Library.

95   **"a bone in my throat":** Thomas Putnam, "The Real Meaning of *Ich Bin ein Berliner*," *Atlantic*, JFK issue, September 19, 2013.

95   **"I am only 44":** Parmet, *JFK*, 198.

95   **Kennedy sought to use the meeting:** Reeves, *President Kennedy*, 137.

95   **"Your job, Mr. President":** William Taubman, *Khrushchev*, 494.

96   **"the young man . . . somewhat fumbling":** Reeves, *President Kennedy*, 153.

96   **"Remember, he's just as scared":** Ibid.

96   **seventy thousand fervent Austrians:** Sidey, *John F. Kennedy, President*, 160.

97   **"We cast the deciding vote":** Reeves, *President Kennedy*, 159.

97   **"If you tell everybody":** Kempe, *Berlin 1961*, chap. 10 (digital version).

97   **"liquidation of the Communist system":** Office of the Historian, "Foreign Relations of the United States, 1961–1963, Volume V, Soviet Union," 83, Memorandum of Conversation, U.S. State Department, State.gov.

98   **"*Miscalculation?*" Khrushchev responded incredulously:** Ibid.

98   **"Tell him I hope they never take it":** Sidey, *John F. Kennedy, President*, 40.

98   **"Are you trying to light me on fire":** Ibid.

99   **"snapping" at Kennedy "like a terrier and shaking":** O'Donnell and Powers, *Johnny, We Hardly Knew Ye*, 342.

99   **In an attempt to clarify:** Schlesinger, *Thousand Days*, 362.

99   **"more than a mistake. It was a failure":** Beschloss, *Crisis Years*, chap. 8 (digital version).

99   **"Certainly, in a speech before the Twentieth Party Congress":** O'Brien, *John F. Kennedy*, 546.

99   **This was exactly what Khrushchev wanted:** Ibid.

100 **"it had been a rough day":** Schlesinger, *Thousand Days*, 365.

100 **"I'm trying to remind myself":** Smyser, *Kennedy and the Berlin Wall*, 65.

100 **In previous generations:** Sidey, *John F. Kennedy, President*, 166–67.

101 **"the most dangerous spot in the world":** *Foreign Relations of the United States, 1961–1963*, vol. 14, *The Berlin Crisis, 1961–1962*, document 32, "Memorandum of Conversation."

101 **"contractual rights":** *Foreign Relations of the United States, 1961–1963*, vol. 14, *The Berlin Crisis, 1961–1962*, document 33, "Memorandum of Conversation."

101   "It is up to the U.S. to decide": Ibid.

101   "like a schoolboy": Kempe, *Berlin 1961*, 234.

101   "naked, brutal, ruthless power": Jacqueline Kennedy, *Historic Conversations*, 210.

102   In diplomatic meetings, Dean Rusk: Beschloss, *Crisis Years*, chap. 8 (digital version).

102   "I never met a man like this": Taubman, *Khrushchev*, 500.

JACKIE

103   "The occasions are few": "Life of Jacqueline B. Kennedy," JFKLibrary.org.

103   "shuffled through": Ibid.

103   "prettiest house in America": John J. O'Connor, "TV: Jacqueline Bouvier Kennedy," *New York Times*, October 14, 1981.

103   "as great a First Lady in her own right": Sidey, *John F. Kennedy, President*, 39.

103   If there had been a bright spot: Margaret Leslie Davis, "The Two First Ladies," *Vanity Fair*, October 6, 2008.

104   "Paris Has a New Queen": Leaming, *Mrs. Kennedy*, 112.

104   "intransigent, insufferably vain": Davis, "Two First Ladies."

104   "Mrs. Kennedy knows more": Leaming, *Mrs. Kennedy*, 111.

104   "First Lady Wins Khrushchev, Too": Ibid., 112–13.

104   "In the pubs, the talk is more of 'Jackie'": Ibid.

104   "I don't think it inappropriate": "Life of Jacqueline B. Kennedy," JFKLibrary.org.

104   "Jack wanted more than looks": Smith, *Grace and Power*, 150.

105   "a darling child, the prettiest little girl": "Life of Jacqueline B. Kennedy," JFKLibrary.org.

105   "Lee was the pretty one": Kelly, *Jackie Oh!*, 18.

105   "not to be a housewife": Collier and Horowitz, *Kennedys*, 95.

105   "happiest and most carefree": Ann Mah, "A Year in Paris That Transformed Jacqueline Kennedy Onassis," *New York Times*, June 28, 2019.

105   "I learned not to be ashamed": Ibid.

105   The same year, she beat out: "First Lady Biography: Jackie Kennedy," First Ladies, National First Ladies Library, firstladies.org.

106   Instead she went on to: Ibid.

106   "Don't pay any attention": Collier and Horowitz, *Kennedys*, 193.

106   "may not be the most appropriate": Klein, *All Too Human*, "Heavy Weather" (digital version).

106   "How perfect it is to be married": Leaming, *Mrs. Kennedy*, 45.

106   "I'm never going back": Andersen, *These Few Precious Days*, 67.

106   According to a 1960 *Time* magazine profile: Ibid., 75–76.

107   "Only one million?": Ibid., 76.

107   "part of a great man's life": Ibid., 15.

107   "Jack could have had a worthwhile life": Ibid., 115.

107   "introvertness [*sic*], stiffness": Janet Auchincloss, Oral History, September 6, 1964, JFK #2, JFKLibrary.org.

107   "The public life is above water": Smith, *Grace and Power*, 8.

107   "Jackie was the only woman": Ibid., 7.

107   "half-bald": Ibid., 163–64.

107   "conveys the idea that women": Ibid.

107   "born and reared" Republican: Beschloss, *American Heritage Illustrated History of the Presidents*, 425.

108   "more Kennedy than thou": Collier and Horowitz, *Kennedys*, 193.

108   "your hair, that you spoke French": Jacqueline Kennedy, *Historic Conversations*, 141.

108   "All the things that I'd always done": Ibid.

108   Her quest to "restore" the White House: Andersen, *These Few Precious Days*, 120.

109   "ashamed of Versailles": Ibid., 114.

109   "Everything in the White House": "The White House Restoration," JFKLibrary.org.

109   In 1962, eighty million American viewers: Ibid.

109   "We had more people today": Jacqueline Kennedy, *Historic Conversations*, 141.

109   "Not since Thomas Jefferson": Arthur and Barbara Gelb, "Culture Makes a Hit at the White House," *New York Times*, January 28, 1962.

110   "to take care of the president": Black, *First Ladies of the United States of America*, 79.

110   "If you bungle raising your children": "Jacqueline Lee Bouvier Kennedy," WhiteHouse.gov.

110   "We better get out of the way": Collier and Horowitz, *Kennedys*, 311.

110   "One of the greatest hits made with state visitors": Letitia Baldrige Oral History, April 24, 1964, JFK #1, JFKLibrary.org.

110   "He liked to see me ride": "Life of Jacqueline B. Kennedy," JFKLibrary.org.

111   "Good night, Mrs. Kennedy": Sidey, *John F. Kennedy, President*, 78.

111   While his paternal delight: Reeves, *President Kennedy*, 322.

111   Though . . . Kennedy had vowed: O'Brien, *John F. Kennedy*, 681.

111   His sexual appetite was ramped: Alan Brinkley, *John F. Kennedy*, 92.

111   "You were on the most elite": Larry Sabato, "John F. Kennedy's Final Days Reveal a Man Who Craved Excitement," *Forbes*, October 8, 2013.

112   All too willing to let Kennedy know: Alan Brinkley, *John F. Kennedy*, 92.

112   What isn't clear is whether Kennedy: Dallek, *Camelot's Court*, 135–36.

112   Beardsley, who lacked secretarial skills: Amy Davidson Sorkin, "Mimi and the President," *New Yorker*, February 10, 2012.

112   On one especially troubling occasion: Bella English, "50 Years On, JFK Intern Tries to Make Sense of Affair," *Boston Globe*, February 16, 2012.

112   "Be sure to lock": Collier and Horowitz, *Kennedys*, 174.

113 "[Jack] was totally open": Smith, *Grace and Power*, 153–54.

113 After losing his virginity: Ibid., 150.

113 "I can now get tail as often": Collier and Horowitz, *Kennedys*, 90.

113 "I don't know how it is with you": O'Brien, *John F. Kennedy*, 682.

113 One of Kennedy's favorite books: Sidey, *John F. Kennedy, President*, 55.

113 "The chase was more fun": Smith, *Grace and Power*, 152.

113 "recreational, not emotional": Ibid., 162.

114 "intrinsic part of his life": Ibid.

114 "And this is the woman": Sabato, "John F. Kennedy's Final Days Reveal a Man Who Craved Excitement."

114 She had not only been mindful: Collier and Horowitz, *Kennedys*, 192.

114 "She wasn't sexually attracted": Ibid., 194.

114 "Kennedy is doing for sex": Smith, *Grace and Power*, 155.

114 "We're a bunch of virgins": Reeves, *President Kennedy*, 291.

115 "a tomb of secrets": O'Brien, *John F. Kennedy*, 827.

115 "Like everyone else, we had heard": Bradlee, *Good Life*, 268.

115 "None of the White House correspondents": Cronkite, *Reporter's Life*, 220.

115 "In the sixties the Washington press": Ibid.

116 "I think the guy had a problem": Author's conversation with Hugh Sidey, January 2001.

116 "our happiest years": Jacqueline Kennedy, *Historic Conversations*, 141.

THE WALL

117 Sirens wailed in the small hours: "Berlin: The Wall," *Time*, August 25, 1961.

117 As the din rose, East German troops: O'Brien, *John F. Kennedy*, 555.

117 Discharged early from Sunday mass: Reeves, *President Kennedy*, 209.

117 Khrushchev's situation, Kennedy knew: Reeves, *President Kennedy*, 208; and Michael O'Brien, "President Kennedy and the Berlin Wall," *History Reader*, August 12, 2011.

118 "The entire East bloc is in danger": Reeves, *President Kennedy*, 208.

118 Kennedy was also of the mind: Dallek, *Unfinished Life*, 425.

118 Despite Khrushchev's initial: Dallek, *Camelot's Court*, 224.

118 Two weeks before it went up: Dallek, *Unfinished Life*, 425.

118 "Why would Khrushchev": Ibid., 426.

118 "the great testing place of Western courage": "President John F. Kennedy, the White House, July 25, 1961," JFKLibrary.org.

119 Though the theory is unproven: Beschloss, *Crisis Years*, 280–81.

119 "Okay, go to your ballgame": Reeves, *President Kennedy*, 210.

119 Three days after the wall went up: Andrea Grunau, "How Did West Germany Respond to the Building of the Berlin Wall?," Deutsche Welle, DW.com, April 11, 2014.

119 Kennedy had ordered 1,600 American: O'Brien, *John F. Kennedy*, 556.

120 "become an inspiration to the entire world": "Visit of Vice President Lyndon Johnson in Berlin 1961," YouTube.com, posted October 10, 2016.

Notes

120 **But Kennedy's response fell:** Daniel Schorr, "Remembering the Construction of the Berlin Wall," *All Things Considered*, NPR, August 12, 2009.

120 **"The Berlin Senate publicly condemns":** Grunau, "How Did West Germany Respond to the Building of the Berlin Wall?"

120 **"hopeless, helpless and harmless":** Dallek, *Camelot's Court*, 229.

120 **As the year closed, the public:** David Coleman, "JFK's Presidential Approval Ratings," History in Pieces, historyinpieces.com.

120 **"the American economy is in trouble":** John F. Kennedy, "Annual Message to the Congress on the State of the Union," January 30, 1961, American Presidency Project, www.presidency.ucsb.edu.

121 **An infusion of domestic and military:** Kimberly Amadeo, "History of Recession in the United States," thebalance.com, updated August 14, 2019.

121 **"Reporters liked Kennedy for being":** Bradlee, *A Good Life*, 236.

121 **Conscious of the infamous photo op:** Associated Press, *The Torch Is Passed*.

121 **"No one ever knew John Kennedy":** Reeves, *President Kennedy*, 19.

121 **"He really kept his life":** Jacqueline Kennedy, *Historic Conversations*, 22–23.

121 **Demand for cigars:** Sidey, *John F. Kennedy, President*, photo insert; and O'Brien, *John F. Kennedy*, 811.

122 **A Georgetown bookstore's increased:** Schlesinger, *Thousand Days*, 105.

122 **"a fanatical reader":** Ibid.

122 **In early 1962, a poll among college:** O'Brien, *John F. Kennedy*, 811.

122 **He actively worked members of the press:** Reeves, *President Kennedy*, 478.

122 **As Kennedy biographer Richard Reeves wrote:** Ibid.

122 **In a late 1962 press conference:** "John F. Kennedy and the Press," JFKLibrary.org.

122 **"They remind me of the ballplayer":** O'Brien, *John F. Kennedy*, 825.

123 **His friendship with Kennedy:** Bradlee, *Good Life*, 128.

123 **A thaw between the president and Bradlee:** Ibid., 128–29.

123 **The White House gave Bradlee:** Ibid., 129.

123 **the president was served up:** Collier and Horowitz, *Kennedys*, 250.

123 **When *Time* incorrectly:** Hugh Sidey, Oral History, JFKLibrary.org; and Reeves, *President Kennedy*, 287.

123 **"I'm getting sick and goddamned tired":** Hugh Sidey, Oral History, JFKLibrary.org.

124 **"I don't agree with Kennedy":** O'Brien, *John F. Kennedy*, 827.

124 **"He took over the [presidency]":** "Man of the Year," *Time*, January 1, 1962.

124 **Did Khrushchev see Kennedy:** Dallek, *Unfinished Life*, 407.

124 **"I tell you, Hugh":** Hugh Sidey, "The Lesson John Kennedy Learned from the Bay of Pigs," *Time*, April 16, 2001.

125 **The bigger-than-life, effusively positive:** Collier and Horowitz, *Kennedys*, 287.

125 **He looked stunned:** Sidey, *John F. Kennedy, President*, 238.

125 **"Dad's gotten sick":** Collier and Horowitz, *Kennedys*, 287.
125 **Bobby took charge, ordering doctors:** Ibid.
125 **Lem Billings recalled Joe:** Ibid.

THE BROTHERS KENNEDY

129 **Bobby was called "the runt":** Thomas, *Robert Kennedy*, 30–31.
129 **"Bobby? Forget it," Eunice said:** Collier and Horowitz, *Kennedys*, 71.
129 **Even his mother fretted that he was "girlish":** Ibid., 70.
129 **"I can't think of anyone who had less":** Chris Matthews, "Once an Awkward Loner, RFK Found Himself on the Football Field," *Boston Globe*, September 28, 2017.
130 **As a boy in Hyannis Port:** Collier and Horowitz, *Kennedys*, 71.
130 **"I can't see that sober":** Thomas, *Robert Kennedy*, 49.
130 **His nickname for Bobby, "Black Robert":** Matthews, "Once an Awkward Loner."
130 **Though Kenny O'Donnell would later:** Thomas, *Robert Kennedy*, 65.
131 **As RFK biographer Evan Thomas wrote:** Ibid., 90.
132 **"For many reasons I believe":** Dallek, *Unfinished Life*, 318.
132 **"Up until that time, Jack more or less":** Collier and Horowitz, *Kennedys*, 241.
132 **"All of us involved made mistakes":** Sidey, *John F. Kennedy, President*, 122.
133 **"The first thing I'm going to tell":** Robert Dallek, "JFK vs. the Military," *Atlantic*, September 10, 2013.
133 **Behind the scenes, he continued to:** Evan Thomas, "We May Owe Our Lives to a Back Channel with Russia," *Washington Post*, June 2, 2017.
133 **In February 1962, he and Ethel:** "More Than a Brother," *Time*, February 16, 1962.
133 **The title of a February 1962:** "Bobby Kennedy: Is He the 'Assistant President'?," *U.S. News & World Report*, February 19, 1962.
133 **"As Robert Kennedy circles the globe":** Ibid.
134 **"We're both cryptic":** "More Than a Brother," *Time*, February 16, 1962.
134 **While their interactions were relatively:** Ibid.
135 **"Get Rusk on the phone. Go get my brother":** Ibid.
135 **"Don't kid anybody about who":** Collier and Horowitz, *Kennedys*, 289.
135 **"his brother's total partner":** Schlesinger, *Thousand Days*, 702.
135 **"prone to look at things more as black or white":** "Bobby Kennedy: Is He the 'Assistant President'?," *U.S. News & World Report*.
135 **"Bobby lacks his brother's easy grace":** "More Than a Brother," *Time*, February 16, 1962.
135 **"Jack Kennedy admired above all":** Bradlee, *Good Life*, 244.
135 **"so obviously untrue":** "More Than a Brother," *Time*, February 16, 1962.
135 **"If he does not want to become President":** Ibid.
136 **"You boys have what you want now":** Ibid.

136   **"I don't want":** Collier and Horowitz, *Kennedys*, 286.

136   **His 1932 birth was met by President Herbert:** John M. Broder, "Edward M. Kennedy, Senate Stalwart, Is Dead at 77," *New York Times*, August 26, 2009.

136   **During his brother's presidential run:** "More Than a Brother," *Time*, February 16, 1962.

136   **He brought the same ethic:** Ibid.

137   **"We're having more trouble with this":** Collier and Horowitz, *Kennedys*, 286.

137   **"demeaning to the dignity":** "More Than a Brother," *Time*, February 16, 1962.

137   **"We're going to take a lot of votes":** Ibid.

138   **"Kennedyism":** Ibid.

KEEPING THE PEACE

139   **"All I want people to say about me":** Boller, *Presidential Anecdotes*, 303.

139   **"I have no firsthand knowledge":** Stern, *Averting "The Final Failure,"* 35.

139   **"All war":** David Talbot, "Warrior for Peace," *Time*, June 21, 2001.

139   **"It turned my father and brothers":** Ibid.

140   **"Ever since the longbow, when man":** Stern, *Averting "The Final Failure,"* 35.

140   **In a press conference late in his presidency:** Burr and Montford, *The Making of the Limited Test Ban Treaty*, George Washington University, August 8, 2003.

140   **"World order will be secured":** John F. Kennedy, "January 11, 1962: State of the Union Address," UVA Miller Center, millercenter.org.

141   **The culprit was the Soviet Union:** U.S. Department of State, "Treaty Banning Nuclear Weapon Tests in the Atmosphere, in Outer Space, and Under Water," archived content, State.gov.

141   **Just over two weeks later, portending:** National Geographic Society, *National Geographic Eyewitness to the 20th Century*, 254.

141   **A January 1961 Gallup Poll reflected:** "Nuclear Test Ban Treaty," JFK in History, JFKLibrary.org.

141   **After the ill-fated summit in Vienna:** Ibid.

142   **"not to an arms race, but a peace race":** "Time to Sheath the Nuclear Sword, but How?," *Daily News*, October 1, 1961.

142   **Before the year was out, they would:** "Nuclear Test Ban Treaty," JFK in History, JFKLibrary.org.

142   **Less than a decade earlier, the Korean War:** Dallek, "JFK vs. the Military."

142   **Not only did the military higher-ups:** Ibid.; and Talbot, "Warrior for Peace."

143   **"If it hadn't been for the Bay of Pigs":** Talbot, "Warrior for Peace."

143   **"JFK's war hero status allowed him":** Ibid.

143   **"a bunch of old men":** Jacqueline Kennedy, *Historic Conversations*, 183.

143 **he worried less about Khrushchev's launch:** Talbot, "Warrior for Peace."
143 **Given the jingoism of the Joint Chiefs:** Lawrence, *Vietnam War*, 72.
144 **True to its name, the policy authorized:** Ibid., 72–73.
144 **Though falling well short of the military's:** Ibid., 72.
144 **Between 10 and 11 million of South Vietnam's:** "Vietnam's Faiths Underlie Rising," *New York Times*, September 14, 1964.
144 **"The thing that bothers me about this":** Ibid.
144 **Charmed by Diem during a visit:** Shesol, *Mutual Contempt*, 89.
145 **"Shit," Johnson replied:** Vandiver, *Shadows of Vietnam*, 9.
145 **Diem's strategic hamlets program, allowing:** Lawrence, *Vietnam War*, 73–74.

"WE CHOOSE TO GO TO THE MOON"

146 **"The life of New York almost stood still":** Nan Robertson, "New York Pauses to 'Watch' Glenn," *New York Times*, February 21, 1962.
146 **nine thousand people crammed into Grand Central:** Ibid.
146 **For the first time in the New York City Transit:** Ibid.
146 **"Colonel John H. Glenn, Jr., has just":** Ibid.
146 **Over 100 million Americans tuned in:** Richard F. Shepard, "$2,000,000 Radio-TV Coverage Carries Story of Flight to Nation," *New York Times*, February 21, 1962.
147 **In keeping with the openness:** Reeves, *President Kennedy*, 285.
147 **Cartoons in the Soviet newspapers mocked:** Theodore Shabad, "Moscow, Unmoved, Gives News of Orbit," *New York Times*, February 21, 1962.
147 **In Washington, John Kennedy awoke early:** Edward T. Folliard, "Kennedy Invites Colonel Here for Public Welcome," *Washington Post*, February 21, 1962.
147 **"If only he were a negro":** Reeves, *President Kennedy*, 286.
148 **Kennedy canceled a planned congratulatory:** Ibid.
148 ***Friendship 7* splashed down safely:** Richard Witkin, "81,000 Mile Trip," *New York Times*, February 21, 1962.
148 **"We have a long way to go":** Folliard, "Kennedy Invites Colonel Here."
148 **Aides saw clearly that he didn't want:** Chaiken, *Man on the Moon*, 340–41.
149 **He was drawn by Glenn's courage:** Reeves, *President Kennedy*, 288.
149 **Shepard, in turn, was taken by Kennedy's:** Chaiken, *Man on the Moon*, 341.
149 **The year prior, before a joint session:** Amy Stamm, "We Choose to Go to the Moon and Other Speeches," Smithsonian Air and Space Museum, July 17, 2019.
149 **On September 12, after touring:** Ibid.
149 **Kennedy had handwritten the reference:** "Address at Rice University, Houston, Texas, 12 September 1962," JFKLibrary.org.
150 **"I think the United States cannot permit":** Alan Brinkley, *John F. Kennedy*, 75.

150   **And, as he had said in his policy address:** NASA, "Excerpt from the 'Special Message to the Congress on Urgent National Needs,'" NASA History, NASA.gov, posted May 24, 2004.

151   **"No sir, I do not":** "Fly Me to the Moon," UVA Miller Center, miller center.org.

152   **Between 1960 and 1973:** Planetary Society, "How Much Did the Apollo Program Cost?," planetary.org.

152   **"Bill, I completely agree with you":** O'Brien, *John F. Kennedy*, 572.

152   **During the course of Kennedy's administration:** Ibid., 571.

152   **By then, NASA had launched three:** Elizabeth Howell, "Gordon Cooper: Record-Setting Mercury & Gemini Programs," Space.com, February 1, 2011.

153   **"one of the great victories of the human":** "May 16, 1963: President Kennedy's Remarks Following the Flight of Astronaut Gordon Cooper," YouTube.com.

153   **"lost a lot of its glamour":** Rachel Day, "JFK Library Releases Recording of President Kennedy Discussing Race to the Moon," May 25, 2011, JFKLibrary.org.

153   **"Why should we spend that kind":** Ibid.

"GOING FOR BROKE"

154   **On the afternoon of April 11:** Sidey, *John F. Kennedy, President*, 247.

154   **"Simultaneous and identical actions":** "Press Conference, 11 April 1962," JFKLibrary.org.

155   **The "non-inflationary" agreement:** Sidey, *John F. Kennedy, President*, 242.

155   **U.S. Steel was the third-largest corporation:** Daniel F. Cuff, "Roger Blough, 81, Dies; Led U.S. Steel for 13 Years," *New York Times*, October 10, 1985.

155   **During a late afternoon Oval Office meeting:** Schlesinger, *Thousand Days*, 635.

155   **By late the following day, Bethlehem Steel:** Cuff, "Roger Blough, 81, Dies"; and Sidey, *John F. Kennedy, President*, 244.

155   **"I think you're making a mistake":** Sidey, *John F. Kennedy, President*, 244.

156   **"He fucked me":** Larry Sabato, *The Kennedy Half Century: The Presidency, Assassination, and Lasting Legacy of John F. Kennedy* (New York: Bloomsbury, 2013), 99.

156   **"This is war":** Alan Brinkley, *John F. Kennedy*, 90.

156   **In order to combat the threat of inflation:** Reeves, *President Kennedy*, 296.

156   **"made a speech about it and then failed":** "From the Rocking Chair," *Time*, December 28, 1962.

156   **"At a time when restraint and sacrifice":** "Press Conference, 11 April 1962," JFKLibrary.org.

Notes

156 **Roger Blough, whose $300,000 annual salary:** Cuff, "Roger Blough, 81, Dies"; U.S. Census Bureau, "Average Family Income Up 4 Percent in 1962," June 26, 1963, census.gov; Sidey, *John F. Kennedy, President*, 247.

156 **Mounting his defense, he called his own:** Cuff, "Roger Blough, 81, Dies."

157 **"Going for broke," Bobby Kennedy set:** Reeves, *President Kennedy*, 300.

157 **"Blough and his people want to know":** Ibid., 301.

158 **Blough learned that his chief competitor:** Rowen, *Free Enterprisers*, 105.

158 **At 5:30 p.m., nearly forty-eight hours:** Ibid., 106.

158 **"We have met the enemy and they":** Reeves, *President Kennedy*, 301.

158 **"Khrushchev said he liked your style":** Ibid., 303.

158 **"The fucking *Herald Tribune* is at it again":** Ibid.

158 **The episode had calmed down:** "The Presidency: Happy Birthday," *Time*, June 1, 1962.

159 **In an iconic fusion of Washington and Hollywood:** Karen Hua, "Marilyn Monroe's 'Happy Birthday, Mr. President' Dress Expected to Bring $3 Million at Auction," Forbes.com, September 7, 2016.

159 **The pricy Jean Louis creation:** Ibid.

159 **"Thanks, Mr. President":** "'Happy Birthday, Mr. President' Sung by Marilyn Monroe to President John F. Kennedy," YouTube.com, posted November 21, 2013.

159 **"I can now retire from politics":** "The Presidency: Happy Birthday," *Time.*

160 **"The stock market careened downward":** Jason Zweig, "Back to the Future: Lessons from the Forgotten 'Flash Crash' of 1962, *Wall Street Journal*, May 29, 2010.

160 **"When the market went down":** O'Brien, *John F. Kennedy*, 646.

160 **A survey conducted in June revealed:** Ibid.

160 **"In winning the victory":** Schlesinger, *Thousand Days*, 639.

OLE MISS

162 **"Negroes are getting ideas":** Reeves, *President Kennedy*, 357.

163 **Among them was a grandson of slaves:** Sidey, *John F. Kennedy, President*, 263.

163 **It was about "power":** "James Meredith Graduates from Mississippi," Learning Network, *New York Times*, August 18, 2011.

163 **As such, he believed its most distinguished:** Debbie Elliot, "Integrating Ole Miss: A Transformative, Deadly Riot," NPR, October 1, 2012.

163 **When the twenty-nine-year-old Meredith showed up:** Eagles, *Price of Defiance*, 316.

163 **"Where's Meredith?" he asked:** Ibid.

164 **Eight minutes later, after telling:** Ibid., 317.

164 **"Thousands Said Ready to Fight":** Haygood, *Showdown*, 143.

164 **"over one black boy . . . backed by the NAACP":** Eagles, *Price of Defiance*, 315.

164 **"white and Negro should go together":** Ibid., 319–20.

164 **"I have no choice. I don't have the power":** Reeves, *President Kennedy*, 357.

164 **Barnett drove 165 miles from Jackson:** Eagles, *Price of Defiance*, 321.

165 **"General," Barnett had said, hoping for:** Reeves, *President Kennedy*, 356.

165 **Barnett had arranged for 220 highway:** "Telephone Conversation Between President Kennedy, Attorney General Kennedy and Governor Barnett," Belt 4C, JFKLibrary.org.

165 **"What can they do to maintain law":** Ibid.

165 **Later that afternoon, Barnett dangled a proposition:** Thomas, *Robert Kennedy*, 198.

166 **The evening prior, Barnett was on hand:** Ibid.

166 **"I love Mississippi," he proclaimed:** "September 29, 1962, Ross Barnett Giving His 'I Love Mississippi' Speech," YouTube.com, posted January 3, 2010.

166 **"Americans are free to disagree":** "Radio and Television Address on the Situation at the University of Mississippi, 30 September 1962," JFKLibrary.org.

167 **As Kennedy spoke, a mob of between two:** Dallek, *Unfinished Life*, 536.

167 **Meanwhile, state senator George Yarbrough:** Sidey, *John F. Kennedy, President*, 264.

167 **It fell to five hundred U.S. marshals, most of them:** Moore, *American President*, 454; and Megan Brodsky, "Ole Miss Riot (1962)," *Black Past*, March 25, 2018.

167 **The horde angrily waved Confederate flags:** Oates, *Let the Trumpet Sound*, 206; and Watson, *Expanding Vista*, 96.

167 **They burned cars and threw rocks:** Brodsky, "Ole Miss Riot (1962)."

168 **Assistant U.S. attorney general Nick Katzenbach:** University of Mississippi Lyceum Building and Civil Rights Monument, Mississippi Hills National Heritage Area.

168 **"No," Kennedy ordered, with specific instructions:** Reeves, *President Kennedy*, 362.

168 **Before daylight, sixteen thousand U.S. Army regulars:** Ibid., 364.

168 **Throughout the night, Kennedy monitored:** Sidey, *John F. Kennedy, President*, 265.

168 **By then, the devastation in Oxford:** Brodsky, "Ole Miss Riot (1962)"; and Dalek, *Unfinished Life*, 517.

168 **Late in the day an unnerving stillness:** Reeves, *President Kennedy*, 364.

168 **James Meredith, flanked by a phalanx:** Brodsky, "Ole Miss Riot (1962)."

168 **"You know, that's General Grant's table":** Goduti, *Robert Kennedy and the Shaping of Civil Rights, 1960–1964*, 150.

169 **"Don't tell them about General Grant's table":** Ibid.

169 "become a battleground for a cause": Oates, *Let the Trumpet Sound*, 207.

169 "made Negroes feel like pawns": Ibid.

169 Appealing to Kennedy's own sense of history: Ibid., 209.

169 "The key to everything is federal commitment": Ibid., 208–9.

169 "the understanding and the political skills": PBS, "Eyes on the Prize: America's Civil Rights Movement, 1954–1985."

"THE GRAVEST ISSUES"

170 On the unseasonably warm morning: Reeves, *President Kennedy*, 368; and Dobbs, *One Minute to Midnight*, chap. 1 (digital version).

170 "Eisenhower Calls President": Tom Wicker, "Eisenhower Calls President Weak on Foreign Policy," *New York Times*, October 15, 1962.

170 "It is too sad to talk about": Ibid.

170 "In those eight years, we lost": Ibid.

171 At 8:45 the same morning: *Foreign Relations of the United States, 1961–1963*, vol. 11, *Cuban Missile Crisis and Aftermath*.

171 "Mr. President," he said: Reeves, *President Kennedy*, 368.

171 "What are we going to do?": O'Brien, *John F. Kennedy*, 659.

171 "Moscow had calculated that the United States": Schlesinger, *Thousand Days*, 798.

171 "right in front of the open jaws of American imperialism": O'Brien, *John F. Kennedy*, 658.

172 Other plots were hatched toward: Max Boot, "Operation Mongoose: The Story of America's Plot to Overthrow Castro," *Atlantic*, January 5, 2018.

172 "broader geopolitical strategy": O'Brien, *John F. Kennedy*, 658.

172 As Khrushchev's support was slipping: Alan Brinkley, *John F. Kennedy*, 115; and Benjamin Schwarz, "The Real Cuban Missile Crisis: Everything You Think You Know About Those 13 Days Is Wrong," *Atlantic*, January/ February, 2013.

173 "Kennedy and his administration, without question": Schwarz, "Real Cuban Missile Crisis."

173 Throughout the balance of the summer: "Cuban Crisis: A Step-by-Step Review," *New York Times*, November 3, 1962.

173 "exclusively for defensive purposes": *Foreign Relations of the United States, 1961–1963*, vol. 11, *Cuban Missile Crisis and Aftermath*, document 61, "Letter from Chairman Khrushchev to President Kennedy."

173 "Were it to be otherwise": Karthik Gopalan, "Kennedy and the Cuban Missile Crisis," *Foreign Policy Journal*, August 16, 2010.

173 On October 14, after reconnaissance missions: "Cuban Crisis: A Step-by-Step Review."

173 If operational, it meant that much: Dobbs, *One Minute to Midnight*, 79.

173 Subsequent intelligence findings would: O'Brien, *John F. Kennedy*, 658.

174 Just one of the SS-4 missiles: Ibid.

174 "Caroline, have you been eating candy": Dallek, *Unfinished Life*, 545.

175   Blown-up photos of the Cuban sites: Dobbs, *One Minute to Midnight*, 79.

175   "How long have we got . . . before": "The World on the Brink: John F. Kennedy and the Cuban Missile Crisis: Thirteen Days in October: Day 1, Oct 16," JFKLibrary.org.

175   "Ken Keating will probably be": Reeves, *President Kennedy*, 370.

176   "an intensive survey of the dangers": Alan Brinkley, *John F. Kennedy*, 115.

176   "One, the quick strike; the other": "The World on the Brink."

176   The secretary of state suspected: Ibid.

176   "For the first time I'm beginning": Ibid.

176   Throughout the crisis, Kennedy: Dobbs, *One Minute to Midnight*, 80.

177   "I realize it's a breach of faith": Reeves, *President Kennedy*, 374.

177   In order to keep the situation under: Sidey, *John F. Kennedy, President*, 273.

177   "We're certainly . . . going to take": "The World on the Brink."

177   Additional military actions: Ibid.

177   "Our major problem overall": Dallek, *Unfinished Life*, 547.

177   "the one who fights the bull": "John F. Kennedy Quotations, Bullfight Poem," JFKLibrary.org.

"BURDEN OF CHOICE"

178   The *Post* reported that 344 editors: Gonzalez, *Nuclear Deception*, 271.

178   Their contention was borne out by: Ibid.

178   At the same time, the poll reflected: Reeves, *President Kennedy*, 378.

179   "they're going to push on Berlin": Thomas, *Robert Kennedy*, 217.

179   "the political action of a blockade": Naftali and Zelikow, *Great Crises*, vol. 2, 597–98.

179   "There's one other factor that I didn't mention": "JFK and the Cuban Missile Crisis," UVA Miller Center, millercenter.org.

180   "Can you imagine LeMay saying": Robert Kennedy, *Thirteen Days*, foreword.

180   "This thing is falling apart": Thomas, *Robert Kennedy*, 217.

180   "Pearl Harbor in reverse": Todd Purdum, "The World: At the Brink, Then and Now; The Missiles of 1962 Haunt the Iraq Debate," *New York Times*, October 13, 2002.

180   "have another look": Thomas, *Robert Kennedy*, 217–18.

180   "very late in the game": McGeorge Bundy, Oral History, March and May 1964, JFKLibrary.org.

181   "Less profile—More courage": "Cuban Crisis: A Step-by-Step Review."

181   "In all those rooms": Thomas, *Robert Kennedy*, 214.

181   "Marine Moves in South Linked to Cuban Crisis.": "Marine Moves in South Linked to Cuban Crisis," *Washington Post*, October 21, 1962.

182   Kennedy was furious: Ibid.

182   "Official Washington yesterday wrapped": Ibid.

182 **"the greatest urgency":** Richard L. Miller, *Under the Cloud*, 346.

182 **"a rolling consensus":** Purdum, "The World: At the Brink."

182 **"burden of choice":** Alan Brinkley, *John F. Kennedy*, 118.

182 **"tolerate any action":** "Letter from Chairman Khrushchev to President Kennedy, October 22, 1962," JFKLibrary.org.

183 **"We've decided to take action":** Purdum, "The World: At the Brink."

183 **"We're either a first-class power or we're not":** Dallek, *Unfinished Life*, 537.

183 **"act of war":** Ibid.

183 **"not actually be an affront to Russia":** Purdum, "The World: At the Brink."

183 **"If I had known the job was this tough":** Dallek, *Unfinished Life*, 537.

184 **"Until this urgent problem is solved":** David Eisenhower and Julie Nixon Eisenhower, *Going Home to Glory*, 96.

184 **"unmistakable evidence":** Dallek, *Unfinished Life*, 537.

185 **The country rallied around Kennedy:** Sidey, *John F. Kennedy, President*, 285.

185 **A Gallup Poll showed that 84 percent:** O'Brien, *John F. Kennedy*, 666.

185 **"one of the most decisive moments":** O'Brien, *John F. Kennedy*, 667.

185 **"extraordinary gravity":** "U.S. Imposes Arms Blockade on Cuba on Finding Offensive Missile Sites: Kennedy Ready for Soviet Showdown," *New York Times*, October 23, 1962.

185 **"From then on":** Jacqueline Kennedy, *Historic Conversations*, 263–64.

THE KNOT

186 **"By what right do you do this?":** *Foreign Relations of the United States, 1961–1963*, vol. 6, *Kennedy-Khrushchev Exchanges*, document 62, "Telegram from the Department of State to the Embassy in the Soviet Union."

187 **"I think you will recognize that":** Alan Brinkley, *John F. Kennedy*, 119.

187 **After asking a lighting technician:** Sidey, *John F. Kennedy, President*, 284.

187 **"If they get mean on this one":** O'Brien, *John F. Kennedy*, 667.

187 **As the quarantine went into effect:** "The World on the Brink."

188 **"At what point are we going to attack":** "JFK Consults ExComm About Growing Missile Crisis," UVA Miller Center, millercenter.org.

188 **"The danger and concern that we all felt":** Schlesinger, *Robert Kennedy and His Times*, 515.

188 **"stopped dead in the water":** Reeves, *President Kennedy*, 401; and Clutterbuck, *International Crisis and Conflict*, 109.

188 **"We're eyeball to eyeball":** Clutterbuck, *International Crisis and Conflict*, 109.

189 **In the eyes of many:** Schwarz, "Real Cuban Missile Crisis."

189 **"annihilation without representation":** Ibid.

189 **"They're sort of like Adlai":** Thomas, "We May Owe Our Lives to a Back Channel with Russia."

Notes

189 **"Do you, Ambassador Zorin, deny":** Michael Dobbs, "The Day Adlai Stevenson Showed 'Em at the U.N.," *Washington Post*, February 5, 2003.

190 **"Terrific," Kennedy said as he watched:** Ibid.

190 **"I don't think America had ever faced such":** Nikita Khrushchev, *Khrushchev Remembers*, 496.

190 **In Buenos Aires, evangelist Billy Graham:** Schlesinger, *Thousand Days*, 819.

190 **"In these critical days":** Leonardo Campus, "Martin Luther King's Reaction to the Cuban Missile Crisis," *European Journal of American Studies*, Summer 2017.

190 ***Time's* Hugh Sidey, after a sobering conversation:** Interview with the author, circa 2003.

191 **Without telling her why, he asked her:** Jacqueline Kennedy, *Historic Conversations*, 263–64.

191 **"Please don't send me anywhere":** Ibid.

191 **Through it all, Kennedy remained cool:** "Cuban Crisis: A Step-by-Step Review."

191 **"He insisted on knowing all his options":** Interview with the author, January 31, 2008.

191 **"I hope you realize there's not enough":** O'Brien, *John F. Kennedy*, 667.

191 **"Everyone needs peace":** "Department of State Telegram Transmitting Letter from Chairman Khrushchev to President Kennedy, October 26, 1962," JFKLibrary.org.

192 **"attack back":** Reeves, *President Kennedy*, 418.

192 **"It looked as if it might be slipping out":** Sidey, *John F. Kennedy, President*, 287.

192 **"This means war with the Soviet Union!":** Dobbs, *One Minute to Midnight*, "National Security Archive," George Washington University, June 11, 2008.

193 **"You have placed destructive missile weapons":** Office of the Historian, *Foreign Relations of the United States, 1961–1963*, vol. 11, *Cuban Missile Crisis and Aftermath*, 91. Message from Chairman Khrushchev to President Kennedy, U.S. State Department, State.gov.

193 **The Cuban missiles added 50 percent capacity:** Ibid.

194 **"We can't very well invade Cuba":** O'Brien, *John F. Kennedy*, 670.

194 **"R. Kennedy and his circle consider":** Thomas, *Robert Kennedy*, 222.

194 **Still, it put the Jupiter missiles on the table:** Ibid., 226.

194 **As Kennedy prepared for a full-scale:** "The World on the Brink."

195 **"no quid pro quo":** Sergei Khrushchev, *Nikita Khrushchev and the Creation of a Superpower*, 620.

195 **"statesmanlike decision":** Maga, *1960s*, 101.

196 **"a traitor":** Garthoff, *Reflections on the Cuban Missile Crisis*, 77.

196 **"To hell with these maniacs":** Ibid.

196 **"a step down":** "The World on the Brink."

196 **"toe to toe on Berlin":** Ibid.

197 **"I know that there is a God and I see":** Dallek, *Unfinished Life*, 470.

197 **"This is the night I should":** Collier and Horowitz, *Kennedys*, 299.

197 **"perhaps the greatest personal diplomatic":** Richard Beatty, "A Magisterial History," *Atlantic*, September 1, 1996.

197 **On the eve of his inaugural, Kennedy:** Sidey, *John F. Kennedy, President*, 22.

197 **"In the final analysis":** Nikita Khrushchev, *Khrushchev Remembers*, 500.

"THE ANTITHESIS OF A POLITICIAN"

198 **To that end, his campaigning across America:** Sidey, *John F. Kennedy, President*, 294.

198 **"Two years ago I said that it was":** Ibid., 296.

199 **"the antithesis of a politician":** Interview with Ben Bradlee and James M. Cannon for *Newsweek*.

199 **"on the way out":** Ibid.

199 **"What the hell am I supposed to do":** Sidey, *John F. Kennedy, President*, 320.

199 **Still, even with Kennedy's magnetism:** Rhodes Cook, "The Midterm Election of '62: A Real 'October Surprise,'" UVA Center for Politics, September 30, 2010.

199 **Traditionally, the midterm elections:** James Reston, "50 Million Vote," *New York Times*, November 7, 1962.

200 **Plus, polls indicated:** Sidey, *John F. Kennedy, President*, 320.

200 **"collective power" and "bloc action":** "From the Rocking Chair."

200 **"This bill serves the public interest":** *Public Papers of the Presidents of the United States: John F. Kennedy, 1962*, 202.

201 **"socialized medicine":** Julian Zelizer, "How Medicare Was Born," *New Yorker*, July 15, 2015.

201 **"one of the traditional methods":** Ibid.

201 **On the eve of the election, November 5:** Reeves, *President Kennedy*, 429; and E. W. Kenworthy, "Kennedy Casts Ballot in Boston and Passes the Day on Cape Cod," *New York Times*, November 7, 1962.

201 **The following morning, he voted:** Ibid.

201 **Kennedy emerged from the voting booth:** Ibid.

202 **House Democrats, meanwhile, had lost just:** Busch, *Horses in Midstream*, 146.

202 **Kennedy described himself as "heartened":** Ibid.

202 **"Losing California after losing":** Jason Schwartz, "55 Years Ago— The Last Press Conference," Richard Nixon Foundation, November 14, 2017.

202 **"Just think how much you're going to be missing":** *Richard Nixon: Speeches, Writings, Documents*, 112.

202 **"Unlike some people":** Ibid.

203 **"barring a miracle [Nixon's] political career":** Schwartz, "55 Years Ago—The Last Press Conference."

203   **"one of the great ladies of the century":** "President Kennedy Leads Nation Expressing Sorrow in Death of Mrs. Roosevelt," *New York Times*, November 8, 1962.

203   **"I listened . . . to your last press conference":** Reeves, *President Kennedy*, 433.

203   **"received a midterm vote of confidence":** Busch, *Horses in Midstream*, 147.

203   **"fit the times":** Bradlee and Cannon interview for *Newsweek*, JFKLibrary.org.

203   **"The outcome of the election demonstrated":** Busch, *Horses in Midstream*, 146.

"GRACE UNDER PRESSURE"

204   **"an updated, visual version of FDR's folksy":** "From the Rocking Chair."

204   **"I would say the problems are more difficult":** "Radio and Television Interview, 'After Two Years: A Conversation with the President': Part 1, 17 December 1962," JFKLibrary.org.

205   **The rocking chair in which Kennedy sat:** "From the Rocking Chair."

205   **Jackie Kennedy bought more than a dozen:** E. L. Hamilton, "Youthful President JFK Relied on Old-Fashioned Rocking Chairs to Relieve Back Pain," *Vintage News*, May 9, 2018.

205   **Determined to maintain an athletic physique:** Jayna Taylor-Smith, "The Weird Thing JFK Never Traveled Without," *Reader's Digest*, updated February 8, 2021.

205   **"Whether it is the astronaut exploring":** "The Federal Government Takes on Physical Fitness," JFKLibrary.org; and Reeves, *President Kennedy*, 576.

206   **his back vertebrae likely started deteriorating:** Lawrence K. Altman and Todd S. Purdum, "In JFK File, Hidden Illness, Pain and Pills," *New York Times*, November 17, 2002.

206   **"How's your aching back?":** "News Conference 40, August 1, 1962," JFKLibrary.org.

206   **"I wish I had more good times":** Jacqueline Kennedy, *Historic Conversations*, 21.

206   **She recalled the "pathetic":** Ibid.

206   **"No one who has the real Addison's":** Schlesinger, *Thousand Days*, 19.

206   **"a distinction between true Addison's":** Altman and Purdum, "In JFK File, Hidden Illness, Pain and Pills."

207   **"excellent" health:** Ibid.; and Robert Dallek, "The Medical Ordeals of JFK," *Atlantic*, November 5, 2013.

207   **"astounding vitality":** Ibid.; and O'Brien, *John F. Kennedy*, 756.

207   **In order to prevent back movement:** Altman and Purdum, "In JFK File, Hidden Illness, Pain and Pills."

207 **To endure news conferences and interviews:** Dallek, "Medical Ordeals of JFK."

207 **"I don't care if it's horse piss":** Ibid.

207 **Kennedy enlisted a legion of medical:** Ibid.

207 **For pain: codeine, Demerol, or methadone:** Altman and Purdum, "In JFK File, Hidden Illness, Pain and Pills."

208 **During times of extreme stress:** Dallek, "Medical Ordeals of JFK."

208 **"Judging from the tape recordings made":** Ibid.

208 **To be sure, the medications seemed to have:** Ibid.

208 **"That's not my face":** Collier and Horowitz, *Kennedys*, 290.

208 **"Vain as always":** Bradlee, *Conversations with Kennedy*, "WASPs go in more for stealing" (digital version).

208 **"Suffering doesn't ennoble, it embitters":** Jacqueline Kennedy, *Historic Conversations*, 102.

208 **" 'Why does this all happen to me?' ":** Ibid.

209 **"He never uttered a word of self-pity":** Altman and Purdum, "In JFK File, Hidden Illness, Pain and Pills."

209 **"He is very restless owing to his back":** O'Brien, *John F. Kennedy*, 756.

209 **"While I was not aware of the exact details":** Ibid.

209 **"that most admirable of human virtues":** John F. Kennedy, *Profiles in Courage*, 1.

209 **"grace under pressure":** Ibid.

209 **Though Hemingway declined to respond:** Stacey Chandler, "JFK & Hemingway: Beyond Grace Under Pressure," July 20, 2018, JFKLibrary.org.

210 **"the seat of all power":** Bradlee and Cannon interview for *Newsweek*, JFKLibrary.org.

210 **"He loved being where the action was":** Dallek, *Unfinished Life*, 632.

BIRMINGHAM

213 **"I guess that's Birmingham down below":** "Man of the Year," *Time*, January 3, 1963.

213 **"In 1963, there arose a great Negro disappointment":** Ibid.

214 **The state's largest city, with a population of:** "Birmingham, Alabama, Population 2020," World Population Review, worldpopulationreview.com.

214 **"the most thoroughly segregated city":** Martin Luther King, Jr., "Letter from Birmingham Jail."

214 **The city had banned a book featuring black:** Oates, *Let the Trumpet Sound*, 210; and O'Brien, *John F. Kennedy*, 834.

214 **"a moral witness to give our community a chance":** *Martin Luther King, Jr., Encyclopedia*, "Birmingham Campaign," Martin Luther King, Jr., Research and Education Institute, Stanford University.

214 **"a year that civil rights was displaced":** Schlesinger, *Thousand Days*, 950.

214 **"needed a victory":** Lewis, *Walking with the Wind*, 195.

215 **"a badge of honor":** "Birmingham Campaign," Stanford.

215 **"Go where Mahatma goes"**: Oates, *Let the Trumpet Sound*, 216–17.

215 **"Martin Luther King of economics"**: David Stout, "A. G. Gaston, 103, a Champion of Black Economic Advances," *New York Times*, January 20, 1996.

215 **"It doesn't do any good to arrive"**: Ibid.

215 **"A Poorly Timed Protest"**: Bass, *Blessed Are the Peacemakers*, 105.

216 **"King is so hot that it's like Marx coming"**: Thomas, *Robert Kennedy*, 250.

216 **"year of great progress on civil rights"**: RFK Report on Civil Rights, submitted January 24, 1963, JFKLibrary.org.

216 **"not only in the South . . . but throughout"**: Ibid.

216 **"Get them out of here"**: Thomas, *Robert Kennedy*, 241.

217 **"more progress"**: "Special Message on Civil Rights, 28 February 1963," JFKLibrary.org.

217 **"no public outcry"**: O'Brien, *John F. Kennedy*, 834.

217 **"They were putting a toe in the water"**: Roy Wilkins, Oral History, August 13, 1964, JFK #1, JFKLibrary.org.

217 **"moral witness"**: "Birmingham Campaign," Stanford.

217 **In the early morning hours**: Oates, *Let the Trumpet Sound*, 219.

218 **After rallying followers at a mass meeting**: Lewis, *Walking with the Wind*, 195.

218 **"the deepest quiet"**: Oates, *Let the Trumpet Sound*, 220.

218 **"I don't know what will happen"**: "Birmingham Campaign," Stanford.

218 **On Good Friday, April 12**: Foster Hailey, "Dr. King Arrested at Birmingham," *New York Times*, April 13, 1962.

218 **"a nightmare of despair"**: Oates, *Let the Trumpet Sound*, 221.

219 **"not in the streets"**: Stout, "A. G. Gaston."

219 **In the murkiness of his small cell**: Oates, *Let the Trumpet Sound*, 229–30.

219 **"paternally believe [they] can set a timetable"**: Martin Luther King, Jr., "Letter from Birmingham Jail."

220 **King and Abernathy were released from jail**: Stout, "A. G. Gaston."

220 **A group of more than nine hundred students**: Foster Hailey, "Dogs and Hoses Repulse Negroes at Birmingham," *New York Times*, May 4, 1963.

220 **"Look at those niggers run"**: Mann, *When Freedom Would Triumph*, 145.

220 **"Don't worry about your children"**: Ibid., 145–46.

220 **"Like the rest of America . . . [I] was absolutely stunned"**: Lewis, *Walking with the Wind*, 197.

221 **"We have the impression"**: Reeves, *President Kennedy*, 488.

221 **It made him "sick"**: Schlesinger, *Thousand Days*, 959.

221 **"I am not asking for patience"**: Ibid.

221 **As he ascended the steps of the state capitol**: Thomas, *Robert Kennedy*, 244.

222 **"The Negroes of this country may never"**: James Baldwin, *New Yorker*, November 10, 1962.

222 "The Root of the Negro Problem": "The Root of the Negro Problem," *Time*, May 17, 1963.

222 Baldwin and the "rowdy" group: Thomas, *Robert Kennedy*, 244.

222 "put it like it was": Frederking, *Reconstructing Social Justice*, 149–50.

222 What Smith was trying to convey: Schlesinger, *Thousand Days*, 962.

222 Bobby sat down reeling, trying to collect himself: Frederking, *Reconstructing Social Justice*, 149–50.

222 As Baldwin took in the attorney general's words: Thomas, *Robert Kennedy*, 244; and Sidey, *John F. Kennedy, President*, 331.

223 Though the meeting lasted three hours: Schlesinger, *Thousand Days*, 963.

223 "After Baldwin": Thomas, *Robert Kennedy*, 245.

223 Initially, Bobby seethed: Ibid.

223 If he had been born Black in America: Ibid.

223 "getting an almost impossible reputation": O'Brien, *John F. Kennedy*, 836.

223 "hopeless": Adam Clymer, "When Presidential Words Led to Swift Action," *New York Times*, June 8, 2013.

223 "around town in a big Cadillac, smoking": O'Brien, *John F. Kennedy*, 836.

224 "outniggered": Lewis, *Walking with the Wind*, 196.

224 "be present to bar the entrance of any Negro": Schlesinger, *Thousand Days*, 965.

224 Another 1,600 troops were put on standby: Reeves, *President Kennedy*, 520.

224 "willingly submit to illegal usurpation": Alabama Department of Archives and History, "George C. Wallace's School House Door Speech," al.com.

224 "I want to go on television tonight": Reeves, *President Kennedy*, 521.

225 "He urged it, he felt it, he understood it": O'Brien, *John F. Kennedy*, 838.

225 "cautious, truly cautious on civil rights": John Lewis, Oral History.

225 Bobby urged his brother to augment the speech: O'Brien, *John F. Kennedy*, 838.

225 "with a moral issue": "Radio and Television Report to the American People on Civil Rights, June 11, 1963," JFKLibrary.org.

226 "Words at great moments of history are deeds": Moran, *Showing How*, 97.

226 "moral passion": Steven Levingston, "John F. Kennedy, Martin Luther King, Jr. and the Phone Call That Changed History," *Time*, June 20, 2017.

226 "Can you believe that white man not only stepped": Jonathan Rieder, "The Day President Kennedy Embraced Civil Rights—and the Story Behind It," *Atlantic*, June 11, 2013.

226 "a compassionate appeal, man-to-man, heart-to-heart": Roy Wilkins, Oral History, August 13, 1964, JFK #1, JFKLibrary.org.

226 **He was carrying T-shirts that read "Jim Crow":** "Life and Death in Jackson," *Time*, June 21, 1963.

LYNDON

227 **"I dreamed about 1960 the other night":** O'Brien, *John F. Kennedy*, 424.

228 **"Now what do we do?":** Unger and Unger, *LBJ*, 244.

228 **"I think everyone was disappointed":** Jacqueline Kennedy, *Historic Conversations*, 85–86.

229 **"I know all the other candidates pretty well":** Stewart Alsop, "The New President," *Saturday Evening Post*, December 14, 1963.

229 **"a man of enormous ambition":** Sorensen, *Counselor*, 241.

229 **"I remember [LBJ's] name":** Edward M. Kennedy, Oral History Interview III, January 21, 1970, LBJ Library.

229 **"I have the feeling that Joe Kennedy":** Lyndon B. Johnson, Oral History Interview, August 6, 1969, LBJ Library.

229 **In fact, the Kennedy patriarch expressed:** Sweig, *Lady Bird Johnson*, 5.

230 **Additionally, he reminded delegates:** W. H. Lawrence, "Johnson Is Nominated for Vice President; Kennedy Picks Him to Placate the South," *New York Times*, July 15, 1960.

230 **Though in January Kennedy said his pick:** Interview with Ben Bradlee and James M. Cannon for *Newsweek*.

230 **"We can carry . . . no southern state":** Hardesty, *Johnson Years*, 136–37.

231 **According to Bobby, in the last:** Unger and Unger, *LBJ*, 245–46.

231 **"raise hell," he recalled saying, "The only":** Lyndon B. Johnson, Oral History Interview.

231 **"Look, let's don't kid ourselves":** Hardesty, *Johnson Years*, 136–37.

232 **"Clare, I looked it up: one out":** Harrigan, *Big, Wonderful Thing*, 687.

232 **"the most insignificant office":** Jaime Fuller, "Here Are a Bunch of Awful Things Vice Presidents Have Said About Being No. 2," *Washington Post*, October 3, 2014.

232 **"a bucket of warm piss":** Ibid.

232 **"The vice president is generally like":** Lyndon B. Johnson, Oral History Interview.

232 **"I wish you'd ask the president":** Melody Barnes (host), *LBJ and the Great Society*, "The Great Unveiling," PRX, February–March 2020.

233 **"the kind of uninhibited young pro":** Geoffrey C. Ward, "A One-Sided Johnson," *American Heritage*, July–August, 1990.

233 **"Uncle Cornpone":** Unger and Unger, *LBJ*, 256.

233 **"like a pebble in [his] shoe":** Peter Grier, "JFK Assassination: Three Feuds in Dallas," *Christian Science Monitor*, November 19, 2013.

233 **scorned them in return as "Harvards":** Ibid., 256.

233 **"I spent years of my life when":** Ibid.

234 **"watch over [the Johnsons] and make sure":** Unger and Unger, *LBJ*, 258.

234 **"saw any indication of anything but friendship":** Interview with Walter Cronkite, "LBJ: Transition and Tragedy," conducted on September 2, 1969, and airing on CBS, May 2, 1970.

234 **"a tormented personality":** Harrigan, *Big Wonderful Thing*, 740.

234 **"a harder personality than his brother":** "Bobby Kennedy: Is He 'the Assistant President'?."

234 **"I can't stand the bastard":** Caro, *Passage to Power*, 244.

235 **"It was southwestern exaggeration":** Dallek, *Lyndon B. Johnson*, 139.

235 **"lies all the time":** Dallek, *Unfinished Life*, 174–75.

235 **"Bob just tore in":** Thomas, *Robert Kennedy*, 245.

235 **For his part, Johnson saw Bobby:** Farquhar, *Treasury of Great American Scandals*, chap. 10 (digital edition).

235 **"Bobby elbowed me out":** Lyndon Johnson, Oral History Interview.

235 **In a February 1963 article:** "The Vice-Presidency: Seen, Not Heard," *Time*, February 1, 1963.

236 **George Reedy, one of his press secretaries:** David M. Shribman, "LBJ's Gettysburg Address," *New York Times*, May 24, 2013.

236 **She saw its possibilities:** Ibid.

237 **Shortly after assuming the vice presidency:** Document signed by Lyndon and Lady Bird Johnson for purchase of home on 4720 Dexter St., NW, Washington, signed on April 3, 1961, owned by Gary D. Eyler, Old Colony Shop, Alexandria, Virginia.

237 **"emotional and intellectual involvement":** Oates, *Let the Trumpet Sound*, 274.

237 **"One hundred years ago":** "May 30, 1963: Remarks at Gettysburg on Civil Rights," UVA Miller Center, millercenter.org.

"TO TURN THE WORLD AWAY FROM WAR"

239 **"The thought of women and children":** O'Brien, *John F. Kennedy*, 550.

239 **"It is insane that two men":** "Nuclear Test Ban Theory," JFKLibrary.org.

240 **he and Khrushchev both faced similar:** Jeffrey Frank, "What Every Candidate Could Learn from JFK," *New Yorker*, February 10, 2016.

240 **"He would like to prevent a nuclear war":** Dallek, *Unfinished Life*, 618.

240 **"misunderstanding":** Reeves, *President Kennedy*, 511.

240 **"But . . . the next step is up to him":** Ibid.

241 **"the most important topic on earth":** "Commencement Address at American University, Washington, D.C., June 10, 1963," JFKLibrary.org.

242 **Importantly, though, the Kremlin had heard Kennedy:** Sidey, *John F. Kennedy, President*, 339; and Dallek, *Unfinished Life*, 621.

242 **"both personal reassurance and a weapon":** Schlesinger, *Thousand Days*, 904.

242 **"courageous":** Henry Raymount, "Khrushchev, in Letter for Archives, Extolled John F. Kennedy as a Statesman," *New York Times*, August 18, 1970.

242 **"pushing back on communism":** Ibid.

243 **"It is mild here compared to what it means":** Sidey, *John F. Kennedy, President*, 340.

243 **On the morning of June 26, he and Kennedy arrived:** Reeves, *President Kennedy*, 535.

243 **"the greatest reception the president had received":** Arthur J. Olson, "President Hailed by Over a Million in Berlin," *New York Times*, June 26, 1963.

243 **Estimates had it that 60 percent:** Dallek, *Unfinished Life*, 624.

243 **"No one is ever prepared for the Wall":** Schlesinger, *Thousand Days*, 884.

243 **Kennedy had hoped to peer into East Berlin:** Olson, "President Hailed by Over a Million in Berlin."

243 **In the distance, well beyond the hundred-yard area:** Reeves, *President Kennedy*, 535.

243 **He asked Major General James Polk, the American:** Olson, "President Hailed by Over a Million in Berlin"; and Reeves, *President Kennedy*, 535.

244 **"This is terrible":** Jesse Greenspan, "JFK Tells Berliners That He Is One of Them, 50 Years Ago Today," History.com, June 26, 2013.

244 **Aided by a translator, Kennedy wrote out the words:** Thomas Putnam, "The Real Meaning of *Ich Bin ein Berliner*," *Atlantic*, JFK Issue, September 19, 2013.

244 **"clapping, waving, crying as if it were the second":** Schlesinger, *Thousand Days*, 884.

244 **"If I told them to tear down the Berlin Wall":** Alan Brinkley, *John F. Kennedy*, 130.

244 **"Does this mean Germany can one day":** Dallek and Golway, *Let Every Nation Know*, 192.

244 **"Two thousand years ago, the proudest boast":** "Remarks of President John F. Kennedy at Rudolf Wilde Plaza, Berlin, June 26, 1963," JFKLibrary.org.

245 **"Other than *ask not*, they were the most famous":** Putnam, "Real Meaning of *Ich Bin ein Berliner*."

245 **"We'll never have another day like this":** Reeves, *President Kennedy*, 537.

246 **"So, let us try to turn the world away":** "Radio and Television Address to the American People on the Nuclear Test Ban Treaty, July 26, 1963," JFKLibrary.org.

SEPTEMBER SONG

247 **At 11:43 a.m., Evelyn Lincoln, Kennedy's secretary:** Thurston Clarke, "A Death in the First Family," *Vanity Fair*, July 1, 2013.

248 **"You'd better haul your ass back":** Steven Levingston, "For John and Jackie Kennedy, the Death of a Son May Have Brought Them Closer," *Washington Post*, October 24, 2013.

248 **"I'm never there when she needs me"**: O'Brien, *John F. Kennedy*, 500.

248 **The infant, doctors told him, was struggling**: Levingston, "For John and Jackie Kennedy, the Death of a Son."

248 **Kennedy was able to briefly**: Gloria Negri, "Whole World Taken by Littlest Kennedy," *Boston Globe*, August 8, 1963; and Levingston, "For John and Jackie Kennedy, the Death of a Son."

248 **"Nothing must happen to Patrick"**: Janet Auchincloss, Oral History.

249 **"Mr. President, we're trying to save"**: Lawrence K. Altman, "A Kennedy Baby's Life and Death," *New York Times*, July 29, 2015.

249 **"He is only 4 pounds, 10 and a half ounces"**: Negri, "Whole World Taken by Littlest Kennedy."

249 **Early Friday morning**: Sally Bedell Smith, "Private Camelot," *Vanity Fair*, July 2004.

249 **"He put up quite a fight"**: Ibid.

249 **Kennedy then retreated to the quiet**: Ibid.

249 **That morning, Kennedy returned**: Jacqueline Kennedy, *Historic Conversations*, 185.

249 **It was only the third time Jackie had**: Ibid.

249 **"There's one thing I couldn't stand"**: Smith, "Private Camelot."

249 **"We must not create an atmosphere"**: Janet Auchincloss, Oral History.

250 **"They'd certainly been through as much"**: Ibid.

250 **"There had always been this wall between them"**: Andersen, *These Few Precious Days*, 255.

250 **"reciprocal forbearance"**: Smith, "Private Camelot."

250 **"re-attach . . . all the lucky things"**: Ibid.

250 **"Jack was getting to the point"**: Collier and Horowitz, *Kennedys*, 310.

250 **"There are two naked women"**: Ibid.

251 **The president sat with him**: Ibid.

251 **On the evening of September 6, the family and close friends**: Andersen, *These Few Precious Days*, 284.

251 **"It was all part of his elegant fatalism"**: Ibid.

252 **"How do you think Lyndon would be"**: Collier and Horowitz, *Kennedys*, 130.

THE MARCH

253 **The president shifted uncomfortably**: John Lewis, Oral History.

253 **"a long, hot summer"**: Sidey, *John F. Kennedy, President*, 337.

253 **"serious fight"**: O'Brien, *John F. Kennedy*, 847.

253 **"The vice president and I know"**: Ibid.

254 **"already in the streets"**: Ibid.

254 **"Mr. President," he said in a rich baritone**: "Transcript: John Lewis on the March on Washington," *Washington Post*, August 23, 2013.

254 **"You could tell by the body language"**: John Lewis, Oral History, JFKLibrary.org.

254 **"peaceful and nonviolent"**: Ibid.

254 **"Frankly, I have yet to see any"**: O'Brien, *John F. Kennedy*, 847.

254 **"Including the attorney general":** Ibid.
254 **"Well, we all have our problems":** Lewis, *Walking with the Wind*, 207.
255 **"We had a meaningful and productive meeting":** "Transcript: John Lewis on the March."
255 **More than half of Americans believed racial:** Andrew Kohut, "From the Archives: JFK's America," Pew Research Center, July 5, 2019.
255 **Immediately after he had proposed:** Ibid.
255 **Not surprisingly, his approval numbers:** Ibid.
255 **"Do you think we did the right thing":** O'Brien, *John F. Kennedy*, 846.
255 **"the largest outpouring of Americans":** A. Philip Randolph to JFK, August 13, 1963, JFKLibrary.org.
256 **"I assume you know you're under":** Goduti, *Robert F. Kennedy and the Shaping of Civil Rights*, 211.
256 **"a conscious agent of the Soviet conspiracy":** Ibid.
256 **"If they shoot you down, they'll shoot":** Ibid.
256 **The preeminent national leader:** Drew Hansen, "Mahalia Jackson, and King's Improvisation," *New York Times*, August 27, 2013.
257 **"There's no way in the world, Martin":** Oates, *Let the Trumpet Sound*, 257.
257 **"Look, Martin":** Ibid.
257 **"about 25,000":** Hansen, "Mahalia Jackson, and King's Improvisation."
257 **"Gentlemen, everything is going exactly":** Ibid.
257 **Just under 6,000 police and 4,000 troops:** Sidey, *John F. Kennedy, President*, 337.
258 **"the moral leader of the nation":** Jakoubek, *Martin Luther King, Jr.*, 81.
258 **"We have come to this hallowed spot":** "'I Have a Dream,' Address at the March on Washington for Jobs and Freedom," Martin Luther King, Jr., Research and Education Institute, Stanford University.
258 **"Tell them about the dream, Martin!":** Hansen, "Mahalia Jackson, and King's Improvisation."
258 **"All of a sudden, this thing came out":** Jakoubek, *Martin Luther King, Jr.*, 81–82.
258 **"I have a dream that my four":** "'I Have a Dream,'" Stanford University.
259 **"He's damn good":** Reeves, *President Kennedy*, 584.
259 **"Washington may not have changed":** James Reston, "I Have a Dream . . . ," *New York Times*, August 29, 1963.
259 **"the cause of 20,000,000 Negroes has been":** Tom Wicker, "President Meets with March Leaders," *New York Times*, August 29, 1963.
259 **"I have a dream":** Reeves, *President Kennedy*, 584.
259 **"It was finally over":** Lewis, *Walking with the Wind*, 229.
259 **The House and Senate had both recessed:** "The Senate and the March on Washington," U.S. Senate, cop.senate.gov.
259 **Kennedy was pleased when he heard:** Reeves, *President Kennedy*, 584.
260 **"appeared to have left much of Congress":** Warren Weaver, Jr., "Congress Cordial But Not Swayed," *New York Times*, August 29, 1963.
260 **"nothing less than a crusade to win approval":** Reeves, *President Kennedy*, 585.

260 **"He could never have passed that bill"**: Author interview with Andrew Young, November 25, 2020.

260 **"Kennedy was not naïve"**: Michael O'Donnell, "How LBJ Saved the Civil Rights Act," *Atlantic*, April 2014.

260 **"It has hurt John F. Kennedy"**: O'Brien, *John F. Kennedy*, 258.

260 **"I may lose the election because of this"**: Goduti, *Robert F. Kennedy and the Shaping of Civil Rights*, 211.

261 **"This is not a matter on which you can"**: "News Conference 61, September 12, 1963," JFKLibrary.org.

261 **"to destroy the man"**: Rick Klein, "Jacqueline Kennedy on Rev. Martin Luther King, Jr.," *ABC News*, December 8, 2011.

261 **"We must mark him now"**: Schlesinger, *Robert Kennedy and His Times*, 353.

A COUP IN VIETNAM

262 ***"Nam mo amita Buddha"***: Jacobs, *Cold War Mandarin*, 147.

262 **Some 350 monks**: Ibid.

262 **"Jesus Christ!"**: Ibid., 149.

263 **"Before closing my eyes to Buddha"**: Cohen, *Two Days in June*, 187.

263 **"I would clap my hands at seeing another"**: O'Brien, *John F. Kennedy*, 859.

264 **In fact, the situation in Vietnam**: Lawrence, *Vietnam War*, 75.

264 **Kennedy was deeply concerned about the matter**: Henry Cabot Lodge, Jr., Oral History, JFKLibrary.org.

264 **"referred to the picture, and to what was"**: Ibid.

264 **"We're going to have to do something"**: Browne, *Muddy Boots and Red Socks*, 12.

264 **"I don't agree with those who say"**: *Foreign Relations of the United States, 1961–1964*, vol. 5, document 50, "Interview with the President."

264 **"to win or lose"**: Ibid.

265 **"the so-called domino theory"**: "Interview on NBC's 'Huntley-Brinkley Report,' 9 September 1963," JFKLibrary.org.

265 **"No, I believe it. . . . If South Vietnam went"**: Ibid.

265 **Kennedy's continued support stood in**: Lawrence, *Vietnam War*, 78–79.

265 **"We don't want to carry on a direct assault"**: "Interview on NBC's 'Huntley-Brinkley Report.'"

265 **"important changes and improvements"**: Alan Brinkley, *John F. Kennedy*, 192.

266 **"basically anti-American"**: "The Diem Coup," a recording of JFK's conversation with National Security Officials, August 26, 1963, UVA Miller Center, millercenter.org.

266 **"we're on the road to disaster"**: Ibid.

266 **"there was no power on earth"**: Lodge, Oral History, JFKLibrary.org.

266 **"not to thwart"**: Ibid.

267 **"We would like to have the option"**: Dallek, *Unfinished Life*, 681.

267 **"however unjustifiably"**: Ibid.

267 **"I do not feel well enough informed"**: Alan Brinkley, *John F. Kennedy*, 143.

267 **"American inspired and manipulated"**: Ibid.

267 **"putting the future of the country and really"**: "The Diem Coup," White House recording of RFK, October 29, 1963, UVA Miller Center, millercenter.org.

267 **"would get the blame for it"**: Ibid.

268 **The U.S. Embassy was given only four minutes**: John Prados, "JFK and the Diem Coup," National Archives, November 5, 2003.

268 **"with a look of shock and dismay on his face"**: Dallek, *Unfinished Life*, 683.

268 **"had not seen him so depressed"**: Schlesinger, *Thousand Days*, 997.

268 **"I feel that we must bear a good deal"**: "JFK's Memoir Dictation on the Assassination of Diem," UVA Miller Center, millercenter.org.

269 **"inexorably"**: John Aloysius Farrell, "He Told Them So," *New York Times*, October 12, 2003.

269 **"I'll be damned as a communist appeaser"**: O'Brien, *John F. Kennedy*, 866.

269 **"directed toward preparing Republic of Vietnam"**: Tim Weiner, "Kennedy Had a Plan for Early Exit in Vietnam," *New York Times*, December 23, 1997.

270 **Bobby replied flatly, "No"**: O'Brien, *John F. Kennedy*, 866.

270 **"to bring Americans home"**: "News Conference 64, 14 November 1963," JFKLibrary.org.

270 **"I can't believe that the Congress"**: Ibid.

270 **"the most damaging event, certainly"**: "Interview on NBC's 'Huntley-Brinkley Report.'"

271 **"If we have to fight, let's fight in Vietnam"**: Moyar, *Triumph Forsaken*, 129.

271 **"How does a president explain a 'defeat'"**: Alan Brinkley, *John F. Kennedy*, 146.

271 **What we do know indisputably is that the war in Vietnam**: Rodney H. Spector, "Vietnam War: 1954–1975," *Encyclopedia Britannica*.

DALLAS

272 **"Oh, probably sell real estate"**: O'Brien, *John F. Kennedy*, 901.

272 **Perhaps half-kiddingly, he suggested to Ben Bradlee**: Jacqueline Kennedy, *Historic Conversations*, 129–30.

272 **In more serious moments he mentioned**: O'Brien, *John F. Kennedy*, 901.

272 **"President of the West"**: Jacqueline Kennedy, *Historic Conversations*, 130.

273 **"they made a rule that would keep you here"**: Ibid., 129–30.

273 **As they discussed Kennedy's prospects**: Sidey, *John F. Kennedy, President*, 350.

273 **The economy was humming along**: Ibid., 351.

273 **Kennedy's approval rating stood at a hardy 59**: Andrew Kohut, "JFK's America," Pew Research Center, July 15, 2019.

273   **"Let's face it, after these many months":** William Styron, "The Short, Classy Voyage of JFK," *Esquire*, September 1983.

274   **Just as encouraging were Gallup Polls:** Dallek, *Unfinished Life*, 686.

274   **He believed that had the New York governor:** Jacqueline Kennedy, *Historic Conversations*, 345.

274   **fall for "that God and country stuff":** Dallek, *Unfinished Life*, 690.

274   **"a low-yield atomic bomb on the Chinese":** Jamieson, *Packaging the Presidency*, 203.

274   **"one into the men's room of the Kremlin":** Ibid.

274   **They helped to explain a March 1963 poll:** Andrew Kohut, "JFK's America."

275   **For Kennedy, a face-off with Goldwater:** Jacqueline Kennedy, *Historic Conversations*, 345.

275   **how "tough" the campaign would be:** Dallek, *Unfinished Life*, 687.

275   **He had seen a steady rise in his disapproval rating:** Ibid.

275   **"Change always disturbs":** "News Conference 61, November 12, 1963," JFKLibrary.org.

275   **"The fact of the matter is that both of these":** Hugh Sidey, "The Presidency," *Time*, November 15, 1963.

275   **"I know he's unhappy in the vice presidency":** Bobby Baker, Oral History, October 23, 1974, LBJ Library.

276   **"Why would I do a thing like that?":** O'Brien, *John F. Kennedy*, 900.

276   **"Hell," Johnson said, "if he wanted to":** Author interview with Larry Temple, August 8, 2020.

276   **As he geared up for 1964:** Author interview with Ben Barnes, July 14, 2020.

276   **Connally opposed the trip:** Author interview with Larry Temple; interview with Ben Barnes; and Reeves, *President Kennedy*, 661.

277   **But when the Kennedy camp pushed:** Author interview with Larry Temple.

277   **Thomas informed him that it was raining:** Reeves, *President Kennedy*, 661.

277   **Originally slated for 8:45 a.m.:** Ronnie Dugger, "The Last Voyage of Mr. Kennedy," *Texas Observer*, November 29, 1963.

277   **"There are no faint hearts":** Ibid.

278   **"Two years ago, I introduced myself":** Ibid.

278   **Reporters surveying those who had come:** Sidey, *John F. Kennedy, President*, 353.

278   **A woman hit him over the head:** "Texas: A Disgraced City," *Time*, November 1, 1963.

278   **"Dallas has been disgraced":** Ibid.

279   **Just prior to the election in 1960:** Cragg Hines, "Racists Spat on Lady Bird," *Times Daily*, July 13, 2007.

279   **"soft on Communists, fellow-travelers and ultra-leftists":** Museum exhibit, Sixth Floor Museum at Dealey Plaza, Dallas, Texas.

279   **"We're heading into nut country today":** Dallek, *Unfinished Life*, 693.

279   **But the visit to Dallas looked promising:** "Assassination Timeline," Sixth Floor Museum at Dealey Plaza, jfk.org.

279   **A hundred and fifty thousand people lined up:** Dugger, "Last Voyage of Mr. Kennedy."

279   **"absorbed":** Ibid.

280   **"You can't say that Dallas isn't friendly":** Hugh Sidey, "Nation: The Assassination," *Time*, November 29, 1963.

280   **"Jack!" the first lady cried out:** Ibid.

280   **It arrived at 12:35:** "Assassination Timeline," Sixth Floor Museum at Dealey Plaza, jfk.org.

280   **Kennedy was stripped of his jacket:** "Dallas Doctor Malcolm Perry, Who Worked on JFK and Oswald, Dies at 80," *Dallas Morning News*, December 8, 2009.

280   **Malcolm Perry, the thirty-four-year-old doctor:** Ibid.

280   **Perry ordered a nurse to get three:** Jimmy Breslin, "A Death in Emergency Room No. One," *Saturday Evening Post*, December 14, 1963.

281   **Before aiding the other doctors, he approached:** Ibid.

281   **"Would you like to leave, ma'am?":** Ibid.

281   **She didn't cry as the doctors fought:** Ibid.

281   **She didn't cry as they stopped:** Ibid.

281   **She held her emotions at bay:** Caroline Graham, "As I Fought to Save JFK, Jackie Slipped Her Ring on to His Finger," *Daily Mail*, November 9, 2013.

281   **"Let us stand together with renewed confidence":** "RNG Draft 11/22/63," Papers of Richard Goodwin, courtesy of Doris Goodwin, Concord, Massachusetts.

"LET US CONTINUE"

283   **"It will never get through":** Merle Miller, *Lyndon*, 337.

283   **"Well, what the hell's the presidency for?":** Ibid.

283   **At 12:30 p.m., five days to the minute:** "Daily Diary, November 27, 1963," LBJ Library, lbjlibrary.org.

283   **"No memorial oration or eulogy":** Lyndon Johnson, "Joint Speech to Congress," November 27, 1963.

EPILOGUE

285   **"So now he is a legend":** William Styron, "The Short, Classy Voyage of JFK."

286   **"A man may die, nations may rise":** "John F. Kennedy Quotations," JFKLibrary.org.

286   **"I see the past more clearly now":** Sorensen, *Counselor*, 524.

287   **"No one has a right to grade":** Ted Widmer, "Profile in Courage," *New York Times*, June 8, 2003.

287   **C-SPAN's 2021 "Presidential Historians Survey":** "Presidential Historians Survey 2021," C-SPAN, www.c-span.org/presidentsurvey2021/.

BIBLIOGRAPHY

Albright, Madeleine. *Fascism: A Warning.* New York: HarperCollins, 2018.

Ambrose, Stephen. *Eisenhower: Soldier and President.* New York: Simon & Schuster, 1990.

Andersen, Christopher. *These Few Precious Days: The Final Year of Jack with Jackie.* New York: Gallery Books, 2013.

Arsenault, Raymond. *Freedom Riders: 1961 and the Struggle for Racial Justice.* New York: Oxford University Press, 2006.

Associated Press. *The Torch Is Passed: The Associated Press Story of the Death of a President.* New York: Associated Press, 1963.

Bass, S. Jonathan. *Blessed Are the Peacemakers: Martin Luther King, Jr., Eight White Religious Leaders, and the "Letter from Birmingham Jail."* Baton Rouge: Louisiana State University Press, 2001.

Beschloss, Michael. *American Heritage Illustrated History of the Presidents.* New York: Crown Publishers, 2000.

———. *The Crisis Years: Kennedy and Khrushchev 1960–1963.* New York: Open Road Media, 2016.

———. *Kennedy and Roosevelt: The Uneasy Alliance.* New York: W. W. Norton, 1980.

Black, Allida Mae. *The First Ladies of the United States of America.* Washington, D.C.: White House Historical Association, 2009.

Blum, John Morton. *Years of Discord: American Politics and Society, 1961–1974.* New York: W. W. Norton, 1991.

Boller, Paul F., Jr. *Presidential Anecdotes.* New York: Penguin, 1982.

Bradlee, Benjamin C. *Conversations with Kennedy.* New York: W. W. Norton, 1975.

———. *A Good Life: Newspapering and Other Adventures.* New York: Simon & Schuster, 1995.

Branch, Taylor. *The King Years: Historic Moments in the Civil Rights Movement.* New York: Simon & Schuster, 2013.

Brinkley, Alan. *John F. Kennedy. The American Presidents Series.* New York: Times Books, 2012.

Brinkley, Douglas. *American Moonshot.* New York: HarperCollins, 2019.

———. *Cronkite.* New York: HarperCollins, 2012.

Browne, Malcolm W. *Muddy Boots and Red Socks: A Reporter's Life.* New York: Times Books, 1993.

Burr, William, and Hector L. Montford, eds. *The Making of the Limited Test Ban Treaty.* Washington, D.C.: National Security Archive, 2003.

Busch, Andrew E. *Horses in Midstream: U.S. Midterm Elections and Their Consequences.* Pittsburgh, Penn.: University of Pittsburgh Press, 1999.

Carelton, Don, and Walter Cronkite. *Conversations with Cronkite.* Austin, Tex.: Briscoe Center, 2010.

Caro, Robert. *The Passage of Power: The Years of Lyndon Johnson.* New York: Alfred A. Knopf, 2012.

Chaiken, Andrew. *A Man on the Moon: The Voyages of the Apollo Astronauts.* New York: Viking, 1994.

Clarke, Thurston. *Ask Not: The Inauguration of John F. Kennedy and the Speech That Changed America.* New York: Henry Holt, 2004.

Clutterbuck, Richard. *International Crisis and Conflict.* London: Macmillan, 1993.

Cohen, Andrew. *Two Days in June: John F. Kennedy and the 48 Hours That Made History.* Toronto: McClelland & Stewart, 2014.

Collier, Peter, and David Horowitz. *The Kennedys: An American Drama.* New York: Summit Books, 1984.

Cronkite, Walter. *A Reporter's Life.* New York: Alfred A. Knopf, 1996.

Dallek, Robert. *Camelot's Court: Inside the Kennedy White House.* New York: HarperCollins, 2013.

———. An *Unfinished Life: John F. Kennedy 1917–1963.* New York: Oxford University Press, 2000.

———. *Lyndon B. Johnson: Portrait of a President.* New York: Oxford University Press, 2004.

Dallek, Robert, and Terry Golway. *Let Every Nation Know: John F. Kennedy in His Own Words.* Naperville, Ill.: Sourcebooks MediaFusion, 2006.

Dobbs, Michael. *One Minute to Midnight: Kennedy, Khrushchev, and Castro on the Brink of Nuclear War.* New York: Alfred A. Knopf, 2008.

Donald, David Herbert. *Lincoln.* New York: Simon & Schuster, 1995.

Duffy, Michael, and Nancy Gibbs. *The Presidents Club: Inside the World's Most Exclusive Fraternity.* New York: Simon & Schuster, 2012.

Duncan, Jason K. *John F. Kennedy: The Spirit of Cold War Liberalism.* New York: Routledge, 2014.

Eagles, Charles W. *The Price of Defiance: James Meredith and the Integration of Ole Miss.* Chapel Hill: University of North Carolina Press, 2009.

Eisenhower, David, and Julie Nixon Eisenhower. *Going Home to Glory: A Memoir of Life with Dwight D. Eisenhower, 1961–1969.* New York: Simon & Schuster, 2010.

Eisenhower, John. *Strictly Personal*. New York: Doubleday, 1974.

Farquhar, Michael. *A Treasury of Great American Scandals*. New York: Penguin, 2003.

Fischer, Heinz-Dietrich, ed. *Facets of the Vietnam War in the American Media: Pulitzer Prize Winning Articles, Books, Cartoons and Photos*. Zurich: Heinz-Dietrich Fischer, 2019.

Frederking, Lauretta Conklin. *Reconstructing Social Justice*. New York: Routledge, 2014.

Garrow, David J. *The FBI and Martin Luther King: From "Solo" to Memphis*. New York: Open Road Media, 2015.

Garthoff, Raymond L. *Reflections on the Cuban Missile Crisis*. Washington, D.C.: Brookings Institute, 1989.

Gitlin, Todd. *The Sixties: Years of Hope, Days of Rage*. New York: Bantam Books, 1987.

Goduti, Philip A., Jr. *Kennedy's Kitchen Cabinet and the Pursuit of Peace: The Shaping of American Foreign Policy, 1961–1963*. Jefferson, N.C.: McFarland, 2009.

———. *Robert F. Kennedy and the Shaping of Civil Rights, 1960–1964*. Jefferson, N.C.: McFarland, 2013.

Gonzalez, Servando. *The Nuclear Deception: Nikita Khrushchev and the Cuban Missile Crisis*. Oakland, Calif.: Spooks Books, 2002.

Goodwin, Richard N. *Remembering America: A Voice from the Sixties*. Boston: Little, Brown, 1988.

Gould, Lewis L. *The Modern American Presidency*. Lawrence: University of Kansas Press, 2003.

Graham, Katharine. *Personal History*. New York: Alfred A. Knopf, 2001.

Greene, Bob. *Fraternity: A Journey in Search of Five Presidents*. New York: Crown, 2004.

Greenstein, Fred I., ed. *Leadership in the Modern Presidency*. Cambridge, Mass.: Harvard University Press, 1988.

Hamilton, Nigel. *Reckless Youth*. London: Random House, 1992.

Hardesty, Robert L. *The Johnson Years: The Difference He Made*. Austin, Tex.: LBJ Library, 1993.

Harper, Brett. *Kennedy*. New York: New Word City, 2015.

Harrigan, Stephen. *Big, Wonderful Thing: A History of Texas*. Austin: University of Texas Press, 2019.

Haygood, Wil. *Showdown: Thurgood Marshall and the Supreme Court Nomination That Changed America*. New York: Alfred A. Knopf, 2015.

Hill, Clint, and Lisa McCubbin. *Mrs. Kennedy and Me: An Intimate Memoir*. New York: Gallery Books, 2013.

Hill, Kathleen Thompson, and Gerald N. Hill. *Encyclopedia of Federal Agencies and Commissions*. New York: Facts on File, 2014.

Jacobs, Seth. *Cold War Mandarin: Ngo Dinh Diem and the Origins of America's War in Vietnam: 1950–1963*. Lanham, Md.: Rowman & Littlefield, 2006.

Jakoubek, Robert. *Martin Luther King, Jr.: Civil Rights Leader*. Philadelphia: Turtleback, 2005.

Jamieson, Kathleen Hall. *Packaging the Presidency: A History and Criticism of Presidential Campaign Advertising*. Oxford, U.K.: Oxford University Press, 1984.

Jenkins, Carol, and Elizabeth Gardner Hines. *A. G. Gaston and the Making of a Black American Millionaire*. New York: Random House, 2003.

Johnson, Lady Bird. *White House Diary*. New York: Holt, Rinehart and Winston, 1970.

Johnson, Lyndon Baines. *The Vantage Point: Perspectives of the Presidency 1963–1969*. New York: Holt, Rinehart and Winston, 1971.

Kelly, Kitty. *Jackie Oh!* New York: Ballantine, 1979.

Kempe, Frederick. *Berlin 1961: Kennedy, Khrushchev, and the Most Dangerous Place on Earth*. New York: G. P. Putnam's Sons, 2011.

Kennedy, Jacqueline. *Jacqueline Kennedy: Historic Conversations on Life with John F. Kennedy, Interviews with Arthur M. Schlesinger, Jr*. New York: Hyperion, 2011.

Kennedy, John F. *The Letters of John F. Kennedy*. Edited by Martin W. Sandler. New York: Bloomsbury Press, 2013.

———. *Profiles in Courage*. New York: Harper, 1956.

———. *Public Papers of the Presidents of the United States: John F. Kennedy; Containing the Public Messages, Speeches, and Statements of the President, 1961–1963*. Washington, D.C.: U.S. Government Printing Office, 1962–64.

Kennedy, Robert F. *Thirteen Days: A Memoir of the Cuban Missile Crisis*. 1971. Reprinted with foreword by Arthur M. Schlesinger, Jr. New York: W. W. Norton, 1999.

Khrushchev, Nikita. *Khrushchev Remembers*. Boston: Little, Brown, 1970.

———. *The Memoirs of Nikita Khrushchev*. University Park: Pennsylvania State University Press, 2007.

Khrushchev, Sergei N. *Nikita Khrushchev and the Creation of a Superpower*. University Park: Pennsylvania State University Press, 2000.

King, Martin Luther, Jr. *Why We Can't Wait*. New York: Signet, 1964.

Klein, Edward. *All Too Human: The Love Story of Jack and Jackie Kennedy*. New York: Pocket Books, 1996.

Lawrence, Mark. *The Vietnam War: A Concise International History*. New York: Oxford University Press, 2008.

Leaming, Barbara. *Mrs. Kennedy: The Missing History of the Kennedy Years*. New York: Thorndike Press, 2001.

Lepore, Jill. *These Truths: A History of the United States*. New York: W. W. Norton, 2018.

Levingston, Steve. *Kennedy and King: The President, the Pastor, and the Battle Over Civil Rights*. New York: Hachette Books, 2017.

Lewis, John. *Walking with the Wind: A Memoir of the Movement*. New York: Simon & Schuster, 1998.

Maga, Timothy P. *The 1960s*. New York: Facts on File, 2003.

Mann, Robert. *When Freedom Would Triumph: The Civil Rights Struggle in Congress, 1954–1968*. Baton Rouge: Louisiana State University Press, 2007.

Matthews, Chris. *Jack Kennedy: Elusive Hero*. New York: Simon & Schuster, 2012.

McCullough, David. *Truman*. New York: Simon & Schuster, 1992.

McNamara, Robert S., with Brian VanDeMark. *In Retrospect: The Tragedy and Lessons of Vietnam*. New York: Times Books, 1995.

Meacham, Jon. *The Soul of America: The Battle for Our Better Angels*. New York: Random House, 2018.

Miller, Merle. *Lyndon: An Oral Biography*. New York: Putnam, 1980.

Miller, Richard L. *Under the Cloud: The Decades of Nuclear Testing*. The Woodlands, Tex.: Two-Sixty Press, 1991.

Moore, Kathryn. *The American President: A Complete History*. New York: Barnes & Noble, 2007.

Moran, Gabriel. *Showing How: The Art of Teaching*. New York: Continuum International Publishing Group, 1997.

Moyar, Mark. *Triumph Forsaken: The Vietnam War, 1954–1965*. Cambridge, UK: Cambridge University Press, 2006.

Naftali, Timothy J., Philip Zelikow, and Ernest R. May, eds. *The Presidential Recordings: John F. Kennedy: The Great Crises*. 3 vols. New York: W. W. Norton, 2001.

National Archives and Records Administration. *Kennedy's Inaugural Address of 1961: Milestone Documents of the National Archives*. Washington, D.C.: National Archives and Records Administration, 1987.

National Geographic Society. *National Geographic Eyewitness to the 20th Century*. Washington, D.C.: National Geographic Society, 1998.

Newfield, Jack. *Robert Kennedy: A Memoir*. New York: E. P. Dutton, 1969.

Nixon, Richard. *In the Arena: A Memoir of Victory, Defeat, and Renewal*. New York: Simon & Schuster, 1990.

———. *Richard Nixon: Speeches, Writings, Documents*. Edited by Rick Perlstein. Princeton, N.J.: Princeton University Press, 2008.

———. *RN: The Memoirs of Richard Nixon*. New York: Grosset & Dunlap, 1978.

———. *Six Crises*. Garden City, N.Y.: Doubleday, 1962.

Oates, Stephen B. *Let the Trumpet Sound: The Life of Martin Luther King, Jr.* New York: New American Library, 1982.

O'Brien, Michael. *John F. Kennedy: A Biography*. New York: Thomas Dunne Books, 2005.

O'Donnell, Kenneth P., and David F. Powers with Joe McCarthy. *"Johnny, We Hardly Knew Ye": Memories of John Fitzgerald Kennedy*. Boston: Little, Brown, 1972.

Parmet, Herbert S. *JFK: The Presidency of John F. Kennedy*. New York: Dial Press, 1983.

Patterson, James. *Grand Expectations: The United States 1945–1974*. New York: Oxford University Press, 1996.

Bibliography

Perrottet, Tony. *Cuba Libre! Che, Fidel, and the Improbable Revolution That Changed the World.* New York: Blue Rider Press, 2019.

Pitts, David. *Jack and Lem: The Untold Story of an Extraordinary Friendship.* New York: Carroll & Graf, 2007.

Reeves, Richard. *President Kennedy: Profile of Power.* New York: Simon & Schuster, 1993.

Reston, James. *Sketches in the Sand.* New York: Alfred A. Knopf, 1969.

Rowen, Hobart. *The Free Enterprisers: Kennedy, Johnson, and the Business Establishment.* New York: Putnam, 1964.

Rubin, Joan Shelley. *Songs of Ourselves: The Uses of Poetry in America.* Cambridge, Mass.: Belknap Press of Harvard University Press, 2007.

Safire, William., ed. *Lend Me Your Ears: Great Speeches in History.* New York: W. W. Norton, 1992.

Schlesinger, Arthur, Jr. *The Cycles of American History.* Boston: Houghton Mifflin, 1986.

———. *Robert Kennedy and His Times.* Boston: Houghton Mifflin, 1978.

———. *A Thousand Days: John F. Kennedy in the White House.* Boston: Houghton Mifflin, 1965.

Shaw, John T. *Rising Star, Setting Sun: Dwight D. Eisenhower, John F. Kennedy, and the Presidential Transition That Changed America.* New York: Pegasus Books, 2018.

Shesol, Jeff. *Mercury Rising: John Glenn, John Kennedy, and the New Battleground of the Cold War.* New York: W. W. Norton, 2021.

———. *Mutual Contempt: Lyndon Johnson, Robert Kennedy, and the Feud That Defined the Decade.* New York: W. W. Norton, 1997.

Sidey, Hugh. "Introduction and Commentary." In *Remembering Jack: Intimate and Unseen Photos of the Kennedys*, by Jacques Lowe. Boston: Bulfinch Press, 2003.

———. *John F. Kennedy, President.* New York: Atheneum, 1963.

———. *Portraits of the Presidents.* New York: Time Home Entertainment, 2000.

———. *The Presidency.* New York: Thornwillow Press, 1991.

Smith, Sally Bedell. *Grace and Power: The Private World of the Kennedy White House.* New York: Random House, 2004.

Smyser, W. R. *Kennedy and the Berlin Wall: "A Hell of a Lot Better Than a War."* Lanham, M.D.: Rowman and Littlefield, 2009.

Sorensen, Theodore C. *Counselor: A Life at the Edge of History.* New York: HarperCollins, 2008.

———. *Kennedy.* New York: Harper & Row, 1965.

Stacks, John F. *Scotty: James B. Reston and the Rise and Fall of American Journalism.* Lincoln, Nebr.: Bison Books, 2006.

Stern, Sheldon M. *Averting "the Final Failure": John F. Kennedy and the Secret Cuban Missile Crisis Meetings.* Stanford, C.A.: Stanford University Press, 2003.

Stossel, Scott. *Sarge: The Life and Times of Sargent Shriver.* New York: Other Press, 2011.

Sweig, Julia. *Lady Bird Johnson: Hiding in Plain Sight*. New York: Random House, 2021.

Talbot, David. *Brothers: The Hidden History of the Kennedy Years*. New York: Free Press, 2007.

Taubman, William. *Khrushchev: The Man and His Era*. New York: W. W. Norton, 2003.

Thomas, Evan. *Robert Kennedy: His Life*. New York: Simon & Schuster, 2000.

Unger, Irwin, and Debi Unger. *LBJ: A Life*. New York: John Wiley & Sons, 1999.

Updegrove, Mark K. *Baptism by Fire: Eight Presidents Who Took Office in Times of Crisis*. New York: St. Martin's Press, 2009.

———. *Indomitable Will: LBJ in the Presidency*. New York: Crown, 2012.

———. *Second Acts: Presidential Lives and Legacies After the White House*. Guilford, Conn.: Lyons Press, 2006.

Vandiver, Frank E. *Shadows of Vietnam: Lyndon Johnson's Wars*. College Station: Texas A&M University Press, 1997.

Waldman, Michael. *My Fellow Americans: The Most Important Speeches of America's Presidents from George Washington to Barack Obama*. Naperville, Ill.: Sourcebooks MediaFusion, 2003.

Watson, Mary Ann. *The Expanding Vista: American Television in the Kennedy Years*. Durham, N.C.: Duke University Press, 1994.

INDEX

Index

Index

China, 12, 16, 175, 240, 242, 265, 270–71
Choate, 25, 36, 37, 58
Churchill, Winston, 38, 226
Civil Rights Act (1957), 81, 237
Civil Rights Act (1964), 238
civil rights movement
 armed forces discrimination and, 13
 Birmingham and, 61, 79–80, 213–26. *See also* Birmingham
 Bobby and, 80–81, 221–23. *See also* Kennedy, Robert Francis "Bobby"
 bus segregation and, 13, 78–80, 82–88
 campaign promises by JFK, 81–82
 college segregation and, 163–69
 Eisenhower and, 13, 14
 federal housing segregation, 81–82
 Freedom Riders, 78–80, 82–88
 inaugural address on, 162–63
 JFK's voting record on, 81
 Johnson and, 236–38
 March on Washington for Jobs and Freedom (1963), 253–61
 modern Emancipation Proclamation and, 169
 Ole Miss radio speech, 167
 reelection plans based on, 275, 277
 Roosevelt and, 13
 school segregation and, 13, 78, 236
 space race and, 147
Clark, William Kemp, 281
Clifford, Clark, 15, 157–58
Cold War diplomacy
 as arms race, 11
 Berlin crisis, 117–20, 243–45. *See also* Berlin
 commitment to peace and, 139–43, 239–46, 286–87
 Cuba crises, 69–77, 171–77. *See also* Cuba
 Eisenhower and, 11–12, 14–16
 espionage and, 12
 Goldwater and, 274
 Joe Sr. on, 124–25

manifesto, 21
"missile gap," 11, 16, 141, 172–73
mutually assured destruction (MAD) and, 140, 239–40
nuclear disarmament as goal, 140–42
Sorensen on, 286
Soviet Union-U.S. summit (1961), 1–3, 5. *See also* Soviet Union-U.S. summit
space race and, 12, 150–52, 153
student demonstrations and, 141
U.S. military commanders on, 142–43
Vietnam and, 143–45. *See also* Vietnam
Committee on Equal Employment Opportunity, 82, 235
communism
 Cold War diplomacy and, 240, 242, 244–45
 in Cuba, 2, 12, 16. *See also* Cuba
 Eisenhower and, 11–12, 14, 15–16
 in Southeast Asia, 2, 15–16. *See also* China; Laos; Vietnam
Conference on the Discontinuance of Nuclear Weapon Tests, 141
Congress of Racial Equality (CORE), 78
Connally, John, 231, 276–77, 278, 279
Connally, Nellie, 278, 279–80
Connor, Eugene "Bull," 214–15, 218, 220
Cooper, Gordon, 152
Cousins, Norman, 240
Crespi, Vivian, 113
Cronkite, Walter, 115, 264
Cuba. *See also* Bay of Pigs; Cuban missile crisis
 Castro's take-over, 2, 12. *See also* Castro, Fidel
 guerilla operations against, 16
 Operation Mongoose, 171–72
 as Socialist nation, 75
 Sorensen on, 286
 Vietnam comparison, 271

Index

Index

Index

Lemnitzer, Lyman, 17, 71–73, 74, 120, 143, 174
"Letter from Birmingham Jail" (King), 217–20, 237
Levison, Stanley, 84, 216, 256
Lewis, John
  on Birmingham march, 220–21
  on Bobby, 225
  on campaign promises of JFK, 82
  on FBI and King, 261
  as Freedom Rider, 78–79, 84
  on JFK as inspiring, 4
  Washington march (1963) and, 253–55, 259–60
Limited Nuclear Test Ban Treaty (1963), 246, 287
Lincoln, Abraham
  assassination premonition of JFK and, 197
  Gettysburg Address, 20, 21
  inauguration address of, 24, 25, 26
  JFK on, 226
  on readiness, 196–97
Lincoln, Evelyn, 247
Lippmann, Walter, 194
Little Rock (Arkansas), 13
Lodge, George Cabot, II, 137
Lodge, Henry Cabot, Jr., 43, 47, 264, 266–67
Luce, Clare Boothe, 232
Luce, Henry, 124

MacArthur, Douglas, 142
Macmillan, Harold, 113, 209
MAD (mutually assured destruction), 140, 239–40
Maguire, Richard, 273
The Making of the President (White), 250
Malcolm, Durie, 123
Malone, Vivian, 224
Mansfield, Mike, 269
March on Washington for Jobs and Freedom (1963), 253–61
Marshall, Burke, 83, 225

Martin, Louis, 162
McCarthy, Joseph, 130–31, 230
McClellan, John, 131
McClellan Committee, 131
McCone, John, 174, 187–88
McCormack, Eddie, 136–37
McGovern, George, 202
McHugh, Godfrey, 244
McNamara, Robert
  American University speech and, 241
  appointment of secretary of defense, 56–57
  Cuba and, 71–73, 188, 192
  ExComm member, 174–75
  steel industry situation and, 157
  transition meetings and, 15
  Vietnam and, 145, 269
Medicare bill, 200–201, 275
Melbourne (book), 113
Menshikov, Mikhail, 90
Meredith, James Howard, 163–68
"Me Too" backlash, 115–16
Meyer, Mary Pinchot, 115
midterm elections, 198–203
Miller, William, 137
Minh, Duong Van, 266, 268
Mississippi, University of, 163–69
Monroe, Marilyn, 114, 159–60
Montgomery (Alabama), 13
Muskie, Edmund, 230
mutually assured destruction (MAD), 140, 239–40

National Aeronautics and Space Administration (NASA), 12, 68–69, 93
National Security Council, 181
Nelson, Gaylord, 202
New Frontier, 47
Newman, Larry, 111–12
New York Herald Tribune, 158, 202
Nhu, Madame, 263, 266
Nhu, Ngo Dinh, 263, 265–68
Nixon, Pat, 21

349

Index

ABOUT THE AUTHOR

Mark K. Updegrove is the author of five books on the presidency, including *The Last Republicans: Inside the Extraordinary Relationship Between George H. W. Bush and George W. Bush.* He currently serves as the president and CEO of the Lyndon Baines Johnson Foundation and presidential historian for ABC News. The former director of the Lyndon Baines Johnson Presidential Library and publisher of *Newsweek*, he has conducted exclusive interviews with seven US presidents.

Deanna,

You are
a true treasure

Maria Manuela
Cabral